TRENDS AND ISSUES IN

TRIBAL STUDIES

TRENDS AND ISSUES IN

TRIBAL STUDIES

EDITED BY

SOUBHAGYA RANJAN PADHI
BISWAJITA PADHY

ABHIJEET PUBLICATIONS
DELHI 110094

ABHIJEET PUBLICATIONS
2/46 Tukhmeerpur Extension
Delhi 110094
Phones: 011-22960492, 65698474
e-mail: abhijeetpublication@gmail.com
abhijeet_singh1@indiatimes.com

TRENDS AND ISSUES IN TRIBAL STUDIES

First Published 2008

ISBN 978-81-89886-45-5

PRINTED IN INDIA

Published by J.K. Singh fo Abhijeet Publications, Delhi 110094, Lasertypeset by Gaurav Graphics, Delhi and Printed as Himanshu Printers, Delhi.

ACKNOWLEDGEMENTS

It gives us immense pleasure to express our sincere thanks to all those who directly or indirectly helped us in completing this book. We cherish our deepest sense of gratitude and indebtedness to our friend Dr. Ajay Kumar Sahoo, Lecturer in Centre for Study of Indian Diaspora, School of Social Sciences, Central University of Hyderabad, for his enthusiastic inspiration, unfathomable interest, valuable suggestions, enlighten and illuminating guidance for the completion of this editorial volume. We will fail in our duty if our indebtedness is not acknowledged to all the authors, who have contributed their valuable papers to bring out this book. Words of gratitude and thanks we definitely owe to our parents, well wishers, friends, children and other family members who have rendered their love, patience, tolerance and thus helped in the process of making this book a reality. Most importantly our thanks are due to Mr. J.K.Singh of Abhijeet Publishers, New Delhi, for his keen interest in publishing this edited book for its wider circulation.

SOUBHAGYA RANJAN PADHI
& BISWAJITA PADHY

PREFACE

Tribal Society is an enigma to the world of culture and heritage. It carries forward a legacy of rich and distinct cultural traits for many decades. Tribal society displays a fascinating profile of ethnic diversity. Most of our contemporary cultures owe origin to tribal and indigenous traditions. Thus it is essential to have a close look on different tribal and ethnic studies in order to understand the matrix of recent societies. The whole tribal societies at present moment are going through the critical state of transition. However the historic isolation of these primitive people has been broken by the diffusion of greater civilization and the process of modernization. Tribal societies have gone through rapid socio-economic transformation in recent days. Time has come to realize the relevance of these social dynamics through various tribal studies.

Tribal communities are aboriginal inhabitants of uneven hilly terrain and forests. They are considered as sons of soil and live in isolation from other communities. It is not far from the truth that we have understood very little about various facets of their life. On many occasion they are ignored as an illiterate iot. The large scale socio-economic transformation in the modern industrialized societies has completely bypassed the tribals. Thus more radical and imperative to us today are to analyze the change brought by the contact of greater civilization and the process of modernization with these primitive people. Against this backdrop this edited volume have focused on the various trends and issues of tribal societies in its immutability and change.

The present publication encompasses a medley of sociological and anthropological research papers written by distinguished writers of India and abroad. The main objective of collating these articles is to provide certain recipe for the student and intellectuals of tribal and ethnic studies regarding the burning socio-cultural issues. Various research studies reported in this volume have focused on eliciting an array of issues of them from their own perspective. The writers hope that this collection of ethnographic, analytical, conceptual and theoretical issues, covering a wide range of subjects in the present array of papers will certainly provide intellectual stimulants.

This volume is structured around two broad themes viz. "Health" and "Tribal welfare". The first section of this book has included several valuable contributions of reputed writers on the theme of "Health". Health is a perquisite for human development and is an essential component for the well being of the mankind. The health problems of tribal community are influenced by interplay of many social, economic, and political factors. The common beliefs, customs, practices related to health and diseases in turn influence the health seeking behaviour of a community. Recent years have witnessed a growing concern with broadening the framework for health. Optimal health has been defined as safe life, control of diseases and that the quality of existing health services required for the total well being of an individual. Presently a number of international and national initiatives have begun to focus attention on the long neglected area of tribal's health aspect. Tribal's health is probably one of the most inadequately researched areas in international public health. The health status of tribal is miserable and this is a neglected field for many years. There are wide gaps in knowledge regarding the levels, determinants and consequences of tribal's health problems.

At present there is little understanding of how the broader circumstances of tribal's lives affect the ability to promote their own health. Ethical and cultural values, belief, attitudes and practices, play an important role in the health processes of tribal. In this context the present book have strived to explore various trends and determinants of morbidity and to obtain a clearer understanding of the socio-cultural and political context in which their health problem arise, how they define their health problems, manage their own as well as family's health and choose their health care options.

In the first article *Dr. A.K. Ravishankar, Dr. S. Ramachandran,* and *Dr. A. Subbiah* have highlighted the dismal state of reproductive health of tribals. They remarked that even though safe motherhood is the right of all women, yet in most of the tribal society, pregnancy and childbirth is a perilous journey. A great disparity exits in the availability, accessibility and utilization of various maternal services among different ethnic groups in India. The maternal health conditions are extremely pathetic among the tribes than the rest of the Indian castes, because of their isolation, remoteness and being largely unaffected by the developmental processes going on in the country. Under this circumstance, they mainly focus on the obstetric care elements, in form of antenatal care for pregnant women, natal care, and postnatal care, which can improve the maternal health conditions of the tribal communities. Their multivariate analysis revealed a positive association of maternal care with education of mother and their standard of living index.

In recent days the Anthropologists, sociologists, missionaries, newsmen, government agencies, ethnic curio seekers, politicians—they have all, from time to time, tried to penetrate the mystery surrounding the *Adivasis* (Original Settlers) of Orissa. Good health constitutes the primary concern for tribal communities, because health care practices which are developed in advanced societies are disseminated world-wide. Emerging issues of health in tribal communities of Orissa is the focus of discussion for *Soubhagya Ranjan Padhi* and *Biswajita Padhy* in their paper. They have employed both the clinical as well as social science perspective in examining the health care issues among tribals of Orissa. The clinical side of tribal health care concerns with examination of "diseases" domain i.e., issues of prevalence of diseases and demographic trends influencing morbidity, nutritional deficiencies, and associated environmental and cultural correlates. In later perspective, the "disease" is seen as illness, in the framework of social and cultural experience of people who suffer and seek health. This domain of health concerns with tribal systems of medicines, tribal healers, rituals, ethno-medicines, influence of cultural factors on health seeking behavior and reaction to public health care programmes. The authors believe that both perspectives compliment each other and will help readers in understanding better the real issues that lie behind failures in improving health conditions of tribes. Another article by *Dr. Rajesh Jaiswal* discusses the health status of the tribal women with special focus on nutritional status and maternal and child health care practices. The author observes that health status of tribal women is found to be lower than that of the non-tribal women. He has identified the gaps in knowledge regarding the health of tribal women and recommends some plan of actions for improving their health.

Prof. Wang has touched upon this very important but neglected dimension of the tribal health issues. He argues that the HIV and STIs in China's tribal groups and ethnic minorities are at a critical stage, which requires urgent, effective and replicable strategies to prevent further expansion. Particularly, it is growing rapidly among the poorest and most socially disadvantaged remote ethnic communities in Tibet, Yi, Jinpou, Dai, Lahu, Laxi, and Zhuang Tribal and ethnic groups of China. In spite of the effort of National and international AIDS society, there has been little progress to tackle the crisis in these ethnic minority communities. Mr. Wang has used an ethnic and linguistically appropriate approach for promoting HIV prevention in different cultural groups in China. The effectiveness was monitored in a pre and post intervention design through testing knowledge, attitudes and practice before and after the intervention in target community. His key findings clearly suggest that the peer-based ethnic/cultural oral story-telling strategy would benefit greatly to promote safe sexual behaviour in different cultural groups of China.

The health status of most of the tribal communities is miserable and there is a lack of awareness towards HIV-AIDS among them. At present there is little understanding of how HIV-AIDS affect tribal's lives. *Dr. P.K. Kar, S.R. Padhi* and *Pujashree Mishra* have focused on various levels, trends and determinants of HIV-AIDS and its consequences on tribal's health problems in Koraput district, which is one of the most underdeveloped regions of our country. He has analyzed the socio-cultural and political context in which tribals experience many stigmas, that affects their physical and mental conditions. The author advocates for a holistic approach to study this issue intensively for effective prevention of HIV among the tribals.

The HIV/AIDS can be effectively prevented only if the deep rooted values and attitudes that drive the risky behavior fuelling the epidemic are changed to understand the risk and vulnerability and thereby resulting in adoption of safe behaviors both sexual and health seeking. The socio-cultural fabric of tribal people may favour the spread of HIV and other communicable diseases. In this context, *Dr. Devesh Kumar Sahu* and *Mrs. Ankita Arya,* observe that the social assessment of HIV/AIDS among tribal people is as an essential requirement and a major tool for understanding the behaviors, practices that drive the vulnerability and risk among the tribal people. They also focus on understanding of the social dynamics underlying the transmission and management of HIV/AIDS in order to mitigate risks and scale up the HIV prevention programme effectively.

Research on indigenous "traditional medicine" is another priority area in contemporary tribal research. *Dr. Bibekananda Nayak* has examined traditional tribal medicine and treatment and suggested for an Ethno-medical model for the better health scenario of tribal society. He advocated for medical pluralism and remarks that demeaning or devaluing any of traditional medication of tribal society would be harmful for the whole arena of medical research.

Dr. Snigdha Mishra, Dr. Pradip Kumar Mishra, Dr. Asbi bin Ali, Dr. Junainah Abdul Hamid and *Seti Haireyah* have conducted the study to assess the nutritional status of ethnic Malay adult females, aged 19-50 years in Tok Muda village, Klang, Selangor Darul Ehsan of Malaysia. Their paper highlights findings on the nutrient intakes, body mass index (BMI) status, socio-economic status, clinical assessment and the micronutrient (iron) status of the adult women. Socio-economic results show that majority of adult women were housewives had attended only secondary school with the moderate incomes. Mean intake of energy and other nutrients of the all groups was found to be lower than the Malaysian Recommended Nutrient Index (RNI). Precisely these authors explore that the nutritional status of adult women of this ethnic group needs to be improved since there is a risk for some major nutritional deficiencies.

The second section focuses on the issues of "Tribal Welfare". Tribal Development has been one of the priority areas of the government ever since independence. However the current developmental scenario has contributed to an increase in economic and social inequalities, notwithstanding its promise of providing improved living conditions. Despite the rosy picture of greater human rights in recent days, tribal people are facing many miseries in every sphere of their life. They are identified to be the most exploited class for obvious reasons of their socio-economic inequalities. Eradication of atrocities against them still remains a distant reality. The tribal communities in the inaccessible regions continue to live in struggling against the element of nature and depending upon its bounty. The contemporary world has been widely characterized by restructuring of economic order and ever increasing interactivity between local and global communities through the social welfare perspective. However the emerging strategies for social welfare by the state and the increasing activism by the civil society to espouse the cause of this marginalized tribal/indigenous people often fall short of their livelihood insecurity, social segregation and alienation, disempowerment, loss of cultural identity etc. Against this backdrop, several authors have expressed their view points on some of the contemporary burning issues of tribal welfare.

Dr. N. Panigrahi, raises his concern about research institutes for their lack of adequate research in tribal field although he observes that at operational level different State and national level agencies are engaged in carrying out their welfare responsibilities as entrusted to them from time to time.

Using the secondary data, he reviewed the role played by Scheduled Caste and Scheduled Tribe Research and Training Institute of Orissa and remarked that the Institute is yet to document and highlight adequately the problems of tribal communities of the State. This has not been able to influence the flow of financial assistance provided by Government of India, so as to carryout research, training, evaluation and document cultures of tribal communities adequately.

In his paper Dr. S.N. Tripathy remarks that, the tribals continued to languish at the bottom of the socio-economic ladder, in spite of rapid industrialization and urbanization in the country. According to the author there is no remarkable diversification of tribal economy with desirable level of social and economic changes in a backward state like Orissa. The dynamics of rural development in the state have hardly changed the quality of life among marginalized groups and mainly the tribes, over period. This is clearly evident from the pattern and trend of growth, employment, poverty, agriculture and infrastructure and social sector development in the state. Keeping in view these challenging situations he finally advocates for appropriate policy actions with special focus on these marginalized groups to tackle this existing alarming situation. He has strongly recommended for the enlightened actions by the state in order to protect the interests of the tribal poor.

Dr. Dibakar Sarangi offers a critical appraisal of educational scenario of tribals in KBK region of Orissa. Education of tribal people had not been paid due attention and these communities are lagging behind in literacy for many reasons. While explaining the dismayed scenario of Secondary Education in K.B.K. region, he focuses on various contours of quality Education in terms of a cluster of indicators viz. within and outside education such as opportunity and access to Secondary Education, infrastructure facilities, human resources, curriculum transaction, assessment of pupils' learning, monitoring, supervision and system feedback, public and stakeholders participation in education, institutional interface and collaboration, pupil productivity and above all interest in Secondary Education. The author suggested that a special package of Secondary Education with distinctive policy directives can mainstream the larger native population and bring forth a sustainable development of the K.B.K. tribal region. Another author *Miss Debjani Dhal,* also consider that education is a prime catalyst of tribal welfare in every society. By reviewing the Tamil Nadu scenario, she remarks that lack of education is a major obstacle of tribal welfare in this state. She finds that these most subordinated, poorest and vulnerable sections of society have been structurally subjected to various kinds of social discrimination including educational deprivation for a long period. Tamil Nadu ranks third among major states with regard to literacy and general education. However, a SC and ST section of society still remains uneducated. Large funds have been allocated for the welfare of S.C's and S.T's education. But in practice, there is a major gap between budget allocation and their due share as envisioned in the Special Component Plan and Tribal Sub Plan.

Development of backward communities has been assigned adequate importance in the planning process of the Indian economy. However *Dr. Nihar Ranjan Mishra* in his study has shown that over the years, the outcome of efforts made by the government does not seem to be quite promising. For instance, the persistence of top-down bureaucratic approach proved disastrous in managing the natural resources, causing harm to the ecosystem and thus threatening the lives of the poor tribal people. In the free market globalize economy, exploitation of natural resources to meet ever increasing requirements of the affluent sections cannot be ruled out. The intervention of modern law and order machinery, and the legal system have affected the functioning of traditional tribal management systems and resulted in conflict resolutions. The author feels grass root level policies through some need based Act like Panchayat Extension to the Scheduled Areas (PESA) Act, could ensure empowerment of tribal people. There is an urgent need of empowering Gram Sabha and Gram Panchayat to make certain provision of grass root level democracy in the Scheduled Areas of India. Against this backdrop, he has broadly made an attempt to examine the correlation between self-governance and management of natural resources in the Scheduled Areas of Orissa.

Dr. S.P. Rout and *P. Patnaik* have emphasized on the role of democratic decentralization as a process of reforming the demographic governance system which can empower the tribals through devolution of power. In their paper they have intensively focused on the issues of inclusion and empowerment of Scheduled Tribes in the democratic local governments or Gram Panchayats. The authors have critically analyzed about the representation, participation and empowerment of scheduled tribes in their panchayat and highlighted the drawback of the decentralized governance in ensuring inclusion and empowerment. In their concluding remarks, they put forth some of the suggestive measures for transforming symbolic inclusion to meaningful representation to ensure an effective decentralized system for inclusion and empowerment of tribals.

Sustainable livelihood has been regarded as a significant catalyst for tribal welfare. The focus of the government in recent years has been on bringing overall development in tribal areas by creating different livelihood avenues for these weakest communities. However, reality shows that many of the development programmes botched due to lack of proper implementation and coordination between various government and non-government departments. An attempt has been made by Dr.J.K. Mohanty to analyze the emerging issues and prospect of tribal development through various livelihood programmes in Koraput district of Orissa. He has extensively focused on various causes responsible for lack of livelihood options and recommended some valuable suggestions to open up various livelihood opportunities in the tribal areas.

Under the auspices of liberalization and globalization tribal continue to be displaced from their own land. The land resources of the scheduled tribes are being rapidly depleted day by day. Exploitation, zilch health care and educational facilities, malnutrition, inhuman torture, rising unemployment, inordinate delay in disposal of land cases are the cruel realities which uncover the development syndrome of the area. The so-called development projects in no way helped the majority of displaced tribal. This, rather, has alienated the rural tribal people and raised their anger towards government policies. Further the frustration of tribals has taken the shape of Naxalite movement in most of the tribal areas. In the perspective of the above facts, Dr. K.C. Pradhan and P.C. Panigrahi have made a humble attempt to study the factors responsible for the tremendous rise of Naxalism in tribal India. Finally they have made attempts to suggest the plausible endeavor which could be helpful to pacify the tribal anger and pave the way for smooth Socio-economic development.

Gender is an important basis of stratification, illustrates that mankind has been willing to give women everything but equal status with their male counter parts. Gender inequality prevents women from acquiring many opportunities, which are indispensable prerequisite for their empowerment. The decade long gender disparities undermines women's rights and decision making power. Truly we are living in a world where gender matters. While human rights itself is about equity, the character of society – its faith and belief system which is for many centuries is dominated by patriarchal and gender bias framework determines the extent of equity that is reflected in reality. Raju Prasad Chapagai, in his paper points out that Empowerment in fact is an outcome of the elimination of the discrimination and violence against women that are being promoted by patriarchal norms and values in society. He observed that in Nepal, defective cultural beliefs prescribed women only limited roles in society. Many people believed that women's natural roles were as mothers and wives. Women were considered to be better suited for childbearing and household work rather than for involvement in the public life. That type of socially constructed gender role resulted in gender imbalance of power between women and men. He has expediently evaluated the role of "Public Interest Litigation"(PIL), which has become instrumental in eliminating discriminatory laws and gender biased customary practices responsible to perpetuate violence and discrimination against women.

SOUBHAGYA RANJAN PADHI
& BISWAJITA PADHY

CONTENTS

SECTION II: TRIBAL WELFARE

LIST OF CONTRIBUTORS

Dr. A.K. Ravishankar, Senior Lecturer, Population Studies Wing, DDE, Annamalai University, Annamalainagar.

Dr. S. Ramachandran, Professor, Department of Population Studies, Annamalai University, Annamalainagar.

Dr. A. Subbiah, Professor and Head, Department of Population Studies, Annamalai University, Annamalainagar.

Soubhagya Ranjan Padhi, Faculty in Sociology, Aeronautic College, Orissa.

Biswajita Padhy, Faculty in Economics, Aeronautic College, Orissa.

Dr. Rajesh Jaiswal, Associate Fellow, National Council of Applied Economic Research, New Delhi.

Dr. Shuguang Wang, Conjoint Professor, School of Psychology, the University of Newcastle, Australia. And also working for Centre for International Program Development in HIV Social Study (CIPD), Institute of Sociology, Sichuan Academy of Social Sciences, China.

Dr. P.K. Kar, Senior Reader, Department of Sociology, F.M. Autonomous College, Balasore, Orissa.

Pujashree Mishra, Scholar, Department of Sociology, University of Hyderabad.

Dr. D.K. Sahu, Programme Manager, MAMTA Health Institute for Mother and Child, New Delhi.

Mrs. Ankita Arya, Research Scholar, Department of Anthropology, University of Delhi, Delhi.

Dr. Bibekananda Nayak, Lecturer in the Department of Sociology, Delhi School of Economics, University of Delhi, New Delhi.

Dr. Snigdha Mishra, Senior Kecturer, School of Health Sciences, Kolej University of Technology & Management, Shah Alam, Malaysia.

Dr. Junainah Abdul Hamid, Vice president, Academic School of Health Sciences, Kolej University of Technology & Management, Shah Alam, Malaysia.

Dr. Pradip Kumar Mishra, Senior Lecturer, School of Business Management & Professional Studies, Kolej University of Technology & Management, Shah Alam Malaysia.

Dr. Asbi bin Ali, Dean & Vice president, Research & Innovations, School of Health Sciences, Kolej University of Technology & Management, Shah Alam, Malaysia.

Seti Haireyah, Research Assistant, School of Health Sciences, Kolej University of Technology & Management, Shah Alam, Malaysia.

Nilakantha Panigrahi, Lecturer in Anthropology, NKC Center for Development Studies (ICSSR supported Center), Bhubaneswar.

Dr. S.N. Tripathy, Professor of Economics, Gokhale Institute of Politics and Economics, Pune (Maharastra).

Dr. Dibakar Sarangi, Lecturer in Education, D.A.V.College of Teacher Education, Koraput, Orissa.

Dr. Debajani Dhal, Department of Humanities and Social Sciences, Indian Institute of Technology, Kanpur- 208016 (U.P.), India

Nihar Ranjan Mishra, Doctoral Fellow, Department of Anthropology, University of Hyderabad.

Dr. Satyapriya Rout, Lecturer, Department of Sociology, University of Hyderabad.

Dr. Pratyusna Patnaik, Research Scholar, University of Hyderabad.

Dr. J.K. Mohanty, Reader in Commerce, D.A.V. College, Koraput, Orissa.

Dr. K.C. Pradhan, Lecturer in Economics, Khemundi College, Digapahandi, Ganjam, Orissa.

Dr. P.C. Panigrahi, Lecturer in Economics, Biju Pattnaik Women's College, Digapahandi, Ganjam, Orissa.

Raju Prasad Chapagai, Public Interest Lawyer, Forum for Protection of Public Interest, Kathmandu, Nepal.

SECTION I: TRIBAL HEALTH

1

SAFE MOTHERHOOD PRACTICES AMONG INDIAN TRIBAL COMMUNITIES: FACTS FROM NFSH-II

DR. A. K. RAVISHANKAR, DR. S. RAMACHANDRAN & DR. A. SUBBIAH

Safe Motherhood is the right of all women. Around the world, people celebrate the birth of a new baby. Societies expect women to bear children, and honour women for their role as mothers. However in most of the world, especially in the primitive societies pregnancy and childbirth is a perilous journey. Worldwide, it is estimated that 515,000 women die annually from maternal causes (World Health Organization, 2001) about one woman every minute and ninety nine percent of these deaths occur in the less developed world, where a woman's lifetime risk of dying from pregnancy-related complications is almost 40 times higher than that of her counterparts in developed countries[1]. However, maternal death is an avoidable tragedy. No mother should die giving life. A little bit of care and awareness can go a long way in preventing this tragedy.

More than fifteen years after the launch of the Safe Motherhood Initiative in 1987, maternal mortality remains to be a major cause of death among women at the reproductive ages in India. Each year in India, roughly 30 million women experience pregnancy and 27 million have a live birth. Of these, over 100,000 maternal deaths and one million newborn deaths occur annually. Millions more suffer pregnancy-related ill-health[2].

India, as a signatory of Millennium Development Summit Declaration (2000), aimed at achieving the MDGs by the year 2015. There are broadly eight development domains that are targeted to bring about qualitative changes in the life of every citizen of the country. The "improve maternal health" element of the Millennium Development Goals envisages to reducing maternal mortality ratic by three quarters between 1990 and 2015.

A diverse set of factors are thought to be associated with maternal mortality; factors that influence delays in deciding to seek medical care, in reaching a place where care is available, and in receiving appropriate care. The links between pregnancy-related care and maternal mortality are well recognized, and over the last decade national programmes and Plans have stressed the need for universal screening of pregnant women and operationalising essential and emergency obstetric care. Proper antenatal care ensures at the end of pregnancy, a healthy mother and a healthy baby.

However a great disparity exits in the availability, accessibility and utilization of various maternal services among different ethnic groups in India. The maternal health conditions are extremely pathetic among the tribes, than the rest of the Indian castes.

In today's modern world, it is difficult to imagine societies that are still socially and culturally isolated from the rest of civilization, however, they do exist. Despite remarkable world-wide progress in the field of diagnostics and curative and preventive health, still there are people living in isolation in natural and unpolluted surroundings far away from civilization with their traditional values, customs, beliefs and myth intact. They are commonly known as "tribals" and are considered to be the autochthonous people of the land. About half of the world's autochthonous people, comprising 635 tribal communities including 75 primitive tribal communities live in India.

According to 2001 census, the population of Scheduled Tribes in the country was 84.32 million representing 8.21 percent of the country's population. The population of tribes had grown at the rate of 24.5 percent during the period 1991-2001. Scheduled Tribes are spread across the country mainly concentrated in the states of Madhya Pradesh, Chhattisgarh, Maharashtra, Orissa, Jharkhand and Gujarat. However, they have their presence in all States and UTs except Haryana, Punjab, Delhi, Pondicherry and Chandigarh.

High level of poverty, inadequate health resources, ignorance and high-risk beliefs and practices among the tribal communities has contributed to the vulnerability of this population. There is a general consensus that the health status of the tribal population is very poor and worst among the primitive tribes because of their isolation, remoteness and being largely unaffected by the developmental processes going on in the country[3].

Even within a particular tribal entity, differences in dialect, health practices, unique customs, values, and traditions are apparent. In rural tribal Indian communities indices of reproductive health are typically very poor: maternal mortality rate is about 230 per 100,000 live births and 61.2 percent of the women was suffer from at least one gynaecologic pathology[4]. Because tribal groups have existed on the fringe of Indian society, they may still be unaware or indifferent to the potential health threats. Ascertaining whether or not tribal communities are potentially a high risk group warranting intervention is a necessary step in India's war on maternal mortality.

In this context, safe motherhood components have been a direct alliance to reduce infant and maternal mortality. The important move toward dropping the maternal mortality included establishment of first referral units for providing emergency obstetric care. This present paper mainly focuses on the utilization of maternal care elements which concentrate on antenatal care for pregnant women, natal care, and postnatal care.

Objectives

Accordingly, this study made an attempt to evaluate the safe motherhood practices among the tribals in India. The study has been designed to

- To study the socio-economic and demographic condition of tribal women in India.

- To analyses the antenatal care service utilization behaviour among the Indian tribals
- To examine the performance of natal (delivery) care services by the tribal communities.
- To study the utilization pattern of postnatal care services in the tribal societies.
- To study the influence of SED characteristics in the utilization of maternal health care services among the tribal communities.

Methods

The data for the present study were drawn from National Family Health Survey, a nationally represented large-scale sample (more than 90,000) survey conducted in India during 1998–99. The structure of the survey is similar to that of the DHS conducted in various Asian and African countries. A total of 10906 married tribal women aged 15-49 years were considered for this analysis. A multivariate analysis technique was used for determining the influencing factors.

Results and Discussion

SED Profile of Tribal women: Indian tribal populations are widely recognized as marginalized and exploited members of society and for centuries have suffered intense and extensive social economic and demographic discrimination.

Tribal people, being essentially ecosystem people, the country's wide ranging diversity in nature and natural resources present a varied tribal population throughout India's length and breath. In general, most tribal populations inhabit under-developed areas of the country which are remote, having low density of population and lacking in adequate access to basic amenities, education, employment opportunities and affordable health care services.

This section presents a profile of the demographic and socioeconomic characteristics of tribal women (ever-married) age 15-49 years, across the country. The Table 1 describes the percentage distribution of ever-married tribal women by age, place of residence, religion, educational level, work status, marital status, co residence with husband and husband's educational attainment.

The age sharing of the tribal ever-married women reflects the normal pyramid shape of the population's age structure. The percentage of respondents in five-year age groups increases from 8.5 percent in the age-group 15-19 years to 21.2 in the age group 25-29 years, and it steadily fall to 7.9 percent among the 45-49 age group.

A similar trend was observed among the rural and urban respondents with some notable exception that the proportion of rural respondent in 15-19 years (9.3 percent) is twofold as compared with urban respondents (4.8 percent). Among the 20-24 age group, it is also fairly higher for rural than the urban respondents (15.5 and 19.6 percent respectively). Thus, the average rural respondents are comparatively younger than the average urban respondents.

In the tribal society, sixty percent of the respondents are belonging to the Hindu religion. The next major share goes to Christian religion (29.0 percent) and less than one percent belongs to Muslims community.

More than eighty percent of the tribals are living in the rural areas and only 17.0 percent were living in the urban area. As the majority of these tribals living in the remote rural areas remain isolated, untouched by civilization, they are largely unaffected by the developmental processes going on in the rest of the Nation. Therefore, these groups remain backward, particularly in health, education and socio-economic aspects.

It is evident from most of the studies that the community's educational level has an influence on the demographic and health-seeking behaviour. According to the NFHS-II, sixty percent of the tribal women aged 15-49 in India are illiterates and only about three percent of the respondents have completed their higher secondary level. However, a notable difference was noticed among the husband's educational level. Just more than one-third of respondents have illiterate husbands, and about 10 percent of them have completed their higher secondary.

About forty percent of the tribal ever-married women did

not participate in any kind work and a major proportion (43.8 percent) was engaged in the agricultural allied activities. Due to these pitiable literacy levels, desolate work status leads to high levels of poverty, in turn these communities are highly vulnerable to various socioeconomic and health problems.

Table 1. Percentage Distribution of Tribal Women by their Socio-Economic and Demographic Characteristics

Characteristics of the Respondents	*Percentage of ST*
Age 5-year groups	
15-19	8.5
20-24	18.9
25-29	21.2
30-34	17.8
35-39	14.8
40-44	10.7
45-49	7.9
Religion	
Hindu	60.5
Muslim	0.9
Christian	28.9
Others	9.7
Type of Place of residence	
Urban	17.0
Rural	83.0
Respondent's Educational level	
Illiterate	60.3
Primary	16.5
Secondary	19.7
Higher	3.4
Respondent's occupation	
Not working	39.8
Agriculture allied activities	43.8
Skilled/Unskilled manual	7.7
Industrial sectors	7.3
Others	1.4
Current Marital Status	
Currently married	92.0

Separated/ Deserted/ Divorced	3.3
Widowed	4.6
Co-residence with husband	
Living with husband	97.2
Not living with husband	2.8
Husband's Educational level	
No education	37.3
Primary	21.7
Secondary	30.9
Higher	10.0
Age at first Marriage	
>15	18.0
15-17	37.9
18-20	27.9
21-22	7.4
23-24	4.2
25+	4.6
Age of respondent at 1st birth	
>14	1.8
14-17	35.4
18 -20	34.7
21-24	20.6
25-30	6.6
30+	0.8
Children Ever born	
0	9.9
1	14.2
2	17.4
3	18.4
4	14.7
5	10.3
6+	15.1
Household Standard of Living Index (SLI)	
Low	42.9
Medium	48.4
High	8.8

In the tribal communities, majority are currently married (92.0 percent) and the proportion of women living with their husbands was 97.2 percent. It pointed out that a greater part of women were living with their husband at the time of the survey.

The table provides the percentage distribution of tribal women who first married by exact age. The results shows that the practices of early marriage was more predominate in the tribal communities, about fifty percent of the marriage was taken place before they reach the legal age at marriage as set by Child Marriage Restraint Act of 1978. The other notable observation made here is that more than one-third of the tribal women given their first birth before they reach the legal age at marriage. Though the mean age at first marriage was 17.5 years, their mean age at first birth was relatively higher (19.0 years) among the tribal women.

The number of children a woman has ever born is a cohort measure of fertility. The number of children that a women will have in her lifetime is strongly associated by the age at she marries. It is evident from the table that one- forth of the tribal women had more than five children (25.4 percent) another one quarter of tribal women had 3-4 children ever born.

A summary household measure called the Standard of Living Index (SLI) was calculated, it reveals that about half of the households (43 percent) living with low standard of living index and only eight percent were living with high standard of living index. It shows that the tribal societies throughout India have remained socially, economically and demographically separated from mainstream Indian society.

Obstetric Care Scenario in the Tribal Communities

Motherhood should be a time of expectation and joy for a woman, her family, and her community. For women in tribal communities, however, the reality of motherhood is often grim. For these women, motherhood is often marred by unforeseen complications of pregnancy and childbirth. Some die in the prime period of their lives and in great distress: from haemorrhage, convulsions, obstructed labour, or severe infection after delivery or unsafe abortion.

Effective health systems make obstetric care available to all women, required to treat life-threatening conditions during pregnancy, delivery, and after childbirth. Antenatal care, among other services, can play a role in detecting and treating some complications of pregnancy.

Antenatal Care

In India ANC services consist of a set of professional pregnancy checkups, tetanus and other immunizations, prophylaxis through iron and folic acid tablets, blood pressure check up and advice and information regarding delivery methods and services, nutrition and postnatal care.

Table 2. Percentage Distribution of Tribal Women by Antenatal Check-ups

Antenatal Check-ups	*Scheduled Tribe*
Antenatal visits for pregnancy	
No antenatal visits	40.2
1	11.0
2	15.5
3	13.0
4+	20.3
Timing of 1st antenatal check (month)	
0	0.2
1	4.6
2	11.1
3	22.8
Before 1st trimester	38.7
4	16.4
5	17.6
6+	27.3
After 1st trimester	61.3

The number of antenatal visits and timing of first antenatal care is imperative for the mother's health and for the foetus. Provision of quality antenatal care services means early registration and (to confirm pregnancy) check-up of the woman at least before twenty weeks of gestation followed by a minimum of three visits for antenatal care[5].

About forty percent of the tribal women who had birth three years preceding the survey receive no antenatal care during their pregnancy episode. Only one-fifth of the tribals made the minimum number of antenatal visits (four visits) which is recommended by WHO to achieve the essential level of antenatal care.

The timing of first antenatal care is imperative for the mother's health and for the foetus. In these tribal communities more than one-fourth of pregnant women visited the antenatal care centre only after the sixth month of their pregnancy period.

Table 3. Percentage Distribution of Tribal Women by Antenatal Check-ups, According to Selected Background Conditions

Background Characteristics	*ANC Visits*			*Timing of 1st antenatal check*	
	No antenatal visits	*Less than four visits*	*More than four visits*	*Before 1st Trimester*	*After 1st Trimester*
Type of place of residence					
Urban	11.6	33.3	55.1	53.2	46.8
Rural	45.2	40.6	14.2	34.6	65.4
Religion					
Hindu	46.6	40.1	13.4	36.7	63.3
Muslim	45.5	29.5	25.0	45.8	54.2
Christian	28.2	41.3	30.5	40.9	59.1
Others	44.0	30.9	25.1	38.8	61.2
Respondents Educational level					
Illiterate	53.5	37.6	8.9	29.5	70.5
Primary	33.5	43.7	22.9	37.4	62.6
Secondary	17.7	42.1	40.3	47.2	52.8
Higher	3.4	34.0	62.6	66.9	33.1
Husband's Education level					
Illiterate	55.6	34.1	10.3	28.4	71.6
Primary	42.6	42.3	15.1	31.9	68.1
Secondary	29.5	43.9	26.6	42.3	57.7
Higher	16.7	39.4	43.9	55.9	44.1

Household Standard of Living Index					
Low	52.1	37.3	10.6	30.7	69.3
Medium	32.9	42.2	24.8	39.8	60.2
High	13.0	34.7	52.3	58.1	41.9
Total	40.2	39.5	20.3	38.6	61.4

Table 3 presents the percentage distribution of Tribal women by Antenatal Check-ups, according to selected background conditions. The table reveals that forty five percent of the rural tribal mothers did not made even a single antenatal visits as against only 11.6 percent of urban tribal mothers. The proportion of mothers who did not receive antenatal check-up sharply decreases with their increasing educational level. Majority of women living in households with a high standard of living had received ante-natal check-ups (87.0 percent) conversely this proportion is low among women living with low standard of living index (47.9 percent). While looking into the recommended minimum number of ANC visits (3 visits), again the educational level and their standard of living index are positively correlated.

In the rural tribal area two-third of mothers receive the first check-up only after the first trimester (65.4 percent) and this proportion was moderate among the highly literate group (33.1 percent) and women living household with high standard of living condition (44.1 percent).

The multivariate analysis also proved the correlation between the minimum number of visits made by the respondents and their SED characteristics. The urban mothers are about four times better than rural mothers with respect to their ANC visits. Similarly the educated mothers (higher) are six times superior to the illiterate mothers. The SLI also shows the well established link between these two variables. The minimum number of visits made by the mother living in the household with high standard is better than (3 times) the women living with low standard of living.

Components of Antenatal Check-ups

The test and measurements done during the antenatal check-ups is ensuring the safe motherhood. The mothers who went for antenatal check-ups were asked whether they received each of several components of antenatal check-ups at least once during their ANC episode and the results are presented in Table 4.

Majority of the women (77 percent) reported that their abdomen was examined during their ANC visits, the next highest proportion (58.5 percent) said that their blood pressure was checked. A reasonable proportion of mothers had the blood test (40.0 percent) and their weight was measured (44.2 percent).

During the antenatal visits, mothers were advised about their diet, the danger sign of pregnancy, delivery care and newborn care to reduce the risk of pregnancy complications and to help the woman prepare for a safe and sound birth. However, most often advice given to the mother was on their diet (47.5 percent). Only one-forth of the mother were received advices on danger signs of pregnancy, delivery care and new born care.

Table No. 4 Percentage Distribution of Tribal Women by Components of Antenatal Check-ups

Components of ANC	*Scheduled Tribe*
Weight measured	
No	55.8
Yes	44.2
Height measured	
No	85.9
Yes	14.1
Blood pressure checked	
No	41.5
Yes	58.5
Blood test	
No	60.0
Yes	40.0
Urine test	
No	64.1
Yes	35.9
Abdomen examined	
No	22.9
Yes	77.1
Internal exam	
No	77.5
Yes	22.5

Antenatal Advices	
Diet	
No	52.5
Yes	47.5
Danger signs of pregnancy	
No	75.4
Yes	24.6
Delivery care	
No	74.0
Yes	26.0
Newborn care	
	77.6
	22.4

TT vaccination: To step up the pace of the immunization programme, the government of India initiated the Universal Immunization Programme in 1985-86. An important objective of the UIP was to vaccinate all pregnant women against tetanus by 1990. However, the coverage of TT injection among the tribal is far from complete. About forty percent of the pregnant women did not receive even a single dose of TT injection during their pregnancy episode.

Table 5: Percentage Distribution of Tribal Women by TT Vaccination

Antenatal Care Services	*Scheduled Tribe*
Tetanus injections before birth	
Received no injection	38.9
Received injection	60.8
Don't know	0 .3
Number of times given tetanus injections	
1	28.6
2	53.3
3+	17.8
Don't know	0.3

According to the National Immunization Schedule, pregnant woman should receive two doses of tetanus toxoid injection, the first when she is 16 weeks pregnant and the second when she is 20 weeks pregnant (Central Bureau of Health Intelligence 1991)[6]. Women who had received TT injection were further asked how many times they had received the injection during their pregnancy period. Among them, more than half of the women received two doses of tetanus toxoid injection and at the same time more than one-fifth (28.6 percent) mothers were received only a single dose.

Folic acid: The U.S. Public Health Service recommends that women of childbearing age get at least 400 milligrams of folic acid each day, through food sources and/or supplements. For women who are thinking about getting pregnant, health care providers recommend supplementing the diet with folic acid for three months before pregnancy, and then for at least the first three months of pregnancy. Prenatal vitamins are a good way to get extra folic acid into the diet. Prenatal supplements often contain high amounts of folic acid and other compounds, such as iron and vitamin A. Findings from research indicate that the right amount of folic acid can help prevent certain types of birth defects and other problems during pregnancy.

Iron deficiency anaemia is the most common micronutrient deficiency in the world. It is a major threat to safe motherhood and to the health and survival of infants. Only half of the tribal mothers received IFA supplements during their pregnancy period. Among women who received IFA supplements during the pregnancy episode, eighty percent women received at least a three months supply and an equal proportion were consumed all the tablets that were supplied to them. As compared with TT coverage, however, IFA coverage is far behind, at the same time those who received the IFA tablets their consumption pattern was fairly good.

Table 6. Percentage Distribution of Tribal Women by Distribution of IFA Tablets

Antenatal Care Services	*Scheduled Tribe*
Given Iron folic tablets during pregnancy	
No	50.8
Yes	49.2
Given enough tablets for at least 3 months	
No	18.8
Yes	80.7
Consumed all tablets given	
No	19.4
Yes	80.6

The coverage of TT vaccination and IFA tablets, according to selected background conditions are presented in the below table. The coverage of TT vaccination among the rural tribal mothers was far from complete. In contrast, among the TT injection received mothers the rural mothers are far better compared to urban mothers.

Table 7. Percentage Distribution of Tribal Women by ANC Services, According to Selected Background Conditions

Background Characteristics	*TT vaccination*			*Given IFA tablets*	
	No injection	*< 1 dose*	*> 2 doses*	*No*	*Yes*
Type of place of residence					
Urban	12.6	28.5	58.5	25.3	74.7
Rural	43.5	15.5	40.5	55.3	44.7
Religion					
Hindu	43.2	12.4	43.7	54.5	45.5
Muslim	43.2	11.4	43.2	56.8	43.2
Christian	28.8	27.7	43.4	45.2	54.8
Others	48.8	12.3	38.6	48.1	51.9
Respondents Educational level					
Illiterate	50.0	13.5	35.9	61.4	38.6
Primary	36.1	20.7	42.9	44.8	55.2
Secondary	18.8	24.5	56.5	34.0	66.0
Higher	3.4	17.7	78.2	17.7	82.3
Husband's Education level					
Illiterate	54.3	13.4	31.7	64.4	35.6
Primary	42.3	18.9	38.4	51.0	49.0
Secondary	28.0	20.6	51.2	43.1	56.9
Higher	14.6	17.8	67.1	29.1	70.9
Household Standard of Living Index					
Low	50.8	13.7	34.9	60.2	39.8
Medium	32.2	20.7	46.7	46.4	53.6
High	8.7	19.9	71.5	20.2	79.8
TOTAL	38.9	17.4	43.2	50.9	49.1

Both the TT vaccination and IFA tablets coverage are substantially lower for births to illiterate mothers and mother living in a household with low standard of living condition.

The results shows that even among women in high SLI receive the recommended two doses of TT are very low (11.2 percent).

Health Problems During Pregnancy

Antenatal care, among other services, can play a role in detecting and treating some complications of pregnancy. The tribal women were asked if at any time during their pregnancy episode she experienced the pregnancy related problems for their most two births in the three years preceding the survey period. Night blindness is the result of chronic vitamin A deficiency and is often seen in pregnant women in areas where vitamin A deficiency is endemic. Convulsion accompanied by signs of hypertension can be symptomatic of eclampsia, a potentially fatal condition. The potential health risk posed by vaginal bleeding during pregnancy varies by when in the pregnancy the bleeding takes place.

Table 8. Percentage Distribution of Tribal Women by Pregnancy Related Health Problems

Health Problems during Pregnancy	*Scheduled Tribe*
Night blindness	
No	80.5
Yes	19.5
Blurred vision	
No	72.6
Yes	27.4
Convulsions	
No	79.1
Yes	20.9
Swelling	
No	68.4
Yes	31.6
Excessive fatigue	
No	52.8
Yes	47.2
Anaemia	
No	73.2
Yes	26.8
Vaginal bleeding	
No	96.0
Yes	4.0

Table 8 presents the percentage distribution of Tribal women by Pregnancy related health problems. It discloses the fact that the most commonly pregnancy-related health problems reported by the tribals are excessive fatigue (47.2 percent), followed by swelling of the legs, and body (31.6 percent). An equal proportion of tribals reported blurred vision and anaemia (27 percent). About one-fifth of the tribals reported the night blindness and Convulsions. The reported prevalence of vaginal bleeding was insignificant.

Reasons for Not Receiving ANC

Effective health systems make obstetric care available to all women, required to treat life-threatening conditions during pregnancy, delivery, and after childbirth. Antenatal care, among other services, can play a role in detecting and treating some complications of pregnancy. However, in the tribal communities more than half of them did not consider that the ANC to be necessary or customary. Another important reason for not receiving the ANC was the costs, distance and lack of transport. It reveals the fact that women and family members should aware the benefits of ANC to help overcome traditional attitudes and other hurdles that prevent mother from seeking antenatal care for their pregnancies.

Table 9. Percentage Distribution of Tribal Women by Reasons Not Receiving ANC

Main reason did not received antenatal checkup	*Scheduled Tribe*
Not necessary	49.7
Not customary	4.2
Cost too much	14.5
Inconvenient/too far	10.6
Poor quality/service	1.3
No time to go	4.4
Family did not allow	3.5
Lack of knowledge	6.0
No health worker visited	2.7
Other	3.0

Delivery Care

Research shows that women's lives can be saved and their suffering reduced if health systems could address serious and life-threatening complications of pregnancy and childbirth when they occur. One of the best ways to do this is to make sure that women receive skilled care at delivery.

The place of delivery is an important determinant for reducing the risk of infant and maternal death. Women were asked whether their last live birth during the three years preceding the survey was born at home or at a health care institution (public hospitals, private hospitals or other health care institutions).

Table 10. Percentage Distribution of Tribal Women by Place of Delivery

Place of delivery	*Scheduled Tribe*
Home	78.5
Govt. hospital/dispensary/PHC/Sub-centre	15.6
Private hosp/clinic/NGO/trust hospital/clinic	5.9
Attendant assisting during delivery	
Doctor	14.5
ANM/nurse/midwife	8.3
Other health professional	0.2
Dai (TBA)	44.4
Others	32.2

Only about half of deliveries in less developed countries take place with the assistance of skilled health personnel. Providing skilled care means ensuring that health professionals such as doctors, nurses, or midwives can manage normal deliveries and treat the life-threatening complications of pregnancy and childbirth. Ensuring that women receive skilled care at delivery is an essential part of safe motherhood programmes.

Nevertheless, more than three-fourth of the deliveries (78.5 percent) are took place at home in the tribal communities. Only five percent of the birth took place at the private sectors and fifteen percent of births were took place at government institutions.

Skilled attendance at delivery and immediately afterward can make a critical contribution to preventing maternal deaths and disabilities. Though, only 53 percent of births in the developing world are professionally attended. This means that every year, by choice or necessity, 60 million women in developing countries give birth cared for only by a family member, a traditional birth attendant, or no one at all[7].

Similarly, more than three-forth of the deliveries among the tribal communities are attended by *Dais* (Traditional Birth Attendant) and other than health personnel (44.4 percent, 32.2 percent respectively). Only about one-fourth (23.0 percent) deliveries are safe in the tribal societies (assisted by Doctor/Nurse/ANM). It reflects the fact that a conspicuous lack of maternal services among the hilly tribal areas and consequently, the tribal demographic scenario is one of high maternal and infant mortality rates.

The proportion of deliveries occurring at home is higher for rural (86.5 percent), Hindu (84.2 percent), illiterate mothers (89.9 percent) and mother's living household with low standard of living (90.2 percent). The proportion of home deliveries decreases as standard of living index increases, from low standard of living index (90.2 percent) to high standard of living index (37.5 percent). Similarly, home deliveries are sharply decreased with the educational attainment of both the women and their husbands (Mother from 89.9 percent to 31.3 percent; Husband 91.4 to 53.6 percent, illiterate to higher level respectively).

Table 11. Percentage Distribution of Births by Place of Delivery, According to Selected Background Conditions

Background Characteristics	*Place of Delivery*		
	Home	*Govt. hospital*	*Private hospital*
Type of place of residence			
Urban	32.5	48.0	19.3
Rural	86.5	10.0	3.5
Religion			
Hindu	84.2	10.5	5.3
Muslim	70.5	11.4	18.2
Christian	68.9	23.8	7.1
Others	78.5	17.9	3.3
Respondents Educational level			
Illiterate	89.9	7.3	2.7

Primary	76.6	18.0	5.2
Secondary	58.4	30.8	10.8
Higher	31.3	40.8	27.2
Husband's Education level			
Illiterate	91.4	6.1	2.4
Primary	83.4	12.9	3.5
Secondary	69.5	22.7	7.8
Higher	53.6	30.9	15.3
Household Standard of Living Index			
Low	90.2	7.6	2.0
Medium	73.3	19.7	7.0
High	37.5	39.0	23.1
Total	78.4	15.7	5.8

The multivariate analysis results shows that urban tribal mothers are performed much better (700 percent) than rural women with respect to the safe delivery (delivery attended at institution). The mother's educational attainment also registered the correlation with respect to institutional deliveries. The attainment of secondary level and Higher level of education have a influence on institutional deliveries (25 and 500 percent).

Postnatal Care

Postnatal care has a stronger element of hospital level care relative to antenatal care that is more focused on information and other basic services. Treatment of complications that might have occurred during the delivery, severe health conditions of the new born, etc. are some of the postnatal care services that require skilled personnel and hospital facilities. The postnatal care services provided at the community level include counselling on family planning, breast feeding practices, nutrition, management of neo-natal hypothermia, early detection of postpartum complications and referral for such problems. The higher-level health care facilities are intended to provide these services as well as take care of post delivery complications.

Just fifteen percent of the home births were followed by a visit to doctor within two months of delivery. Among these births, one-third took a postpartum check-up within two days and two-third took place within a week.

Table 12. Percentage Distribution of Tribal Women by Place of Delivery

Postpartum Check-ups	*Scheduled Tribe*
Saw doctor within 2 months of birth	
No	85.3
Yes	14.7
Within two days	33.4
Within one week	66.0
Components of Postpartum check-ups	
Abdomen examined	
No	70.7
Yes	29.3
Family planning advice	
No	86.7
Yes	13.3
Breastfeeding advice	
No	88.0
Yes	12.0
Baby care advice	
No	76.0
Yes	24.0

Further the mothers who went for postpartum check-up asked whether they had received specific components of postpartum care. Twenty-nine percent of mother reported that their abdomen was examined at the time of postpartum check-up. About one-fourth of them received advice on baby care and family planning and breastfeeding advices were given at the time of postpartum check-up was very poor.

Conclusion

The health of the mother and new born infant constitutes one of the most serious health problems affecting the tribal community. To improve this problem maternal and child health services have seen a spectrum of changes dating from antiquity to the most recent development of reproductive and child health programme.

In India, maternal and child health care is an important component of the public health system. Government hospitals and primary health centres provide free antenatal and delivery services. Besides, paramedical professionals, usually female health workers, provide extension services. They visit houses, identify pregnant women, and provide antenatal, delivery, and post-natal services at home to the extent possible.

However, the use of health services is a complex behavioural phenomenon. It is related to the organization of the health-delivery system and is affected by the availability, quality, costs, continuity and comprehensiveness of services; social structure and health beliefs also affect the use.

Despite substantial public investments in health infrastructure the supply of such services continues to be inadequate and of poor quality among the tribal communities. The high level of poverty, inadequate health resources, ignorance and high-risk beliefs and practices among the tribal communities has contributed to the vulnerability of this population. There is a general consensus that the health status of the tribal population is very poor and worst among the primitive tribes because of their isolation, remoteness and being largely unaffected by the developmental processes going on in the country.

It is well-known from the analysis that the maternal health conditions among the tribal communities, with respect to most of the indicators discussed above is quite distressing. The salient findings from the study are:

Majority of the Indian tribals (83 percent) living in the remote rural areas remain isolated, untouched by civilization, they are largely unaffected by the developmental processes going on in the rest of the Nation.

About forty percent of the tribal women did not receive any kind of antenatal care during their pregnancy episode. Only one-fifth of the tribals received the minimum number of antenatal visits (four visits) which is recommended by WHO to achieve the essential level of antenatal care.

Among the tribal communities more than half of them did not consider that the ANC to be necessary or customary. Another important reason for not receiving the ANC was the costs, distance and lack of transport.

More than three-fourth of the deliveries (78.5 percent) are took place at home in the tribal communities and more than three-forth of the deliveries among the tribal communities are attended by *Dais* (Traditional Birth Attendants) and other than health professional (44.4 percent, 32.2 percent respectively). Just fifteen percent of the home births were followed by a visit to doctor within two months of delivery. Multi variate analysis revealed a positive association of maternal care with place of residence, education of mother and her husband and their standard of living index.

As a whole, it is very clear from the above analysis that the care received at each and every stage of the pregnancy episode and at the child birth in the tribal communities are far from the national averages. Therefore, appropriate/ alternate strategies should be taken to strengthen the existing maternal care service packages to ensure a healthy mother and healthy baby at the end of each pregnancy in the tribal communities.

Policy makers, planners and care providers need to think not only the resources of the health care system, but also keep in their mind about the tribe's unique customs, values, beliefs and traditions pursuing in the maternal health practices and also their isolation, remoteness. So a "differential approach" is to be launched for tribal areas, with differential norms for establishing facilities to gear up the existing programmes to suit their specific requirements.

Tribal Women by Recommended ANC Visits (>3) and Their SED Background Conditions: Multivariate analysis

	B	*S.E.*	*Wald*	*df*	*Sig.*	*Exp(B)*	*95.0% C.I. for EXP(B)*	
							Lower	*Upper*
Rural (ref)						1.0		
Urban	1.314	.107	151.818	1	.000	3.722	3.020	4.587
Hindu(ref)			2.462	3	.482	1.0		
Muslim	.275	.370	.550	1	.458	1.316	.637	2.718
Christian	.019	.093	.040	1	.842	1.019	.849	1.223
Others(3)	.180	.130	1.926	1	.165	1.198	.928	1.546
Res Illiterate (ref)			116.066	3	.000	1.0		
Primary	.768	.109	50.097	1	.000	2.156	1.743	2.667
Secondary	1.086	.113	91.715	1	.000	2.962	2.371	3.698
Higher	1.763	.245	51.741	1	.000	5.829	3.606	9.423

	B	S.E.	Wald	df	Sig.	Exp(B)	Lower	Upper
Hus Illiterate (ref)			17.799	3	.000	1.0		
Primary	.069	.112	.380	1	.537	1.071	.861	1.334
Secondary	.325	.106	9.340	1	.002	1.384	1.124	1.705
Higher	.557	.151	13.674	1	.000	1.746	1.299	2.345
SLI low (ref)			21.921	2	.000	1.0		
Medium	.301	.085	12.610	1	.000	1.352	1.144	1.596
High	.709	.170	17.448	1	.000	2.032	1.457	2.834
Constant	-.513	.128	16.071	1	.000	.598		

Model Summary

Step	*-2 Log likelihood*	*Cox & Snell R Square*	*Nagelkerke R Square*
1	4352.450	.189	.262

Tribal Women by Place of Delivery: Multivariate Analysis

	B	*S.E.*	*Wald*	*df*	*Sig.*	*Exp(B)*	*95.0% C.I. for EXP(B)*	
							Lower	*Upper*
Rural (ref)	-				-		1.0	
Urban	2.037	.109	349.750	1	.000	7.665	6.192	9.409
Hindu (ref)			3.514	3	.319	1.0		
Muslim	.461	.435	1.125	1	.289	1.586	.676	3.722
Christian	-.155	.112	1.904	1	.168	.857	.688	1.067
Others(3)	-.136	.163	.690	1	.406	.873	.634	1.202
Res Illiterate (ref)			65.329	3	.000	1.0		
Primary	.605	.137	19.638	1	.000	1.831	1.401	2.393
Secondary	.948	.136	48.683	1	.000	2.581	1.978	3.369
Higher	1.614	.245	43.531	1	.000	5.024	3.110	8.115
Hus Illiterate (ref)			16.924	3	.001	1.0		
Primary	.281	.147	3.635	1	.057	1.325	.992	1.769
Secondary	.543	.139	15.277	1	.000	1.721	1.311	2.259
Higher	.594	.181	10.795	1	.001	1.811	1.271	2.581
SLI low (ref)			50.208	2	.000	1.0		
Medium	.533	.109	23.705	1	.000	1.704	1.375	2.112
High	1.256	.183	46.961	1	.000	3.513	2.452	5.032
Constant	-.862	.147	34.458	1	.000	.422		

Model Summary

Step	*-2 Log likelihood*	*Cox & Snell R Square*	*Nagelkerke R Square*
1	3183.421	.232	.359

NOTES

1. World Health Organization (WHO), United Nations Children's Fund (UNICEF), and United Nations Population Fund (UNFPA), Maternal Mortality in 1995: Estimates Developed by WHO, UNICEF and UNFPA (Geneva: WHO, 2001).
2. Ministry of Health and Family Welfare (MOHFW). 1997. Reproductive and Child Health Programme: Schemes for Implementation. New Delhi: Department of Family Welfare, MOHFW.
3. *Health of Tribal Population in India*; Results of Some ICMR Studies. Indian Council of Medical Research, New Delhi, p.1, 1998.
4. Kumar, R., Singh, M.M., Kaur, A., Kaur, M.: Reproductive health behaviour of rural women. *J Indian Med Assoc* 1995, 93:129-31.
5. Ministry of Health and Family Welfare (MOHFW). 1998b. Manual on Community Needs Assessment Approach in Family Welfare Programme. New Delhi: Department of Family Welfare, MOHFW.
6. Central Bureau of Health Intelligence (CBHI). 1991. *Health Information of India – 1991*. New Delhi: CBHI, Directorate General of Health Services, Ministry of Health and Family Welfare.
7. World Health Organization: *Safe Motherhood*. Online at http://www. Safe motherhood.org/init_what_is.htm. May 2005.

REFERENCES

Basu, S.K., *Health problems and health care of the tribal population of India. In: Tribal Economy, Health and Wasteland Development*. Ed. N. Mahanti, Inter-India Publications, New Delhi, p.137, 1994

Bardhan, A., Sinha, A.K., Gopinath, K. and Brahmbhatt, A.K., *A Diagnostic Study of Factors Responsible for Less or No Utilization of Health Facilities among the Bhuls of Madhya Pradesh*. PAC Report, (Mimeo), National Institute of Health and Family Welfare, New Delhi 1989.

Bhatia, H.M., Rao, V.R., *In Genetic Atlas of Indian Tribes*, ICMR Publication, Mumbai (1988).

Central Bureau of Health Intelligence (CBHI), 1991. *Health Information of India*– 1991. New Delhi: CBHI, Directorate General of Health Services, Ministry of Health and Family Welfare.

Government of India. *Scheduled Tribes, Scheduled Areas and Tribal Areas in India.* Ministry of Social Justice and Empowerment (Tribal Division), 1998.

Health of Tribal Population in India, Results of Some ICMR Studies. *Indian* Council of Medical Research, New Delhi, p. 1, 1998.

Kumar, R., Singh, M.M., Kaur, A., Kaur, M., Reproductive health behaviour of rural women. *J Indian Med Assoc* 1995, 93: pp. 129-31.

Ministry of Health and Family Welfare (MOHFW). 1997. *Reproductive and Child Health Programme: Schemes for Implementation.* New Delhi: Department of Family Welfare, MOHFW.

Ministry of Health and Family Welfare (MOHFW). 1998b. *Manual on Community Needs Assessment Approach in Family Welfare Programme.* New Delhi: Department of Family Welfare, MOHFW.

World Health Organization (WHO). *Safe Motherhood.* Online at http://www. safe motherhood.org/init_what_is.htm. May 2005.

World Health Organization (WHO), United Nations Children's Fund (UNICEF), and United Nations Population Fund (UNFPA), *Maternal Mortality in 1995: Estimates Developed by WHO, UNICEF and UNFPA* (Geneva: WHO, 2001).

2

HEALTH STATUS OF TRIBALS IN ORISSA

SOUBHAGYA RANJAN PADHI & BISWAJITA PADHY

1. Introduction

Tribal Society carries forward a heritage of distinct and diversified cultural traits for many decades. The forces of modernization have largely by passed them. Despite remarkable global development in the health, there are many tribal people living in isolated or remote places. About half of the world's indigenous people, comprising 635 tribal communities including 75 primitive tribal communities live in India. Orissa, the most scenic state in eastern India, occupies a unique place in the tribal map of the country having largest number of tribal communities (62 tribal communities including 13 primitive tribes) with a population of 8.15 million constituting 22.3% of state's population (Census of India, 2001). This constitutes 9.7 per cent of the total tribal population of the country. The state holds 3rd and 11th rank among the States/UTs in terms of ST population and the proportion of ST population to total population of the State respectively. The decennial growth of ST population has been 15.8 per cent, which is 0.5 per cent lower than the growth of population (16.3 per cent). This indigenous tribal population has chiefly concentrated in the north-western and south–western districts.

The Scheduled Tribe population in the State is overwhelmingly rural, with 94.5 per cent residing in villages.

District wise distribution of ST population shows that Malkangiri district has the highest proportion of STs (57.4 per cent) followed by Mayurbhanj (56.6 per cent), Rayagada (55.8 per cent) and Nabarangapur (55 per cent). Puri district has the lowest by proportion of STs (0.3 per cent).

Out of sixty two (62) STs, Khond is the most populous tribe with a population of 1,395,643 constituting 17.1 percent of the total ST population. Gond is the second largest tribe, having a number of 782,104, i.e. 9.6 per cent of the total ST population. Six other tribes namely, Santal, Kolha, Munda, Saora, Shabar and Bhottada along with Khond and Gond constitute 64.2 per cent of the total ST population of the State. Bhumij, Bhuiya, Oraon, Paroja and Kisan having a population ranging from 248,144 to 321,592. Together, they form 18.1 per cent. Five STs, namely, Bhumia, Binjhal, Koya etc. having population in the range of 103,537 to 196,846 constitute 9 per cent of total ST population. Remaining forty four (44) tribes along with the generic tribes constitute the residual 8.8 per cent of total ST population of the State. Five tribes namely Chenchu, Mankidi, Desua Bhumij, Ghara, Tharua are very small groups having less than 500 population. (Census of India, 2001).

District wise distribution of the individual ST shows that Khond have the highest proportion (93.3 per cent) in Kandhamal district, followed by Nayagarh (76.9 per cent), Baudh (76.4 per cent) and Rayagada (71.1 per cent) districts. Gond has the highest concentration in Nabarangapur districts followed by Nuapada district whereas Santal and Kolha are primarily concentrated in Mayurbhanj district. Other four STs, Munda, Saora, Shabar and Bhottada are primarily concentrated in Sundargarh, Bargarh, Gajapati and Nabarangapur districts respectively.

Health is a perquisite for human development and is an essential component for the well being of the mankind. The health problems of any community are influenced by interplay of many social, economic, and political factors. The common beliefs, customs, practices related to health and diseases in turn influence the health seeking behaviour of the community (ICMR Studies, 1998). Recent years have witnessed a growing concern with broadening the framework for health. Optimal health has been defined as safe life, control of diseases and that the quality of existing health services required for the total well being of an individual. Presently a number of international and national initiatives have begun to focus attention on the long neglected area of tribal's health aspect. Tribal's health is probably one of the most inadequately researched areas in international public health. The health status of tribal is miserable and this is a neglected field for many years. There are wide gaps in knowledge regarding the levels, determinants and consequences of tribal's health problems in Orissa, which is one of the most underdeveloped regions of our country.

1.1 Objective

At present there is little understanding of how the broader circumstances of tribal's lives affect their ability to promote their own health. Ethical and cultural values, belief, attitudes and practices, play an important role in the health processes of tribal. In this context the present paper would like to explore various trends and determinants of morbidity and to obtain a clearer understanding of the socio-cultural and political context in which their health problem arise, how they define their health problems, manage their own as well as family's health and choose their health care options.

1.2 Method

The study is conducted using a combination of qualitative and quantitative methods. The information is collected from health records of tribals maintained by various health workers, government officials and social workers of the area who have expertise and first hand knowledge in the field. Besides this, data is also collected from official records, census materials and other precious published materials.

2. Some Critical Issues in Understanding Health

In the study of health the most perplexing and ambiguous issue has been its definition. However the most widely accepted definition is what is stated in the Constitution of World Health Organization, which defines health as a "state of complete physical, mental and social well-being and not merely the absence of disease or infirmity". In a broader perspective health refers to the promotion of social and related services and prevention of the barriers for the realization and maintenance of one's physical, mental and social well-being. The challenges of securing tribal's health direct attention not simply to physical and mental health services, but to the justice of the foundations upon which societies function.

The broader perspective of health prescribe for giving attention to the full range of human rights that go beyond the provision of medical, nursing and related health services and to contribute in different ways and at different levels to the achievement and maintenance of health. (Cook, 2004). Therefore the rights relevant to the promotion and protection of tribal's health include:

- The right of tribals to be free from all types of discriminations.
- The right with regard to survival and safety.
- The right to information and education.
- The right regarding tribal's empowerment, including right to freedom of thought and the right to political participation.
- The right to health care and the benefits of scientific progress.

The familiar WHO concept that health is determined by reference to "physical, mental and social well-being and not merely the absence of diseases or infirmity" emphasizes the significance of social welfare of populations and not merely the medicalization of diseases. Medical science occupies a central position in health, but health is the outcome of a combination of factors – biological, genetic, environmental, political social and economic. The elements that condition a population's health go beyond physiological factors to include economic condition, literacy level, accessibility to different opportunities, exposure to the larger society, developmental processes, political and bureaucratic inventiveness. Circumstances affecting health of tribes can be analyzed through various statistical indicators and other socio-economic functioning of their community.

3. Health Indicators of Tribals

Various indicators undertaken by the World Health Organization (WHO)—can be divided into two broad approaches viz. understanding health in relation to "social indicators" such as literacy, better housing, water supply, health care facilities etc. and "health indicators" in relation to the level of health such as mortality, morbidity and disability. Nevertheless one can take some of these commonly used indicators to understand the health scenario of tribal communities.

The health problem of tribals may be dichotomized as urgent health need problems and emerging health problems. The first category includes maternal health, nutritional status, sexually transmitted diseases, malaria, IMR, MMR etc. And the other socio-demographic aspects, which contribute to health status, may be included within the second category. Thus status of women, sex ratio, literacy, marriage pattern, age at marriage, fertility and mortality etc. comes under emerging health problem.

Orissa is known to have poor health indicators in comparison with many other states of India. As far as health status of the poor tribals is concerned, it also bears the dubious distinction of being among the more iniquitous states of our country. This underscores the fact that there is a tremendous burden of morbidity and mortality, which is borne almost largely by the tribals.

Efforts have been made to collect available literature on the health studies among different tribal in the light of several health indicators i.e. Sex ratio, female literacy, marriage practices, age at marriage, fertility, mortality, life expectancy at birth, nutritional status and health, child bearing and maternal mortality, maternal and child health care practices, family welfare programme, sexually transmitted diseases and genetic disorders. However, it may be mentioned that health related information on tribals in particular found to be limited, most of the available studies fragmentary in nature without an adequate sample size and standard methodology. Nevertheless the research findings of few available studies are discussed in the context of following parameters:

3.1 Fertility and Mortality

Studies on fertility and mortality trends among the tribal population of Orissa have been observed to be very inadequate. However Fertility and mortality among tribal groups of Orissa is very high and attributed to the low level of education, low income, lack of knowledge of family planning method and poor medical facilities, lack of proper sanitation and drinking water.

3.1.1 Mortality

Basu and Kshatriya (1993) studied the mortality trends among the Dudh Kharia of Sunderagarh district Orissa. They reported that the estimated crude death rate is very high i.e. 11.80 per thousand as against National average of 9.8 per thousand. The crude death rate (per 1000 population) is of 19.2 in Bondo, 23.7 in Didayi, 21.2 in Juang and 20.9 in Kondha population. These demographic data showed higher values than the Indian national population level. The life expectancy at birth in Juang tribe of Orissa is only 35.9 years (Roy and Rath: 1991). The life expectancy rate is 48.7 years in Bondo, and 50.7 years in Kondh. (RMRC, Bhubaneswar). However, Kharia's life expectancy based on q5 values is 52.03 years which is comparable tc (58.6) Indian National population (Census of India, 1991).

3.1.2 Fertility

Roy & Rath (1991) studied the fertility pattern of Juangs of Orissa. It was observed that the marital age specific fertility rate was highest (3.36%) among mothers in the 20-24 year age group whereas it was lowest (0.44%) among the 45-49 year age group. The total marital age-specific fertility rate was 1.157 among the Juang mothers. It was also observed that the Index of Overall Fertility and the Index of Marital Fertility among the Juangs were 0.49 and 0.50 respectively. Basu and Jindal (1990) made an in-depth study of a primitive tribal group i.e. Kuttiya Kondhs of Phulbani district, Orissa. The average age at menarche among Kuttiyas was found to be 14.5 years. There is a prevalence of early marriage among them and it is also observed that the average number of pregnancies per mother is 5.09 and 3.89 among mothers of completed and incomplete reproductive life cycles respectively. The fertility record of Kuttiya Kondh mothers in various age groups indicated a total fertility of 5.0 estimated from the average fertility of the women. Basu and Kshatriya (1993) studied the fertility trends among the Dudh Kharia of Sunderagarh district Orissa. They reported that the estimated total fertility, and crude birth rate are 5.39 and 38.5 (per thousand) respectively. These demographic features show higher values than the general population of Orissa. The crude birth rate (per 1000 population) is 18.31 in Bondo, 24.3 in Didayi, 22.3 in Juang and 21.6 in Kondha. The population growth rate of 2.67 percent for the Kharias is much higher than Indian National population which stands at 2.05 percent and is closer to the growth rate of Scheduled Tribes of India recorded as 2.57 percent. Satish Kumar (1993) reported that the average pregnancies per mother among the Desia Kondhs of Orissa are 3.89. Khan (1993) while investigating the Dongria Kondhs of Orissa found average pregnancies per mother as 4.07.

3.1.3 Infant Mortality Rate (IMR)

IMR is a key indicator of health reflects the combined effects of economic development, health interventions, technological change and the socio-cultural environment. It refers to the death of infants (below the age of one year) per 1000 live births per year. Orissa has the dubious record of highest IMR i.e. 96 in comparison to 68 of the country in 2000. (Orissa HDR- 2004). It is 91 in 2001 and 87 in 2002 (Orissa Human Development Report, 2004). IMR among tribal groups of Orissa is very high and attributed to the low level of education, low income, lack of knowledge of health services, poor medical facilities, lack of proper sanitation and drinking water.

Respiratory infection, pre-maturity, anaemia, diarrhoea, birth injury, Pneumonia, malnutrition, fever and other diseases are some of the important causes of IMR among the tribes of Orissa. With all these, malaria has been one of the additional reasons for high IMR among tribals. Pregnant women are more susceptible to malaria than others. Malaria in pregnancy can cause abortions, pre-term delivery, still births and low birth-weight babies and leads to infant deaths.

The IMR of the tribal population in Orissa is worse than the national average. Under five mortality rates among them are 126.6. There is a high prevalence of infant mortality among specific tribal groups in Orissa, i.e. 102.4 per thousand live birth found among the Dudh Kharia of Sunderagarh district, Orissa, as against 80 per thousand live births for Indian National population. (Basu and Kshatriya, 1993). Infant mortality is observed to be very high i.e. 179.75/1000 among Kuttiya Kondh of Phulbani district, Orissa (Basu and Jindal, 1990). Infant mortality rate among the Desia Kondhs of Orissa are 151.28 (Satish Kumar, 1993) and 153.11 among Dongria Kondhs of Orissa (Khan, 1993).

IMR is 97 in 1999 in Koraput district, and most of the deaths are found among tribals. However data on IMR among the tribes of Orissa are not comparable because these studies are conducted in different years. One can also find that tribal population living in a particular district also shows variation in IMR. But it shows that the mean IMR among tribal people is much higher than the general population of state.

According to RMRC, Bhubaneswar IMR (per 1000 live birth) is 139.5 among Bondo, 131.6 in Didayi, 132.4 in Juang and 128.7 in Kutia Kondha. IMR among the Kondha is very high due to inadequate vaccination, lack of early diagnosis and prevention of diseases.

However studies on IMR among the tribal population of Orissa have been observed to be scrappy and remote. It is therefore necessary to conduct several well-designed studies at micro level among different tribal groups to understand the magnitude of the IMR in proper perspective.

3.1.4 Maternal Mortality Rate (MMR)

MMR in Orissa was 367 (per 100,000 live births) in 1998 in comparison to 407 of the country (Orissa HDR – 2004). The maternal mortality rates are also very high among the tribes of Orissa. A study carried out by RMRC, Bhubaneswar among four primitive tribes of Orissa revealed that maternal mortality rate (per 1000 female population) is 12 among

Sl. No.	Tribe's Name	Crude Birth Rate (CBR)	Crude Death Rate (CDR)	Sex Ratio	Total Fertility Rate (TFR)	General Fertility Rate (GFR)	Infant Mortality Rate (IMR)	Authors
1	Santal	3.6	13	1019	4.6	-	127	Kshatriya(1999)
2	Konds	-	-	-	3.6	-	105.5	Sharma(1979)
3	Kutia Konds	-	-	-	5.03	-	179.7	Chetlapalli(1999)
4	Dudh Kharia	38.5	11.8	1098	5.39	164	102.4	Kshatriya &Basu (1987)
5	Desia Kondh	-	-	-	3.89	-	151.28	Chetlapalli(1993)
6	Dongaria Kondh	-	-	-	3.87	-	153.11	Khan(1993)
7	Mirdha	-	-	-	3.14	-	116	Choudhury(1994)

Bondo, 10.9 in Didayi, 11.4 among juang and 11.2 among kondha tribe. The unhygienic and primitive practices of giving birth to a child are responsible for high maternal mortality. It is observed that among Kutia Kondhas the delivery is conducted by the mother herself in a half squatting position holding a rope tied down from the roof of the house. This helped her in applying pressure to deliver the child. In complicated labour cases, it might lead to maternal as well as child mortality.

3.3 Diseases

3.3.1 Malaria

Malaria is one of the major health problems of the rural and tribal communities of Orissa, causing 23% of malaria cases, 40% of Plasmodium falciparum cases and 50% of malaria deaths in the country. More than 60% of tribal population of Orissa lives in high-risk areas for malaria. It is observed that the undivided Koraput district is endemic for malaria and is hyper endemic in top hills where Bondo primitive tribes are residing. A prospective study conducted by RMRC, Bhubaneswar during 2000-2003 in Malkangiri, Kandhamala and Keonjhar districts, showed slide positive rate (SPR) is 14.2% in Bondo, 14.4% in Didayi, 10.5% in Kondha and 9.5% in Juang tribes.

In some of the tribal dominated districts like Koraput, 92,566 malaria positive cases are found between 2002 to July 2006. During this period 126 have died due to malaria. In Kalahandi district 10,19,533 positive cases are found between 2002 to August 2006. During this period 26 have died due to malaria. In Reygada district 1,28,203 malaria positive cases are found between 2002 to July 2006. During this period 61 have died due to malaria. In Malkanagiri district 81,050 malaria positive cases are found between 2002 to July 2006. During this period 120 have died due to malaria. In Nabrangpur district 95,421 malaria positive cases are found between 2002 to July 2006. During this period 35 have died due to malaria. In Nuapada district 1,26,075 malaria positive cases are found between 2002 to July 2006. During this period 38 have died due to malaria. In Kandhamala district 1,49,704 malaria positive cases are found between 2002 to August 2006. During this period 111 have died due to malaria. In Boudha district 16,423 malaria positive cases are found between 2002 to May 2006. During this period 60 have died due to malaria (DHARITRY, Local News Daily). The number of death due to malaria found by government departments in fact is very less than the actual death. Most of the people died in malaria are tribals in these districts. Because of communication problem, the health department even can not reach many areas of these districts to prevent malaria and create awareness against malaria. It is observed that due to the unavailability of health workers and doctors, tribals are not getting information and necessary help to prevent malaria.

3.3.2 Prevalence of HIV-AIDS

The deadly HIV/AIDS diseases are rapidly spreading among tribals, due to their lack of awareness. The State AIDS Cell (SAC) observe that there are 4,193 HIV positive cases in Orissa. The killer AIDS is slowly taking in its grip in the state. One can imagine that the unofficial and unreported HIV-AIDS must be much more than this. Even the surveys conducted by voluntary organizations reveal that the number is a lot more than what is mentioned in the government records.

Knowledge of HIV/AIDS and of STIs among tribals is very low and the safe sex is not practiced. As elsewhere in India, it is poor and marginalized tribal people, especially tribal women are most vulnerable to this hazardous epidemic.

With lower literacy rate among most of the tribal, the risk of HIV has increased. Most of tribals practice polygamous marriages, which also increase the risk of HIV- AIDS and other infections. Furthermore virginity is not very much valued in their society. Many of the tribal communities are slack towards pre marital and post marital sex relations. This brings many infections and sometimes causes HIV- AIDS. Along with the cultural practices there are some other factors like lack of HIV- AIDS awareness, less access to contraceptive, migration of tribals from their native place and engage in unsafe sexual practices, dearth of modern health facility, absence of other supporting agencies etc. also causes HIV among tribals.

Government health centres provide low quality of service. Lack of basic infrastructural facilities, absence of qualified doctors and non-availability of essential instruments and lab-testing facilities, disposable injections and others are also responsible for the spread of HIV. No wonder that tribals like to access the services of quacks (*Disari*) and traditional birth attendants (TBA) for all their health problems, which cannot prevent but spread HIV/AIDS.

Government has not provided the Anti-retroviral Therapy (ART) facility for the AIDS infected people of tribal districts of KBK region. The only Art centre for southern Orissa is located at Berhampur but the centre is not easily accessible by the poor tribals as it is situated at a far distance place from their locality. Though treatment is provided free of cost, most of the HIV positive and AIDS infected tribals can not afford the transportation charges to Berhampur. An ART centre needs to be set up at each district headquarters.

Anti-retroviral (ARVs) significantly slow downs the progress from infection to disease. But it is provided by government only to states in which there is a high prevalence of HIV. Whatever drugs are there for the prevention of HIV-AIDS are only available at district headquarters. One of the key high-risk group i.e. mobile tribal labourers is not showing their interest for travelling to district headquarters hospital to pick up these drugs. Because this means losing one day's wages, paying for the travel up and down and food. There is an urgent need of availability of these drugs at the block and village level.

The Voluntary Confidential Counselling Testing Centre (VCTC) although exist at district headquarters hospital, still that is not adequate enough for the treatment of HIV-AIDS patient. The infrastructure and facilities at this centre should increase for the better prevention of HIV-AIDS at tribal region. The state government should extend testing and treatment facilities at all the public Health centres. Often the district AIDs cell does not receive adequate funds to treat the HIV patients. Government should provide adequate funds for combating AIDS among the tribals.

3.3.3 Other Diseases

The upper respiratory tract infection was more commonly prevalent 14.9% in Bondo, 16.6% in Didayi, 13.6% in Kondha and 8.3% in Juang. The prevalence of genetic disorders like sickle cell haemoglobin plays important role in the health status of many tribal populations (Kshatriya, 1992). As they sleep on untidy floors and do not regularly wash their bodies most of them suffer from various types of skin diseases like ringworm, eczema, scabies etc. Apart from this fever, swelling of body, hook-worm infection, round worm infection, dysentery, jaundice, goitre, syphilis, tuberculosis and conjunctivitis are also frequently found among the tribals.

3.4 Sex Ratio

Sex ratio (females per thousand males) measures the balance between males and females in human population. Large imbalances in this aspect affect the social, economic and community life in many ways. The sex ratio is an indicator of the sex differential in mortality. A higher or lower sex ratio reflects the status of the socio-cultural, maternal and child health care programmes existing in the population.

The sex composition of the population in India is found to be favourable to males. Female disadvantage in mortality attributed as the cause for the low sex ratio (F/M over the last 30 year i.e. 941 (1961), 930 (1971), 935 (1981), 927 (1991).

As compared to the general population, there appears to be a more even distribution of males and females among the Scheduled Tribes in India i.e. 987 (1961), 982 (1971), 983 (1981), 972 (1991), 978(2001). This suggests that the preference of male child over female child does not exist in the tribal society. The social and cultural values of tribal society also give equal importance to female child. However, it may he pointed out that their sex ratio (972) in 1991 census shows a definite decline when compared to the 1981 census figure of 983.

The sex ratio of the Scheduled Tribes varied within the country. Among the States it was highest in Orissa (1003) and lowest in Uttar Pradesh/Sikkim (914); among the Union

Territories, it was highest in Dadra and Nagar Haveli (1022) and lowest in Daman and Diu (931).

Statement -1: Sex Ratio

Age Group	*All STs (India)*	*All STs (Orissa)*	*Khond*	*Shabar*	*Saora*	*Gond*	*Bhottada*	*Kolha*	*Munda*	*Santal*
All ages	978	1003	1027	1008	1007	1005	993	990	982	976
0-6 yrs	973	979	990	982	971	980	998	973	974	955

It shows the preponderance of females and is higher than the national average (978) for all STs. At individual tribe level, almost the major tribes of the state have over all sex ratio higher than that of the national average. Females outnumber the males among Khond, Shabar, Saora and Gond tribes. The sex ratio among the STs, in the age group 0-6 years (979) is slightly higher than that of all STs at the national level.

While conducting health related studies by the scholars among the individual tribal population groups, the sex ratio was found to exhibit a variable picture. According to 1991 census, Kutia Kondhs, a primitive tribal group of Phulbani district, Orissa, had a low sex ratio of 920 females per thousand males as compared to the Scheduled Tribes of India (972) (Basu, Kshatriya, 1990). This indicated a prevalence of female deaths among the Kutia Kondhs. One of the ascribed social reasons for this sex difference was the utter neglect and apathy towards proper rearing of the female children among them.

Although higher sex ratio indicating a comparatively better status among the tribal women, in recent days because of the interaction of tribal society with the broad society, the preference of male child and negligence of girl child is also frequently increasing among tribals. As a result the sex ratio is gradually decreasing in tribal society.

3.5 Maternal and Child Health Care

In tribal society women get health catastrophe due to

nutritional deficiency. Because of this nutritional paucity anaemia is frequently found among the tribal women. U.N report states that in developing countries half of the non-pregnant and two thirds of the pregnant women are anaemic. According to Health and Family Welfare Department, Govt. of India, 64.9 per 1000 women in tribal population of Orissa suffers from anaemia. But unlike their counterparts of larger society tribal women work very hard within and outside household and as a result anaemia has a harmful effect on their psychological and physical health. It lowers their resistance to fatigue, reduce working capacity and increases vulnerability to other diseases. The nutritional insufficiency directly influences the productive performance of tribal women and the birth weight of their children.

High incidences of nutritional deficiencies are found in various research studies. Prevalence of malnutrition is observed among some of the primitive tribes in Phulbani, Sundergarh and Koraput districts. (Ali, 1980; Basu, 1993; Mahapatra and Das, 1990). Bonda, one of the most primitive and backward tribe of Malkangiri district of Orissa also fight with malnutrition for their survival (Haque, 1990). It has observed that ecological imbalance caused by shifting cultivation, extensive deforestation that resulted not only in declining food resources but also in prolonged drought, causes hunger and malnourishment. Foods contain protein, iron, vitamins and calcium are lacking in the diet of tribal women. Average calorie consumption is found to be below than the recommended level for normal and pregnant women.

Anaemia is also found to be very common to tribal children. ICMR bulletin shows that malnutrition, and other diseases like goitre, Sickle cell, intestinal problem etc. highly prevails among children of tribal people. Anaemia in children is 79.8, acute respiratory infection is 22.4, and children with diarrhoea are 21.1 (Health and Family Welfare Department, Govt. of India, 2003).

Most of the primitive tribes of Orissa viz. Bondo, Didayi, Kondha and juang had different grades of anaemia. The severe anaemia (Hb<7g/dl) ranged from 0.6 to 2.3%, moderate (Hb7-9g/dl) from 7.4 to 13.6% and mild (Hb9-11g/dl) from 30.7 to 48.2% of population. Anaemia was more frequently found among women than men. A study conducted by RMRC in 1999-2000, reported 85% of Paudi Bhuyan primitive tribes of Sundergarh district to be suffering from different grades of anaemia. Most of these studies explored a positive connection between hookworm infection and anaemia.

3.6 Reproductive Health

The tribal women of Orissa form a salient and often invisible group, making-up a significant strata of society, performing most of the economic activities, producing and rearing their children; but most of them remain out of reach of even the most basic health care. Women internalized this suffering and discomfort emanating from their reproductive and sexual roles and various socio-cultural stigma attached to it is perceived as a way of life of tribal women.

Reproductive health has been defined as safe motherhood, child survival, maternal well-being and child's development to it's full potential, family planning, absence of unwanted pregnancy, control of sexually transmitted diseases and provision of better health services. The broader implications of sexual and reproductive health approach centres on people and their well-being.

There is a wide intra district variation in reproductive health index (RHI) values. 13 districts in Orissa have RHI values less than the state average. It is obvious that the less aware, primitive and illiterate tribal communities have a very low RHI values. Reproductive health cares, though the most essential of every family, yet it is not given the serious attention it deserves. Taboos, misconceptions, misunderstanding, and misbelieves are found more among tribals in relation to reproductive health than any other diseases.

In the hilly and forest tribal areas the health infrastructure facility are either nonexistent or inadequate. Even though health facilities are available in some tribal areas the cultural taboos put obstacle for availing those facilities. Due to this there is an extremely high rate of infant and maternal mortality found in tribal society. 90% of deliveries are conducted non-institutionally by traditional birth attendants (TBA). Because of illiteracy and availability of TBA and DISHARIES (tribal priest) at the doorstep of the villagers, they recognize them as the health catalyst and health service provider. Lack of awareness leads to risk of early pregnancy, complications in pregnancy, reproductive tract infections, contraceptive side effects etc. among them.

3.7 *Marriage Practices*

The cultural ethics that mostly influence women's health are attitudes towards marriage, marriage practices, age at marriage, values attached to fertility and sex of the child and the pattern of family organization. (Kshatriya, 1992). All these determine her placc in the family, her access to medical care, education, nutrition and other health resources.

Tribal community does not confer much weight to the regulation of sex life. Many of the tribal societies were lax towards pre-marital sex relations, which were considered as training in the art of love and sex life and often ended in marriage (Vidyarthi and Rai, 1977). The socio-cultural values determine the age at which a girl is given in marriage. In tribal communities girls (*Dhangidi*) marry at a very early age. Girls in tribal societies were given in marriage generally after puberty. The mean age at marriage of the tribal females in Orissa is less than 15 years.

There were a few micro-level studies, which dealt with the age at marriage of individual tribes like Santhals is below 18 years (Basu, 1993). Most of the primitive tribals have the mean age at marriage below 14 years. The mean age at marriage of Koraput, one of the tribal district of Orissa is 17.1 years and teenage pregnancy is common. Poverty, communicable diseases, low food availability and hard physical labour by women have combined to produce high rates of maternal malnutrition and low birth weight.

It was further observed from research investigations that the frequency of abortions, miscarriages, and stillbirths were found to be much higher in younger mothers below the age of 18 years. The major life threatening complications for very young mothers during pregnancy are high blood pressure, anaemia and difficulty in delivery.

3.8 Lack of Accessibility to Health Care

The poor tribal people are unable to afford and access hospitalization even when it is required. The per capita public health expenditure in tribal communities is awfully low. In comparison to the general mass, tribals are less exposed to various immunization programmes. Similarly very less percentage of them receives antenatal care from a medically trained person. Untrained women of their community mostly conduct the delivery of tribal mother at home. All these factors elevate many health problems for them.

3.9 Dilemma Between Modern and Ethnic Medicine

Health, sickness and their indigenous methods of treatment are all deeply rooted in the cultural history of tribal people. Tribal communities in Orissa and even other parts of the country still depend heavily on their traditional ethnic and cultural resources for preventing the problems of health. In tribal societies, which are hitherto observed in the realm of traditionalism, their first option is ethnic healing methods and treatment of ethnic healers for any diseases and modern medication system have not yet considered as useful for tribals.

By and large tribals reside in forest and hilly tracts, which are very isolated and inaccessible. They are reasonably secluded and relatively self-sufficient people. Their socio-economic organization is simple, homogeneous and somewhat closed. Their techno-economic base is also very remote and often below substance level. This background forces the tribals to believe that diseases are either predetermined or occur according to violation of supernatural powers. Gods, goddesses, and various spirits are approachable for the prevention of diseases only through specialist functionaries *(Disaries)* who are intermediaries between human powers and supernatural powers. This kind of belief system restricts them to avail modern medical facilities and motivates to rely on traditional medicines for their health treatments.

3.10 Environmental Sanitation and Personal Hygiene

The state of public health is measured not merely from

absence of diseases but from a variety of physical and cultural factors, which encompass the physical environment, sanitary practices, food habits and drinking facilities. The environment of tribal villages is polluted and dirty for many reasons. The village street is littered with animal dung, household rubbish, swamps of human and bovine urine. Tribals believe that the health is ensured by supernatural powers and other hygienic factors like regular bathing, washing of clothes, cleaning of head hair, washing of cloths, cutting of nails, are not regarded as essential from the point of view of good health.

Tribal people inhabiting forest and hilly areas mostly depend on natural water recourses like hilly streams, gorges, ravines etc. These sources are used for bathing of human and livestock. Dirty clothes are cleaned in these streams water. When this source of water is used for drinking purpose, it causes havoc on health condition of tribals.

3.11 *Impact of Religion and Nature*

Among a plethora of factors, impact of religion is observed as the most dominant one, responsible for the low health status of tribal. Tribal worldview is full of different benevolent and malevolent supernatural forces such as *Jogini, Devis* etc. Health is realized in great mysteries. Various diseases are attributed to supernatural or religious forces (*Dharma diseases*) and effects of ancestral deeds (*Karma diseases*) or evil spirits. This may be viewed as a built in cause of their health problem.

Witchcraft, sorcery and evil eye, have a greater impact on the health of tribals. The belief in witchcraft and magic are deeply rooted in the traditional customary ideas. Tribal system of medicines is largely magico-religious, under which the tribals subscribe to supernatural agencies through traditional healers (*Disaries*) and perform a wide variety of rituals and sacrifices in order to propitiate the angry spirits. This excessive dependence on supernatural form of treatment is primarily due to its easy accessibility and absent of other alternatives. In some areas even though health facilities are available, they consult local healers.

Tribals are strong believers of natural theory of diseases. They feel when man falls out of harmony with nature suffers from illness and becomes susceptible to diseases and accidents.

Hence various rituals are observed to restore harmony with nature. The prevention of diseases includes use of charms, amulets, animal sacrifices for the propitiation from diseases attributable to nature and evil spirits.

The religious and herbal treatment of Saora and Koya tribe for instance shows they depend more on traditional medicine system than the modern medical facility. Malaria is known as *YANANGBASUM* among the Saora and *WASA-EDEK* among the Koya. The Koya believe that the disease is caused through witchcraft, but the saora believe that it is caused by the intrusion of spirit called, *YANANGBASUM*. The Koya *Wadde* or *Shaman* (priest) nullifies the influence of witchcraft on the patient and among saora the *Kudanboi* or shamanin (priest) blows out the influence of the spirit through magico-religious rite. The Saora *Reggammar* (medicine man) prepares a therapeutic powder out of *Bahada* (Terminalia balerica), *Pippala bark* (Ficus religiosa) and *Kendu seeds* (Azadir achta indica) that the patient is supposed to take thrice daily. The Koya Shaman prepares medicine out of *Neem leaves*, seeds and *Pippali* (Piper longum) and prescribes the same to patient twice daily. These treatments often do not prevent the diseases; rather it increases the diseases and endangers their life.

3.12 Poverty

In fact, for the vast majority, the key huddles to good health are not the lack of modern medical facility but poverty. Acute poverty, a manifestation of social inequality, leads to large sections of the tribal population being denied adequate nutrition, clean drinking water and sanitation, basic education, good quality housing and a healthy local environment, which are all prerequisites for health. At the same time, we have a highly inequitable health system which denies quality health care to all those who cannot afford it. According to the Human Development report, 2004, 75% of tribals in Orissa live under poverty. Many of the poor tribals depend on forest for their livelihood. Because of growing deforestation, poor natural resources management system and change of forest rights, most of tribals are highly vulnerable to natural shock and have limited access to public services. Orissa is a food insecure state, where 57% of general population suffers from Chronic

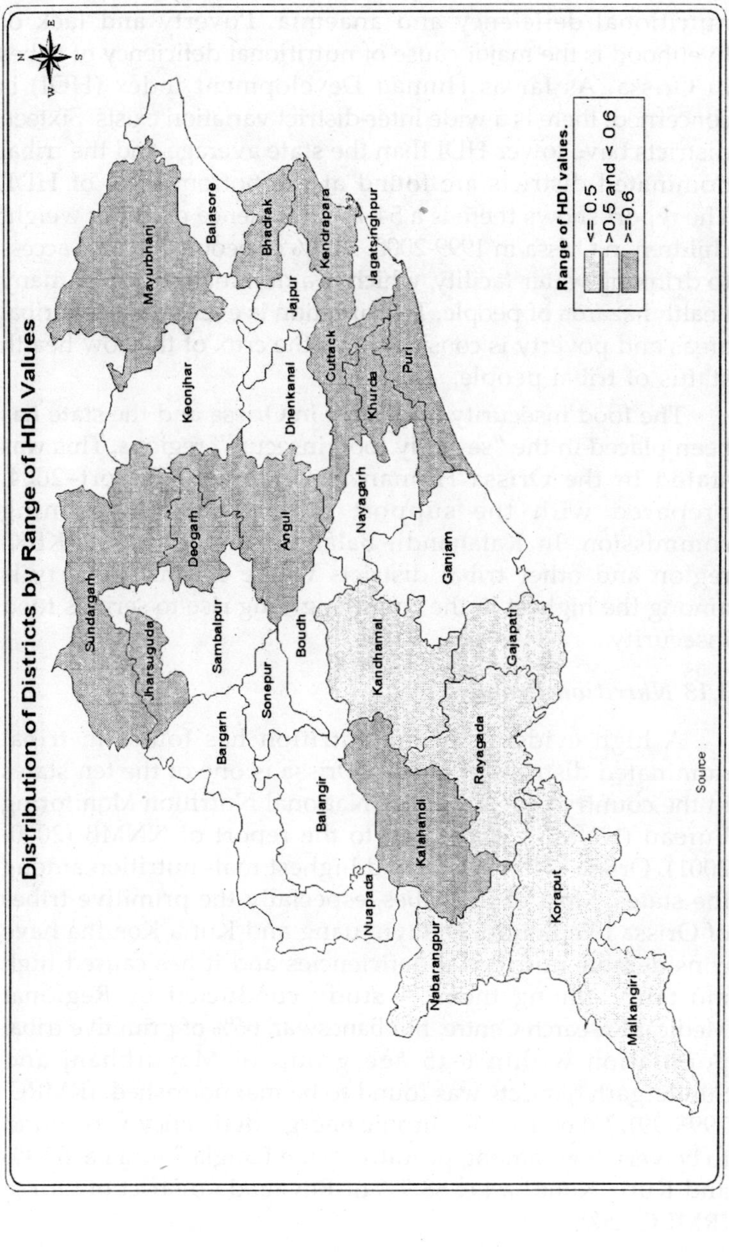
Distribution of Districts by Range of HDI Values
Range of HDI values.
<= 0.5
>0.5 and < 06
>=0.6
Mayurbhanj
Balasore
Bhadrak
Kendrapara
Jagatsinghpur
Jajpur
Keonjhar
Dhenkanal
Cuttack
Khurda
Puri
Sundargarh
Jharsuguda
Deogarh
Angul
Nayagarh
Sambalpur
Bargarh
Sonepur
Boudh
Kandhamal
Ganjam
Gajapati
Balangir
Nuapada
Kalahandi
Rayagada
Nabarangpur
Koraput
Malkangiri
Source :

Energy Deficiency (CED). Majority of tribals suffer from nutritional deficiency and anaemia. Poverty and lack of livelihood is the major cause of nutritional deficiency of tribes in Orissa. As far as Human Development Index (HDI) is concerned, there is a wide inter-district variation exists. Sixteen districts have lower HDI than the state average and the tribal dominated districts are found at the bottom level of HDI. The report shows there is a 54.4% prevalence of under weight children in Orissa in 1999-2000. 34.7% of people have no access to drinking water facility, which is a dominant cause of many health hazards of people. The situation is even worse for tribal areas and poverty is considered as the crux of this low health status of tribal people.

The food insecurity is chronic in Orissa and the state has been placed in the "severely food insecure" regions. This was stated in the Orissa Human Development Report–2004, prepared with the support of UNDP and planning commission. In Kalahandi, Balangiri and Koraput (KBK) region and other tribal districts where chronic poverty is among the highest in the country, giving rise to serious food insecurity.

3.13 Nutrition Problem

A high evidence of malnutrition has found in tribal dominated districts of Orissa. Orissa is one of the ten states in the country covered under National Nutrition Monitoring Bureau (NNMB). According to the report of NNMB (2000-2001), Orissa is having second highest mal- nutrition among the states. Most of the tribes, especially the primitive tribes of Orissa like Bondo, Didayi, Juang and Kutia Kondha have considerable nutritional deficiencies and it has caused high mortality among them. A study conducted by Regional Medical Research Centre, Bhubaneswar, 66% of primitive tribal population within 6-15 age group of Mayurbhanj and Sundergarh districts was found to be mal nourished. (RMRC: 1998-99). Likewise the chronic energy deficiency was found to be very high among primitive tribe Langia Saura i.e. 89.4% and Kutia Kondha i.e. 88.9% of Rayagada district of Orissa (RMRC: 2000-01).

Literacy Rate of Some Tribes of Orissa

Literacy rate	*All STs (Orissa)*	*Gond*	*Saora*	*Santal*	*Munda*	*Shabar*	*Khond*	*Kolha*	*Bhottada*
Persons	37.4	47.0	41.1	40.5	39.7	35.4	31.9	27.1	24.3
Females	23.4	30.8	25.7	24.7	27.6	19.9	18.0	14.3	11.1

3.14 Literacy Rate

Basic social services are now being recognized as fundamental rights. The 93rd amendment, of the constitution accepts education as a fundamental right. Education is the chief defence of a society. A poor state like Orissa need mass education on the right line to improve the health status of people. The educational level is dismal in the state of Orissa. As per 2001 census figures the rate of general literacy in Orissa is 63.61%, with male literacy being 76% and female literacy 56%. But literacy among the tribals is found to be very low i.e. 22.3 per cent and especially miserable among the tribal females (10.2 per cent). The overall literacy rate of the STs has increased from 22.3 per cent in 1991 to 37.4 per cent in 2001. Despite this improvement, the literacy rate among the tribals is considerably below the national average (47.1 per cent). Male literacy has increased from 34.4 per cent to 51.5 per cent while female literacy has gone up from 10.2 per cent in 1991 to 23.4 per cent during 1991-2001.

Among the numerically major tribes, Gond have the highest percentage of literates (47 per cent) followed by Saora, Santal, Munda, Shabar etc. Gond has also registered the highest female literacy. Bhottada have the lowest percentage of female literates, preceded by Kolha and Khond.

Among tribal literates in Orissa, 44.7 per cent are either without any educational level or have attained education below primary level. The proportions of literates who have attained education up to primary and middle levels constitute 28.7 per cent and 13.7 per cent respectively. Literates, who are educated up to matric/secondary/higher secondary etc. have a share of 11 per cent only. Graduates and above are 1.5 per cent while non-technical & technical diploma holders constitute less than half per cent (0.4 per cent).

Levels of Education Among the Major Scheduled Tribes

Name of the STs	*Literate without educational level*	*Below primary*	*Educational levels attained by major the STs*				
			Primary	*Middle*	*Matric/ Secondary Higher Secondary/ Intermediate etc.*	*Technical &Not-technical diploma etc.*	*Graduate and above*
All STs	4.4	40.3	28.7	13.7	11 0	0.4	1.5
Khond	5.8	47.7	28.2	10.4	6.9	0.2	0.8
Gond	5.4	40.4	29.4	12.8	10.3	0.4	1.3
Santal	2.6	34.6	27	17.7	14.8	0.6	2.6
Kolha	3.7	40	27.5	16	11.1	0.4	1.4
Munda	2.7	35.7	30.8	15.4	13.3	0.5	1.6
Saora	4.6	43.9	30.6	11.4	8.3	0.3	0.9
Shabar	5.1	46.2	28.6	11.2	7.8	0.3	0.8
Bhottada	9.4	47.3	27.4	9.8	5.5	0.1	0.4

Source: Office of the Registrar General, India.

The level of literacy is indisputably one of the most important indicators of social, cultural and health development among the tribal communities. Education is important for the young girl because it has correlations with the survival of her children. But despite this, the tribes of Orissa have a very low exposure to education. Most of the literates among the Scheduled Tribes were literate only up to the primary level. Literacy among tribals in general had improved slightly over time. But improvement in literacy level was still less, which adversely affect women health in tribal society. In general the tribal population, which lacks education and adequate income generating assets, suffers from nutritional deficiency and other health hazards.

3.15 Social Status

Tribal women are hard working contributing immensely to the family income by means of doing multiple domestic and income generating tasks. Although they are the backbone of their economy, they tend to neglect their health and thus suffer from adverse health consequences.

4. Promoting Right to Health: A Panacea to Improve the Health Status of Tribals

The right to basic health care is recognised internationally as a human right. The time has come to ask as to how these human rights related commitments and concerns will be translated into action in a realistic, time-bound and accountable framework.

The massive burden of morbidity and mortality suffered by the underprivileged tribals is of deep structural injustice, within and beyond the health sector. This denial needs to be addressed in human rights framework, by systematically establishing the right of every citizen of this country, to a healthy life. More specifically, health care can no longer be viewed as just a technical issue to be left to the experts and bureaucrats, an issue of charity to be dealt with by benevolent service delivering institutions, or a commodity to be sold by private doctors and hospitals. The role of all these actors needs to be redefined and recast in a framework where every person, including the most marginalized tribal people is assured of basic health care and can demand and access this as a right.

It is clear that achieving a decent standard of health for all requires a range of far reaching social, economic, environmental and health system changes. There is a need to bring about broad transformations both within and beyond the health care sector, which would ensure an adequate standard of health for all.

Given the gross inequities in access to health care and inadequate state of health services today, one important component of promoting the Right to Health would be to ensure access to appropriate and good quality health care for all. This would involve reorganization, reorientation and redistribution of health care resources on a societal scale. The responsibility of taking forward this issue seems to lie primarily with agencies working in the health sector, though efforts in this direction would surely be supported by a broad spectrum of society.

5. The Constitutional and Legal Justification of Right to Health – An Important Component of Fundamental Rights

The negative impact of Globalisation-Liberalisation and Privatization policies on various social sector services, especially since the early 1990s has been widely experienced. With the growing withdrawal of the state from the social sector and encouragement to the private medical sector, raising the issue of health rights has become extremely relevant today. The ongoing abdication of basic obligations by the Public Health system needs to be countered by a strong movement to establish Health rights. Only a determined effort to establish these rights can roll back the trend of weakening the Public health system, and can provide a framework for rejuvenation of this system with increased accountability.

The right to life is acknowledged as a fundamental right in the constitution (*Article 21*) and this right has been treated as a basis for preventing avoidable disease producing conditions and to protect health and life. It imposes an obligation on the State to safeguard the right to life of every person. ... the Government hospitals run by the State and the medical officers employed therein are duty bound to extend medical assistance for preserving human life. Failure on the part of a Government hospital to provide timely medical treatment to a person in need of such treatment results in a violation of his right to life guaranteed under Article 21.

The *directive principles of the Indian constitution* include article 47, which specifies the duty of the state in this regard: the state must raise the level of nutrition and the standard of living to improve health. It is now widely recognised that besides being a basic human right, provision of adequate health care to a population is one of the essential preconditions for sustained and equitable economic growth. Basic education, good health and other human attainments are not only directly valuable ... these capabilities can also help in generating economic success as well.

6. Suggestion to Improve the Health Conditions of Tribals

- Making the right to health care a legally enforceable

entitlement by legal enactment:

- Providing basic health services to all communities and persons; focusing on equity so as to improve the health status of poor and neglected communities and regions.
- Adopting a comprehensive strategy based on a gender perspective so as to overcome inequalities in women's access to health facilities.
- Adopting measures to identify, monitor, control and prevent the transmission of major epidemic and endemic diseases.
- Making reproductive health and family planning information and services available to all persons and couples without any form of coercion
- Availability of certain basic medications free of cost through the public health system.
- A National Essential Drug Policy ensuring the production and availability of an entire range of essential drugs at affordable prices.
- There is an urgent need for a comprehensive legislation to regulate qualification of doctors, required infrastructure, investigation and treatment procedures especially in the private medical sector.
- Maintaining complete patient records, notification of specific diseases and observing a ceiling on fees also needs to be observed by the medical sector.
- No doctor or hospital, *including those in the private sector*, can refuse minimum essential first-aid and medical care to a citizen in times of emergency, irrespective of the person's ability to pay for it.
- Our overall goal should be to move towards a system where every citizen has assured access to basic health care, irrespective of capacity to pay.
- Developing essential public health infrastructure is an important catalyst for health care. Investing sufficient resources in health and allocating these funds in a cost-effective and fair manner in tribal areas would definitely reduce the gloomy health conditions of them.

Conclusion

Right to Health Care for all is not an unrealistic scenario, but has become an imperative for a nation, which is the 'world's largest democracy' claims to accord certain basic rights to its citizens, including the right to life in its broadest sense. Health and Health Care should form one of the components of our dream for a more just and humane society. The reproductive health framework for tribal women should go beyond the narrow confines of maternal and child health and family planning to encompass all aspects of human sexuality and reproductive health needs during the various stages of women's lives and takes a life cycle approach. There is a need to explore varied information in the areas, where there are information gaps. Various studies should highlight on the ground reality experience of what works and what does not and why, in different socio-cultural contexts.

The tribal health issue unfortunately has not taken seriously. For a meaningful understanding of tribal health, it is important to understand the people themselves and their indigenous medicinal system and understand how under the social, economic, and cultural setting these needs can be best met to the satisfaction of these people.

REFERENCES

1. Ali, A. (1980), Health and genetic problems of Kutia kondhs of Bulubaru village, Phulbani district, Orissa, *The Newsletter* (Gove. Of India, Ministry of Home Affairs, Tribal Development Division, New Delhi, 1(2) 103-114.
2. Basu and Kshatriya (1993), *Demographic Features and Health Care Practices in Dudh Kharia Tribal Population of Sundergarh District Orissa.*
3. Basu, S.K. (1993), *Tribal Health in India* (Edited), Manak Publishers, New Delhi.
4. Basu, S.K., Kshatriya, G.K. (1990), Growth trends and adolescent spurts among Kutia-Kondha—A primitive tribal group of Phulbani district, Orissa. *Acta Medica Auxologica.* 22 (3): 153-164.
5. Basu, S.K. and G.K. Kshatriya (1992), *Fertility and Mortality Trends in the Dudh Kharia Tribal Population of Sundargarh District,*

Orissa, Paper presented at 18th National Conference on Human Genetics in Hyderabad.

6. Basu, S.K. and A. Jindal (1990), Genetic and socio-cultural Determinants of tribal Health: A primitive Kuttiya-Kondhs tribal group of Phulbani district, Orissa, ICMR final report, NIHFW.
7. Chaudhuri, Buddhadeb (1990), Social and environmental dimensions of tribal health, in *Cultural and Environmental Dimensions of Health* (ed. by) B. Chaudhuri, Inter-India Publications.
8. Chetlapalli (1991), Estimates of fertility and mortality in Kutia kondhs of Phulbani district, *Orissa J. Hum. Ecology*, 2 (1): 117-120.
9. Chetlapalli, Satish Kumar (1993), A study of relationship between blood group polymorphism, red blood cell enzymes and scrum proteins interactions thereof and their impact on reproductive performances among... Desia Kondh of Phulbani district of Orissa. Unpublished Ph.D. Thesis.
10. Haque, M. (1990). Height, Weight, and nutrition among the six tribes of India. (In) *Cultural and Environmental Dimensions of Health*, (eds.) Chaudhuri, B., Inter-India Publications, New Delhi, pp. 192-206.
11. Kshatriya, G. (1992). Health as parameter for women's development in National workshop on Education and women's development, National Institute of Education Planning and Administration. New Delhi.
12. Khan, Abdul Samad (1993), Genetic structure of Dongria Kondh of Koraput district of Orissa with special references to its impact of mortality and morbidity (unpublished Ph.D. thesis).
13. Mahapatra, D.K., J.Das (1990), Nuritional Ecosystems of Orissa tribal, in *Cultural and Environmental Dimension on Health* (ed.) Buddhadeb Chaudhuri.
14. Mann, K. (1987), *Tribal Women in A Changing Society*, Mittal Publications, Delhi.
15. Prema, L. and Thomas, F. (1992). Nutrition and health problems faced by Kanikkar women, in *Dimensions of Scheduled Tribes development in India*, (Eds) P.D. Tiwari and R.S. Tripathi, Uppal Publishing House, New Delhi.
16. Ray, A. and A. Rath (1991). Indian tribal's fertility patterns from Orissa, *Man in India* 1991 (special) 71(1):235-239.
17. Regional Medical Research Centre for tribal health (RMRC) (1992), *Tribal Health Bulletin*, Bhubaneswar.

18. Regional Medical Research Centre for Tribal Health (RMRC) (1998-99), *Tribal Health Bulletin*, Bhubaneswar.
19. Regional Medical Research Centre for Tribal Health (RMRC) (2000-01), *Tribal Health Bulletin*, Bhubaneswar.
20. Sharma, Krishan (1979), *The Kondhs of Orissa: An Anthropometric Study*, Concept Publishing Company, New Delhi.
21. Singh, K.S. (1988), Tribal women: An Anthropological Perspective, in *Tribal Women and Development* (eds.) Singh, Vyas and Mann, Rawat Publications, Jaipur.
22. Swain, S., S.C. Jena and P. Singh (1990), Morbidity status of the Kondha tribes of Phulbani (Orissa), in *Cultural and Environmental Dimensions on Health*, (ed.) Buddhadeb Chaudhuri), Inter-India Publications, New Delhi.
23. Vidyarthi, L.P. and Rai, B.K. (1977), *The Tribal Culture of India*, Concept Publishing Company, Delhi.
24. *ICMR Bulletin* (1998), "Health Status of Primitive Tribes of Orissa", Vol. 33, No. 10.
25. *ICMR Bulletin* (2003), "Health Status of Primitive Tribes of Orissa", Vol. 33, No. 10.
26. Cook, R.J (1994), "Women Health and Human Right", Switzerland, World Health Organization.

3

DIMENSIONS OF FEMALE TRIBAL HEALTH IN INDIA

DR. RAJESH JAISWAL

Introduction

The tribals constitute nearly eight per cent of the total population of India comprising nearly sixty eight million Scheduled Tribes as per 1991 census. There are a number of studies on the impact of acculturation on the tribal society. There are studies on the status of women relating to their food, health, etc. But these issues have not been properly focused for the tribal women. There are only a few studies on the status of tribal women in India (K. Mann, 1987; J.P. Singh, N.N. Vyas and R.S. Mann, 1988; A. Chauhan, 1990). It becomes important because the problems differ from area to area (A. Chauhan, 1990). Therefore, there is a need to understand their problems. There is a need to undertake a region-specific study of the status of tribal women which can throw up data that will make planning for their welfare more meaningful and effective (K.S. Singh, 1988).

The status of women reflects the level of social justice in the society. Women's status is primarily described in terms of their health and fertility in addition to their role within the family, the community and society (Ghosh, 1987).

A tribal woman occupies an important place in the socio-economic structure of her society. The Dhebar Commission Report (1961) mentions that the tribal women is not drudge or a beast of burden, she is found to be exercising a relatively free and firm hand in all aspects related to her social life unlike in non-tribal societies. The tribal women in general and in comparison with casts, enjoy more freedom in various walks of life. Traditional and customary tribal norms are comparatively more liberal to women.

The status of tribal women is found to be better than non-tribal women. However, their status is comparatively lower than that of tribal men. Moreover, the status of tribal women has gone from bad to worse as a result of the impact of social change which has affected the social structure of tribal society (Chauhan, 1990).

In the present paper, an attempt has been made to review the available literature on health and its correlates among tribal women, to indicate their existing health status, to identify the gaps of knowledge and to suggest a possible plan of action besides pointing out the debatable issues.

Health and its Linkages

Health is dependent on medical care, socio-cultural, economic, education, and political factors. These indicators have strong influence on health. Therefore, it is not possible to improve the health and quality of life unless efforts are made to bring about the overall change in the society. Good health and good society go together (Basu, 1992). This is possible only when services like nutrition and education are improved substantially.

The common beliefs related to health are related to the treatment of disease. It is, therefore, necessary to analyze all the cultural dimensions of the health of a community. In tribal communities, there is a fortune of folklore related to health. Documentation of this folklore available in different socio-cultural systems may be very rewarding and could provide a model for appropriate health and sanitary practices in a given eco-system. Maternal and childcare is an important aspect of health seeking behaviour, which is largely neglected among the tribal groups (Basu et al., 1990).

Health and treatment are closely interrelated with the environment, particularly the forest ecology. Many tribal groups use different parts of a plant not only for the treatment of diseases, but for population control as well (Chaudhuri,

1990). There exists a definite nexus between forests and nutrition. It has been noted by many that tribals living in remote areas have a better overall status and eat a more balanced diet than tribals living in less remote, forest free areas. The mode of utilization of available natural resources often determines the long term impact on health.

Nutritional Status and Mother's Health

The health and nutrition problems of the tribals are as varied as the tribal groups themselves. The nutritional problems of tribal communities are full of obscurities and hardly any scientific information on dietary habits and nutrition status is available. Malnutrition is common and affects the ability to resist infection, lead to chronic illness and in the post weaning period lead to permanent brain impairment. Good nutrition is a requirement throughout life and is vital to women for their health and work. Nutritional anaemia is a major problem for women especially in the rural and tribal belt. In developing countries, it is estimated that at least half of the non-pregnant and two thirds of the pregnant women are anaemic (U.N., 1984).

The situation is serious because both rural and tribal women have a heavy workload and anaemia has a profound effect on their psychological and physical health. Anaemia lowers resistance to fatigue, affects working capacity under conditions of stress and increases susceptibility to other diseases.

Maternal malnutrition which is quite common among the tribal women is also a serious health problem, especially for those having multiple pregnancies too closely spaces, and reflects the complex socio-economic factors that affects their overall situation. The nutritional status of pregnant women directly influences their reproductive performance and the birth is crucial to an infant's chances of survival and to its subsequent growth and development. Nutrition also affects location and breast feeding which are key elements in the health of infants and young children and a contributory factor in birth spacing. It is observed that among most of the tribal groups, the staple diet is rice or minor millets except the

Mompas of Assam who consumes wheat also (Basu et al. 1985). The tribals also consume birds, fish and other meat products occasionally.

Diet of not a single tribal is fully satisfactory. Tribal diets are grossly deficient in Calcium, Vitamin A, Vitamin C, riboflavin and animal protein. Diets of South Indian tribes are deficient in calories and protein. Studies carried out at the National Institute of Nutrition (1971) and Planning Commission of India (Sixth Five Year Plan, Government of India) reported a high protein calorie malnutrition along the rice-eating belts. Studies available on the dietary status and health of the Bihar and Maharashtra found deficiency calorie as well as protein and essential amino acids in their diets though major signs of nutritional deficiencies were not observed (Chitre, 1976). Surveys on the nutritional deficiencies (Gopalan, 1971) among the tribals reported a high incidence of goitre, angular stomatitis among the Mompas of Assam and Vitamin A deficiency among the Onges. A high incidence of malnutrition was observed (Ali 1980, Basu *et al*., 1990, Mahapatra and Das, 1990) in some primitive tribal groups (Haque, 1990). Studies of tribal communities in Orissa conducted by Ali (1992) found that an ecological imbalance caused by rapid deforestation had resulted not only in depleting food resources, but in prolonged droughts, adding to hunger and starvation.

Other Studies carried out among the tribal groups of Bastar district, showed the following trends (Basu *et al*., 1989, 1993).

a) The average protein calorie intake is much less in the Gond children as compared to the Bhattra and Halba children.

b) Higher frequencies of Bitot's spot, angular stomatitis and mottling of teeth are found among the Gond children as compared to the Bhattra and Halba children.

c) Muscular wasting is higher among the Gond children as compared to the Bhattra children. Consumption of milk or milk products are taboo in pre-school tribal children because milking of cow was a taboo among these groups.

The nutrition and health problems faced by Kannikar tribal

women of Trivandrum district, Kerala in normal and physiological conditions like pregnancy and lactation were studied (Prema and Thomas, 1992). Pulses, milk and milk products and other animal foods, which are the source of protein are lacking in their diets. Average calorie consumption is found to be below the recommended level for the normal, pregnant as well as lactating women. Consumption of calcium is highest in normal women, whereas it is poorest in the lactating women. Similar deficiency of calcium in the diets of pregnant and lactating tribal women of western and central India is reported by Gopaldas (1987). The intake of iron and vitamin are found to be low. Detailed clinical examination of the Kannikar tribal women showed that anaemia (90 per cent), vitamin A deficiency (30 per cent) and niacin deficiency (10 per cent) are prevalent. The morbidity status of the tribal women revealed the prevalence of pyrexia, respiratory complaints, gastro-intestinal diseases and rheumatic diseases. Among the adult women gynecological complaints and deficiency diseases are common.

Nutrition

A diet and nutrition survey of the tribal populations living in the Integrated Tribal Development project (ITDP) areas, in the States of Kerala, Tamil Nadu, Karnataka, Andhra Pradesh, Maharashtra, Gujarat, Orissa and West Bengal was done during 1985-87. A repeat survey was carried out during 1998-99 among tribal population living in the same ITDP areas to assess time trends in food and nutrient intake, nutritional status as assessed by anthropometric indices of nutritional status and prevalence of nutritional deficiency signs.

Comparison of data between the two surveys in tribal population showed that over time there has not been any improvement in the food and nutrient intake. The tribal population is more under nourished than their rural counterparts.

Table: Average Intake of Foodstuffs (g/day) Among the Tribal Population

Age group	*Cereals & Millets 1985-87*	*Cereals & Millets 1998-99*	*Pulses 1985-87*	*Pulses 1998-99*	*Food grains 1985-87*	*Food grains 1998-99*	*Decline in consumption during 1985-99 in %*
1-3 years	187	155	13	14	200	169	15.5
4-6 years	276	224	18	18	294	242	17.7
7-9 years	334	282	21	18	355	300	15.5
10-12 years	408	335	23	19	431	354	17.9
10-12 years	373	333	22	20	395	353	10.6
13-15 years	465	405	24	21	489	426	12.9
>16 years	521	518	29	23	550	541	1.6

Impact of Forest on Women's Health

The forest based tribal economy is primarily women-centred (Menon, 1987-1991). Women make provisions for basic necessities like food, fuel, medicine, housing material etc. from the forest produce. Food is obtained from shifting cultivation and from minor produce (MFP) like flowers and fruits collected from the forest. Extracts from herbs, roots and animals are used for medicine. All these efforts incur an excessive workload on women. In a study on the Garos of Meghalaya, Kar (1982) calculated the ratio of male or female investment in labour in shifting cultivation as 100:136 days per year. The contribution of women is more in almost all activities like clearing (169:120), sowing (102:60), weeding (272:182) and cotton harvesting (56:6).

Because of the extensive cutting of trees by vested interests, the distances between the villages and the forest areas had increased forcing the tribal women to cover longer distances in search of minor forest produce and firewood. A study on the Kondhs revealed (Dasgupta, 1988) that women put on an average of 14 working hours per day as compared to 9 hours by men. Given this additional workload, even women in advanced stages of pregnancy are required to work in the agricultural fields or covei more distance to collect fuel and minor forest produce. The overstrain on tribal women however, is not adequately compensated due to the non-availability of minor forest produce and reduction in food grain production. A study among the Pauri Bhuniyas of Orissa (Ali, 1980) showed that 19.0 per cent women as against 6.0 per cent men suffered from malnutrition. As a result of deforestation, additional distance and less fertile soil, the availability of food for the tribal family was reduced. This had negative implications for the housewife who is responsible for arranging the food. Studies have shown that tribals are undernourished. Another study has shown that over 55 per cent of Kondhs consumed less than 2000 calories per day (Patel, 1985) and most of them as little as 1700 calories (Sharma, 1979) compared to the ICMR recommended dose of 2400 calories a day.

In addition to malnutrition and additional workload, there is lack of access to modern medicine. This, combined with the increasing ecological imbalance, has resulted in diseases such as TB, stomach disorders and malaria (Menon, 1987).

Child Bearing and Maternal Mortality

Childbearing imposes additional health needs and problems on women, physically, psychologically and socially. The complications of pregnancy, childbirth and abortions have resulted in large numbers of female deaths (U.N. 1984). In India, the maternal mortality is quite high (UNICEF, 1983). Poor nutritional status and problems of poor body weight, poor weight gain during pregnancy, low haemoglobin levels, is one of the underlying causes of maternal mortality in India. More maternal deaths occurs in India in a week as compared to maternal deaths in entire Europe in a year. Generally malnourishment, poor medical facilities and unfavorable social conditions are the major causes for high maternal mortality in India. Nutritional anaemia, a serious problem in pregnancy, affects 50 per cent of the women of childbearing age in South East Asia. (Shiva, 1992). The situation is all the more aggravated among women in the tribal belt of India because of the prevailing magic-religious and socio-cultural practices.

Maternal mortality is reported to be high among various tribal groups but no exact data is available. The main causes of maternal mortality are found to be unhygienic and primitive practices. For example, it is observed that among the Kutia Kondhs (Basu, *et al.*, 1990), the delivery is conducted by the mother herself in a half squatting position holding a rope tied down from the roof of the hut. This helps her in applying pressure to deliver the child. In complicated labour, obviously it might lead to maternal as well as child mortality. Similar crude births practices do exist in other tribal groups too.

Health Care Practices

Maternal and child health care practices are largely neglected in various tribal groups. Expectant mothers to a large extent are not immunized against tetanus. From the inception of pregnancy to its termination, no specific nutritious diet is consumed by women. On the other hand, some pregnant tribal women (i.e., Dudh Kharias, Santals) reduce their food intake because of the fear of recurrent vomiting and also to ensure that the baby may remain small and the delivery may be easier. The consumption of iron, calcium and vitamins during pregnancy is poor. The habit of taking alcohol during pregnancy is common among the tribal women and almost all of them continue their regular activities including hard labour even during advanced pregnancy. More than 90 per cent of the deliveries are conducted at home attended by elderly ladies of the household. No specific precautions are observed at the time of conducting deliveries, which results in an increased susceptibility to various infections. Services of paramedical staff are secured only in difficult labour cases.

Maternal mortality related to pregnancy and childbirth is high among the tribal population groups of Bastar district. In addition, a lot of females suffers from ill health due to pregnancy and child-birth in the absence of health consciousness. As far as child-care is concerned, both rural and tribal illiterate mothers breast-feed their babies. But, most of them adopt harmful practices like discarding of colostrum. Giving prelacteal feeds, delayed introduction of breast feeding and delayed introduction of complementary feeds. Vaccination and immunization of infants and children are inadequate among tribal groups. In addition, extremes of magico- religious beliefs and taboos aggravate the problems.

Family Welfare Programme

While evaluating the impact of the family welfare programme on tribal women through a study of 300 tribal women of Tamian development block of Chindwara district of Madhya Pradesh, it is observed that tribal women gave more attention to child welfare and child development programmes rather than mother care or family planning programmes (Tekhre, 1989). This may be because of their inherent maternal instinct and protectiveness towards their children. They contacted doctors more for antenatal care than postnatal care because of their concern with the welfare of the foetus in the womb and preparing for a safe labour. More than 90 per cent of the eligible couples of Jaunsaris and Santals are found to be aware of family planning methods whereas only 16 per cent Dudh Kharia couples are aware of family planning methods.

Necessity of Knowledge Updating

While scanning through the available literature on the health status of the tribal women in India, it is observed that comprehensive area specific health related studies are limited, Most of the available studies are isolated, fragmentary and did not cover the various dimensions of health affecting the status of tribal women like sex-ratio, female literacy, marriage practices, age at marriage, age of mother at first conception, life expectancy at birth, etc. It has been noted that there is hardly any study on many urgent issues affecting the health status of tribal women. Detailed information is called for on maternal malnutrition, nutritional anaemia, nutritional status of pregnant women and their nature of workload, the distribution of food within the family and its effect on the nutritional status of women, the complications of pregnancy and of childbirth, maternal mortality, birth weight of children, infant and childhood mortality and their sex differentials, nature, of maternal and child health care practices, attitude towards family planning, prevalence of sexually transmitted diseases and effect of degradation of forest ecology.

Policy Implications

Tribal women in India have specific problems, some of these are built-in problems of these tribal communities and some are imposed upon them which jeopardize their overall development and progress inclusive of their health. Therefore, in order to improve the health status of the tribal women, the health care delivery should be designed for each specific tribal group in such a way to cater to their specific needs and problems by ensuring their personal involvement. The following strategies may be pursued.

Formulation of realistic development health plans based on needs as felt by tribal women of the specific tribal groups.

- Need for promoting nutritional and health education among working, lactation and pregnant tribal women.
- Healthy nutrition should be encouraged through local produce and local recipes. The tribal women themselves needs should solve Nutritional through better utilization of their locally available cheap nutritious food.
- Development of poultry and fisheries need to be encouraged.
- The local tribal women should impart health education with guidelines provided by health functionaries.
- The nutritional and health status of pregnant tribal women need to be improved by adequate intake of nutritious diet, including iron and minerals and also by hundred percent Immunization.
- Tribal women in their advanced stage of pregnancy should be advised to reduce their workload and take adequate rest.
- The habit of taking alcohol and drugs during pregnancy should be discouraged.
- The children should be properly immunized, the harmful practices of discarding colostrum, delayed initiation of breastfeeding an complementary feeds should be discarded and health education aspects should be properly explained to tribal women.
- Tribal girls should be properly trained as "*dais*"/nurses.

Specific precautions need to be observed at the time of conducting deliveries at home, aseptic conditions need to be followed for cutting the umbilical cord.

- Primitive practices are to be discarded and necessary health education should and tribal nurses should impart necessary health education.
- Tribal nurses or "*dais*" should properly explain maintenance of personal hygiene in connection with childbirth, abortion or menstruation in order to prevent the infections of the female genital tract.
- Periodic examination of tribal women by qualified technicians of primary health centre should be carried out to detect the presence of sexually transmitted diseases, if any.
- The staff of the Primary Health Centre should be properly trained to detect the presence of two commonly prevalent genetic disorders i.e. sickle cell and Glucose-6-Phosphate Dehydrogenates Enzyme Deficiency (G-6-PD). Identified tribals (male and female) can be tattooed with dot marks.
- A Genetic Health Card needs to be maintained for each tribal family where vital information like blood group status, haemoglobin level, presence/absence of genetic disorders will be mentioned.

REFERENCES

1. Ali, A. (1992) *Nutrition [In] State of India's Health* [ed. Alok Mukhopadhyay]. Voluntary Health Assoc of India. New Delhi.
2. Baryam, S., (1982). Biodemographic factors associated with offspring morality among the Jahongs of Meghalaya, *J. Ind. Anthropol. Soc.*, 17(2): 143-146.
3. Basu and Kshatriya (1993), *Demographic features and health care practices in Dudh Kharia Tribal Population of Sundergarh district Orissa* [communicated].
4. Basu, S.K. (1993), Study on fertility and mortality trends among the tribal population of India—A review, Monograph ICSSR (in press).
5. Census of India (1991), *Paper-1 of 1992: Final Population Totals*, Registrar General and Census Commissioner of India, New Delhi.

6. Chaudhuri, Buddhadeb (1990), Social and environmental dimensions of tribal health (In) *Cultural and Environmental Dimensions of Health* (ed. by) B. Chaudhuri, Inter-India Publications.
7. Chauhan, Abha (1990), *Tribal Women and Social Change in India*, A.C. Brothers, Etawah.
8. Chetlapalli Satish Kumar (1993), A study of relationship between blood group polymorphism, red blood cell enzymes and scrum proteins interactions thereof and their impact on reproductive performances among Desia Kondh of Phulbani district of Orissa. unpublished Ph.D. Thesis.
9. Datta, U. (1990), Demographic investigation among the Koras of Midnapur district, West Bengal Ph.D. Thesis (unpublished).
10. Gopalan, C. (1971). *Nutritional Atlas of India*. ICMR, New Delhi.
11. Gurumurthy, G., Naidu, V. Nagraja (1990), Demographic and health determinants of infant death among Sugalis—a study of community of Andhra Pradesh. In National Seminar on Population Programme Towards 2001, Vol. II, 23-25 Aug 1990, 8 pp centre for population studies, Annamalai University. Annamalai Nagar.
12. Khan, Abdul Samad (1993), Genetic structure of Dongria Kondh of Koraput district of Orissa with special references to its impact of mortality and morbidity (unpublished Ph.D. thesis).
13. Menon, Geeta (1991), Ecological transitions and the changing context of women's work in tribal India. *PURUSARTHA, 14* pp. 291-314.
14. Pandey, A.K. (1990), Ecology and Tribal Demography: A comparative study of Idu and Digaru Mishmis of Arunachal Pradesh, Ph.D. Thesis, Delhi University.
15. Parsuraman, S. and S. Rajan (1990), On the estimation of vital rates among the Scheduled Tribes in Western India. In: *Demography of Tribal Development* (eds. A. Bose, U.P. Sinha and R.P. Tyagi).
16. Prema, L and Thomas, F. (1992). Nutrition and health problems faced by Kanikkar women, (In) *Dimensions of Scheduled Tribes development in India* (eds P.D. Tiwari and R.S. Tripathi), Uppal Publishing House, New Delhi.
17. Regional Medical Research Centre for Tribal Health (ICMR) (1992), *Tribal Health Bulletin*, Vol. 1, No. 4, Jabalpur.
18. Sinha, U.P. (1990), Demographic profile of tribal population in India, in *Demography of Tribal Development* (eds. Bose et *al.)* B.R. Publishing Corporation, Delhi.

4

ORAL-STORY NARRATIVES: A TRIBAL AND ETHNIC RESPONSE TO EPIDEMICS IN TIBET AND YI OF CHINA

DR. SHUGUANG WANG

1. Introduction

By the end of 2003, Over 650,000 HIV/AIDS cases had been publicly reported in China (Gao, 2003; UNAIDS/WHO, 2004). Epidemiologist estimates the true figure for these figures have since been overtaken, also that the actual incidence is very much higher (Mao, 2006). The five Provinces of Yunnan, Sichuan, Henan, Xinjiang, and Guangxi have been especially hard hit with HIV/AIDS (Ministry of Public Health of China, 1999; UNCHINA, 1999, UNAIDS/WHO, 2004). Except for Henan, the other four regions are major traditional residential areas for most of the Chinese ethnic minorities. The HIV/AIDS epidemic in these regions has therefore had a significant impact upon ethnic minorities.

China has fifty-six officially recognised ethnic minorities, ranging in size from several thousands up to over five million, accounting for about 10% of the nation's population of presently 1.3 billion people (Zhang, 2001). Yunnan, Sichuan, Xinjiang and Guanxi, with over 25 minority groups, have the highest reported HIV-rate in China (UNAIDS/WHO, 2002; UNCHINA, 1999; Wubuli, A-li, Ma, & Hai, 2002; Mao, Re, Zheng, Pan, Liu & Wang, 2002). Epidemiological evidence (Sichuan Centre of Disease Control, 2001) has indicated that HIV prevalence among the Yi ethnic community of Sichuan and Jinpou, Dai and Lahu ethnic and tribal groups in Yunnan are the highest compared with all other cultural and socio-demographic groups in two provinces China. The potential epidemics are also impacting upon the other ethnic groups and those majority Han people who are living in Yi and Tibetan communities in Sichuan, Yunnan and Tibet Autonomous Region (TAR) (Keats & Wang, 2002; Gong, Cheng, Li, Jian, Han, & Feng, 2003). Studies by Luo & Wu (1996) among members of the Naxi ethnic group in Sichuan, by Luo, Wu, & Chen (1999) among the Naxi, Dai and Han cultural groups in Sichuan and Yunnan, and by Wang & Zhao (2002) among the A-Ba Tibetan group in Sichuan have all shown that the prevalence of reproductive transmitted infections/sexually transmitted infections (RTIs/STIs) was generally higher in the ethnic minority groups than in the majority Han people living in the same local areas. Furthermore, STIs and potential HIV threaten the broad home provinces of the Tibetans, Gansu, Qinghai, and the TAR. However, the actual situation for STIs/HIV prevalence for the Tibetans living in these areas is unclear due to the lack of testing sites and the limitation of official surveillance program of behaviour and serostatus, which has focused only on currently acknowledged high-risk groups such as drug users, sexual workers and those suffering from transmission from blood transfusions in urban and town areas (Liu, *et al.*; 2003; Xing & Zhang, 2002).

China's ethnic minority communities are experiencing STIs and escalating HIV epidemics that are divers in socio-cultural dynamics. Many of the tribal groups and ethnic minorities reside in some of the poorest and most socially disadvantaged rural areas. Amongst these people there is not only widespread poverty that mitigates against the purchase of condoms, but also no tradition of condom use. Traditional sexual customs at collective practice level across communities in various tribal and ethnic groups have been greatly facilitated the vulnerability to epidemics. In the recent rapid development of the marketing economy, the high degree of poverty in the ethnic communities has had a demoralising effect on many young people, leading to massive cross-regional migration to seek work earning extra income in towns and urban centres.

By joining the ranks of the self-employed these young minority people may escape the tight conventional cultural norms imposed on the rest of their communities, but their freer life-style also provides more opportunities to become involved in risk-taking activities, such as drug traffic and selling, intravenous drug use, illegal blood sales, "unconventional" sexual practices and prostitution (Wang & Zhao, 2002; Wang, 2006).

The empirical evidence in previous studies (Wang, 1998; Wang & Keats, 1999; Liao, 2001; Wang, 2001) showed not only that threatening moralistic official messages were having little effect, but also that the many currency approaches of "official-led" social campaigns and messages and international Behaviour Change Communication (BCC), Information Education Communication (IEC) and Behaviour Communication Intervention (BCI) projects with their uniform prescription of officially approved media materials, could not in practice reach into the various ethnic minority cultural groups with hundreds of local languages. The data from these surveys showed that the traditional official anti-STIs/HIV campaign not only has an infrequent effect in improving health behaviour, but also that it is difficult to adopt a monocultural approach to target different cultural and language groups in areas where official Chinese is not widely read or spoken.

It was apparent from these findings that culturally appropriate strategy needs to develop, fulfil and practice effective HIV/AIDS interventions in the ethnic community of China. Although many BCC, IEC and BCI programs have been widely conducted in various ethno-cultural groups and communities from both government organised and non-government organised levels (Sichuan China-UK HIV/AIDS Prevention and Care Project, 2004), only a few intervention program have been evaluated, largely because of the lack of following up and comparable data and, moreover, the confounding factors such as exposure to other non-targeted intervention programs were not taken into account. Clearly there is undoubted to develop a transferable and replicable model which is linguistically and culturally appropriate and which makes use of the interpersonal communication networks to spread correct rather than incorrect information.

The theoretical approach taken here takes a cross-cultural perspective, drawing upon the previous research cited above, the collectivistic, group-centredness of the Chinese culture (Bond, 1986; 1991; Ho, Spinks, & Yeung, 1989) which has also helped to maintain the identity of the ethnic minorities, Fishbein's (1995) integrative model of behavioural prediction, and Corby & Wolitski's (1997) use of role model stories in HIV prevention with African, Asian and Latino Americans. However, neither the Fishbein nor the Corby & Wolitsky model addresses the specific Chinese cultural context.

The aim of this research is to develop and test the effectiveness of an intervention program which will be transferable to a number of different cultural contexts among the ethnic groups of China. The program will use a small core of trained volunteers to spread safe-sex messages among their peers using oral communication based on role model stories/narratives with themes of improving knowledge, attitudes and behavioural intentions. A key feature of the program is to use local, tribal and ethnic languages, carried out and modified as required by the participants themselves, in an indirect, non-moralistic, style adapted to the local cultural tradition.

The effectiveness of this program was examined in a cross-cultural study of HIV/AIDS prevention carried out in three contrasting cultural groups from Sichuan Province: a Yi ethnic minority group, an A-Ba Tibetan ethnic minority group, and a Han majority cultural group from the town of Yaan. Sichuan Province is the hub of much transit between the remote southern and western regions of China and the cities of the eastern seaboard. The Yi communities in this study are found in the Shi-Mian district, a mountainous region of South-Western Sichuan. The traditional activity is farming, but many of the young men are engaged in transport, mainly long distance haulage. Poverty is widespread, and education is only available locally up to elementary school level. Few can afford to send children to distant towns to attend school. Few people can speak Chinese. Their local Yi language has only recently been written down, so that oral traditions are the dominant modes of communication. The A-Ba communities are a large and diverse Tibetan group of over 300,000 inhabitants, situated in a remote and impecunious mountainous area of North-Western Sichuan, strategically placed as the major passageway to the Yi areas and to Tibet. It has been documented that STDs have been found to have a significant impact among these ethnic groups and that a potential HIV epidemic has threatened to do likewise. In both these ethnic minorities sex before marriage with casual sexual partners is culturally acceptable, consequently the risk is increased when they leave their own villages for mobile occupations and life in urban environments. The many differences in community languages and cultural traditions among these diverse Tibetan groups are a major barrier to their access to AIDS education.

2. Method

2.1 Selection of Participants

The study was conducted in a cohort of 450 male participants with matched comparisons of three groups: Group A (direct training group); Group B (indirect intervention group), Group C (comparison group). Using a cluster sampling approach, 150 male volunteers were drawn from the Yi ethnic group, 150 from the Tibetan ethnic group, and 150 from the majority Han cultural group in the three target areas. To allow for possible attrition during the second stage of the procedure, the study actually began 480 participants with 160 in each cultural group. Cluster sampling was used as there was no available sampling frame for all units of the two ethnic groups or the Han group, nor was any sampling frame available to reach all socio-geographical areas of ethnic people living in frontier mountainous regions. The 50 participants from each cultural group who were assigned to the direct training group were selected on the basis of their popularity with their community and willingness to become volunteers with the program. The 50 participants in the indirect intervention group were selected from those contacted by the volunteers in the direct training group. All 150 participants from the Yi cultural group were self-employed young males living in their own villages in the Yi Minority Autonomous Region of Shi-Mian county, and all 150 of the Tibetan participants were self-employed young men living in their own villages in the villages in the Tibetan Autonomous Region of the A-Ba Wen Chuan county of Sichuan. All 150 majority Han participants were self-employed young male trishaw drivers from Yaan town. The three intervention areas were situated 400-600 km away from each other in different prefectures.

Locations selected for the comparison groups were identified through a pilot study (Keats & Wang, 2002) as being reasonably comparable to the matching intervention groups in ethnic and cultural characteristics, socio-demographic and socio-geographic status. All 150 participants assigned to the comparison groups were located about 50–70 kms from the intervention places and separated from the intervention group participants by different villages or county district, main traffic roads and mountains.

2.2 *Procedure*

A pre-test post-test design was used for evaluating the difference in HIV-related knowledge, attitudes and sexual behaviour in the three groups. Participants in Group A were pre-tested, given the intervention program with direct peer and professional training activities, and tested again approximately 5 months later. Participants in Group B were pre-tested, received indirect intervention information of the program from Group A participants through the communication networks, and were tested again approximately 5 months later. Participants in Group C were pre-tested, received no direct or indirect intervention information, and were tested again approximately 5 months later. All responses were obtained by individual interviews. The analysis of differences between those exposed and those unexposed to the program was used to assess the impact of the program. Estimates for this sample size are based on the results of earlier studies on situational analysis of sexual health among male risky populations in Sichuan (Wang, 1998; Wang, 2001).

2.3 Intervention Program

2.3.1 Recruitment and Training of Peer Volunteers (Group A)

The vanguard peer volunteers (Group A: direct training group) were selected on the basis of their popularity with other peers, having attended primary school up to year 6 or higher in the Han community or up to year 3 or higher in the two ethnic communities, having some previous experience in community social work or health promotion, good communication skills, connectedness to the peer network, and willingness to be involved in peer education activities in a voluntary capacity. All were male in ages ranging from 18 to 35 years. They received remuneration on average of approximately equal to US$ 20 for their initial involvement in the training program. Barriers to recruitment were mainly the sensitive nature of the work for these volunteers in ethnic communities and limited reimbursement for involvement the training program in Han trishaw drivers. The training program consisted of two 2-hour small group sessions and two 2-hour small group workshops for each cultural group in their own community. Training sessions were conducted by community health professionals and the first author. The training sessions and subsequent workshops focused on developing understanding of the health messages in each role model story in the community language and improving peer communication and negotiation skills to promote condom use. Groups of about 15–20 volunteers with varying attitudes and practices with regard to safe sex (condom protected sex) were organised to ensure that a range of views and experiences could be discussed, and to provide support to each other. Role-play was employed to develop multiple skills about how to deal with potential difficulties in persuading condom use. The training program was also designed to improve skills through continued feedback.

2.3.2 The Role Model Stories Strategy

Because there was general difficulty in reading health-related printed materials among most self-employed populations in small towns and remote rural areas, due to their low levels of schooling and official Chinese not being widely used (Wang, 1998), the oral story-telling tradition was used as the major communication strategy in the study. A sex-related humorous story-telling narrative (Qing Gang Gushi) is a ubiquitous and popular communication mode in these communities. Safe sex role-model stories were therefore used as a major educational tool to focus on developing peer negotiation skills to promote condom use. The intervention message and delivery strategies were shaped by the findings from the ethnographic study of HIV-related sexual behaviour assessment in the region (Wang *et al.*, 1995;), sociological and psychological research into self-employed youth subcultures and their concomitant vulnerability to STIs and HIV (Wang & Keats, 1999), communication study on local oral story-telling traditions with effective health promotion for such communities (Wang & Zhao, 2000), drawing on behaviour change theories in HIV prevention (Ajzen & Fishbein, 1994; Bandura, 1994; Corby & Wolitski, 1997; Fishbein, 1995; Fisher & Fisher, 1992; Fishbein, Middlestadt, & Hitchcock, 1991; Fisher, & Misovich, 1990; McAlister, 1997; Nucifra, Gallois & Kashima, 1993; and Prochaska & DiClemente, 1986). The stories were further developed in in-depth case studies, focus groups and special workshops conducted by the project team, volunteers and peer educators, and were tested in pilot work aimed at improving linguistically and culturally appropriate relevant contexts (Keats & Wang, 2002). In addition, practice in adopting the role-model stories strategy to promote safe sex among a majority Han cultural group has been also documented in elsewhere (Wang & Van de Ven, 2003).

The four stories covered different situation of target groups with their sexual practices. The information within the four stories was constituted around representative experiences from the target groups describing how they communicate their experiences to change their attitudes, beliefs and practices related to their own risk-taking sexual behaviour for HIV infection. Changing thinking, risk-reducing behaviour (condom use for vaginal or anal sex with casual sexual partners) and negotiation skills are addressed in the stories. The themes in the four stories were: Story 1. Protecting My Family from AIDS (emphasizing positive information toward developing HIV/AIDS-related knowledge); Story 2. A

Cautious Friend (attitudes toward safe sex; belief and perceived social norms); Story 3. Getting Used to Condoms (decision to try to use condoms); and Story 4. Always Carry a Condom (sustaining safe sex).

To support the story-based intervention, other activities included a training program in communication skills for the volunteers, developing safe places for peers to get together in small group workshops, a drop-in centre/room for counselling and support in each intervention community, and peer outreach to enrol additional volunteers to distribute a small sticker highlighting key points from the role-model stories.

2.3.3. Peer-Led Diffusion of Role-Model Stories (Group B)

In the Han community of Yaan, each peer educator who was directly involved in the initial training program (Group A) was asked to tell the role model stories to at least 3 to 8 of his peers within the first two weeks as potential future volunteers and at least 8 to15 of his peers within three months. These became Group B. A small sticker, listing key points from the role-model stories in simple language, a condom cartoon, and the address (and hours) of the drop-in centre, was pasted on the front of a new volunteer's trishaw after he had been told all the stories and instructed in how to communicate them to others. The registration number of the trishaw of the new volunteer was recorded and relayed to the program manager.

Because of the smaller population size and more widespread socio-geographic situation, each peer educator in the initial training program (Group A) in both Yi and Tibetan ethnic communities was asked to diffuse the role model stories to at least 3 to 4 of his peers who were potential future volunteers (Group B) within the first two weeks, and at least to 4 to 8 of his peers within three months. A badge of red ribbon was worn and a sheet of key points from the role model stories in the Yi or Tibetan community language was distributed when a new volunteer had been told all the stories and instructed in how to communicate them to others. The code number of the new volunteer was recorded and reported to the program managers and volunteer team leader in the two ethnic communities. One hundred and fifty of these volunteers, 50 for each of the three target cultural communities were later sampled and interviewed to evaluate the program effectiveness. Table 1 shows the total number of people contacted.

Table 1. Total Numbers for Involved in the Study Among Three Cultural Groups

Study groups	*Group A* *Direct training*	*Group B* *Indirect intervention*		*Group C* *Comparison*	*Total*
Different cultural groups		*three months period for process evaluation*	*within five months*		
Shi-Mian Yi ethnic group	55	193	769	53	1012
A-BaTibetan ethnic group	55	124	774	53	982
Yaan-Han group	55	287	992	54	1334
Actual number involvement in the program	165	604	2535	160	3493
Actual number involvement interviewed	160	—	160	160	480
Final numbers included in the statistical analysis	150		150	150	450

2.4 Measures and Data Analysis

The responses to the face-to-face interviews were used as the major data source. An interview schedule of 35 questions was prepared. Topics included questions relating to demographic, social and education background variables, social contexts, HIV-related knowledge and attitudes, sexual practices, condom use and HIV education promotion. The interview schedule was worded in simple, colloquial and slang local Yi, Tibetan and Han languages. All interviewers were from local communities and took part in a training program to develop their interviewing skills in probing ambiguous responses, interpreting individual items and controlling bias in responses.

Exposure to the intervention program was checked by surveying interview respondents. Respondents were particularly asked to describe anything they had been involved in or heard about the activity in broadcasting "safe sex role-model stories" to prevent HIV. in the past months around their local community. Based on information about the role model stories, respondents were coded by the interviewer as exposed or unexposed to the program. The differences between those directly exposed (Group A), those indirectly exposed (Group B) and those unexposed to the program (Group C), were used to assess the effects of the program.

The aims of the data analysis were statistically to determine: *a)* the cultural suitability in diffusing health message through safe sex role-model stories; *b)* the promotion of HIV.-related knowledge, positive attitudes and condom use from before intervention to after intervention between the intervention group and comparison group. Initially, two core-related criteria were considered to detect the intervention effects: *1)* always use condoms for vaginal sex when having sex with casual partners, and *2)* always use condoms for anal sex when having sex with casual partners. However, only the first of these was finally adopted as very few participants reported having engaged in anal sex (two Yi, one Tibetan and two Han).

Accuracy of knowledge on HIV./AIDS-related safe/unsafe sex and condom use was assessed by scores developed from 28 items in the interview schedule with a maximum score of 56. The proportion of participants who reached a basic scoring standard of 46 out of 56 (82.1% accuracy) for HIV./AIDS knowledge was examined to determine the change rate of improved knowledge on HIV./AIDS between baseline and post-intervention.

Level of correct attitudes toward AIDS-related safe sex was scored using a Likert-type scale with four levels of response—"agree strongly", "agree", "disagree", "disagree strongly", —scored four, three, two and one respectively. Scores for safe sexual practice were developed from 14 items about condom use both for vaginal sex anal sex with both casual partners and regular partners. All scored 1 if response was "yes", otherwise 0 for safe sexual scales (SSS) in relevant items about always using a condom when having sex. A high score in SSS denotes a high level in regard to safe sexual behaviour for STIs and HIV. The proportion of participants who reached a basic scoring standard of 11 out of 14 (78.6 % accuracy) was examined to determine the change rate.

Condom use every time with casual or regular sexual partners and the numbers who reported having sex with more than one sexual partners were recorded. Chi-square tests (c^2) were used to test the difference in frequency distribution of a) socio-demographic characteristics and b) stories diffusion between the three comparison groups in each cultural group. Paired *t*-tests were used to examine changes in knowledge, and attitudes towards HIV infection, safe/unsafe sex and condom use between before and after intervention.

3. Results

3.1 Participants in Baseline

As data in Table 2 show, there were no significant baseline differences in socio-demographic characteristics among the three cultural groups. The mean age for the three different groups was 26.37 with a range of 17–39 years. Most were of similar marital status, had very low income levels, with 357 (79.3%) under the standard national poverty line of ¥300 or less monthly income, and low levels of education, with 373 (82.9%) having less than six years of schooling. Differences between the intervention groups and the comparison groups were not found.

Table 2. Socio-Demographic characteristics of Yi, Tibetan and Han cultural groups at baseline (*n*=450)

Characteristics	*Frequency* Yi ethnic group (n =150)	*Tibetan ethnic group (n =150)*	*Han cultural group (n =150)*	*Total sample (n =450)*
Age				
Mean	26.59	25.66	26.88	26.37
SD	6.54	4.63	7.99	6.39
χ^2 = 0.183; p = 0.988				
Current marital status				
Married	62(41.3)	58(38.7)	52(34.6)	172(38.2)
Never married/single	72(48.0)	76(50.7)	63(42.0)	211(46.8)
Divorced	6(4.0)	8(5.3)	14(9.3)	28(6.2)
Separated	8(5.3)	7(4.6)	13(8.6)	28(6.2)
Committed relationship	2(1.3)	1(0.6)	8(5.3)	11(2.4)
χ^2 = 7.286; p = 0.328				
Monthly income (Chinese Yuan)				
¥ 100 and less	72(46.6)	58(36.6)	42(32.6)	172(38.2)
¥ 101- 300	58(38.6)	66(44.0)	75(51.3)	199(44.2)
¥ 301-500	20(13.3)	24(16.0)	26(21.3)	70(15.6)
¥ 501-1000		2(1.3)	7(4.6)	9(2.[illegible]
¥ 1000 +				
Kruskal-Wallis Test (Z) (Mean Rank) = 9.214; p = 0.021				
Education				
Never attended school	11(7.3)	9(6.0)	3(2.0)	23(5.1)
Less than 3 years primary schooling	84(56.0)	63(42.0)	54(36.0)	201(44.6)
Completed year 6 primary schooling	40(26.7)	50(33.3)	59(39.3)	149(33.1)
Completed middle school	12(8.0)	21(14.0)	25(16.7)	58(12.8)
Completed high (or technical high) school	3(2.0)	7(4.6)	9(6.0)	19(4.2)
Completed college or university	0	0	0	0
χ^2 = 11.022; p = 0.097				

Table 3

Attitudes Toward the Four Safe Sex Role-Model Stories Over Three Months Period

Role-model stories:	*1. Protecting my family from AIDS*		*2. A cautious friend*		*3. Getting used to condoms*		*4. Always carry a condom*	
Themes:	*Knowledge and safe sex strategies to prevent HIV transmission*		*Attitudes toward safe sex; beliefs and perceived social/behavioural norms*		*Decision to try to use condoms*		*Self-efficacy to consistently reduce risk*	
Attitudes and evaluation toward stories diffusion *Shi MianYi ethnic groups*	*Training group n=50 (%)*	*Indirect intervention group n =193 (%)*	*Training group n=50 (%)*	*Indirect intervention group n =193 (%)*	*Training group n=50 (%)*	*Indirect interven-tion group n =193 (%)*	*Training group n=50 (%)*	*Indirect intervention group n =193 (%)*
Easy to understand	50 (100.0)	172 (89.1)	36 (72.0)	179 (92.7)	48 (96.0)	177 (91.7)	46 (92.0)	176 (91.1)
Suitability in using community language	46 (92.0)	182 (94.4)	35 (70.0)	175 (90.6)	45 (90.0)	180 (93.4)	45 (90.0)	175 (90.6)
Easy to remember	41(82.0)	155 (80.3)	37 (74.0)	179 (92.7)	46 (92.0)	175 (90.6)	46 (91.0)	174 (90.1)
Easy to relate to peers	47 (94.0)	174 (90.5)	35 (70.0)	174 (90.1)	47 (94.0)	174 (90.1)	45 (90.0)	175 (90.6)
Easy to put into practice	45 (90.0)	163 (84.5)	38 (76.0)	176 (91.1)	45 (90.0)	162 (83.9)	34 (68.0)	113 (58.5)

A-Ba-Tibetan ethnic groups								
Attitudes and evaluation toward stories diffusion	*Training group n=50 (%)*	*Indirect interve-ntion group n =193 (%)*	*Training group n=50 (%)*	*Indirect interve-ntion group n =193 (%)*	*Training group n=50 (%)*	*Indirect interve-ntion group n =193 (%)*	*Training group n=50 (%)*	*Indirect interve-ntion group n =193 (%)*
Easy to understand	50 (100.0)	113 (91.5)	37 (74.0)	113 (91.1)	48 (96.0)	115 (92.7)	47 (94.0)	116 (93.5)
Suitability in using community language	47 (94.0)	118 (95.1)	35 (70.0)	112 (90.3)	46 (92.0)	117 (94.3)	47 (94.0)	117 (94.3)
Easy to remember	41(82.0)	101(81.4)	37 (74.0)	115 (92.7)	46 (92.0)	117 (94.3)	46 (91.0)	114 (91.9)
Easy to relate to peers	47 (94.0)	112 (90.3)	36 (72.0)	112 (90.3)	47 (94.0)	114 (91.9)	46 (92.0)	112 (90.5)
Easy to put into practice	46 (92.0)	108 (87.1)	37 (74.0)	109 (87.9)	45 (90.0)	116 (93.5)	35 (70.0)	83 (66.9)
Yaan-Yunjin Han cultural groups								
Attitudes and evaluation toward stories diffusion	*Training group n=50 (%)*	*Indirect interve-ntion group n =193 (%)*	*Training group n=50 (%)*	*Indirect interve-ntion group n =193 (%)*	*Training group n=50 (%)*	*Indirect interve-ntion group n =193 (%)*	*Training group n=50 (%)*	*Indirect interve-ntion group n =193 (%)*
Easy to understand	50 (100.0)	277 (96.5)	48 (98.0)	266 (92.6)	49 (98.0)	278 (96.8)	49 (98.0)	278 (96.8)
Suitability in using community language	46 (92.0)	267 (93.0)	47 (95.0)	273 (95.1)	46 (92.0)	279 (97.2)	45 (90.0)	265 (92.3)
Easy to remember	45 (90.0)	257 (89.5)	44 (88.0)	267 (93.0)	47 (94.0)	263 (91.6)	47 (95.0)	266 (92.2)
Easy to relate to peers	48 (96.0)	260 (90.7)	47 (94.0)	261 (90.9)	47 (94.0)	259 (90.2)	46 (92.0)	261 (90.9)
Easy to put into practice	49 (98.0)	262 (91.5)	48 (96.0)	267 (93.0)	47 (94.0)	262 (91.5)	39 (78.0)	205 (71.7)

3.2 Attitudes Toward the Role Model Stories

Data in Table 3 show attitudes toward the stories in terms of ease of understanding; suitability of the language used, i.e. culturally appropriate expression using local idiom in ethnic community languages; ease of remembering the content of the stories; ease of relating the stories to peers; and ease of incorporating the story message into one's own sexual practice. Data in Table 3 include these participants who heard the stories from their peer volunteers, a total of 193 Yi, 124 Tibetans and 287 Han, within three months. Some small variations within topics may be noted where responses were incomplete.

The results of this analysis show that all fore stories were easy to understand by Han respondents. Stories 1, 3 and 4 were easy to understand by the Yi and Tibetans but Story 2 was not so easy to understand. It can be seen, however, that Story 2 was easier to understand in the peer-led indirect training than in the indirect intervention group.

Table 3 also shows that the language suitability was high in all three cultural groups, and greater in the peer-led indirect training than in the indirect intervention group. Except for Story 2, ease of remembering was high in all groups and all stories were easy to relate to peers. The exception to these results is shown in the responses relating to ease of putting the message into practice.

Changes from pre-test to post-test over a five months period after the intervention for all intervention groups and comparison groups are shown in Table 4. Scores are presented in percentages for comparability and confidence levels for significance of the change.

Table 4. Changes from Baseline to Post test after 5 Months

Knowledge, attitudes and behaviour characteristics		*Baseline, % (Pre-test)*	*Post-Interve., % (Post-test)*	*Observed change, (95% CI)*
<u>*Correct knowledge about safe/unsafe sex*</u>				
Direct training groups	Yi (n=50)	16.0	86.0	.70.5 (54.6, 86.4)***
	Tibetan (n=50)	18.0	88.0	70.0 (53.8, 86.2)***
	Han (n=50)	22.0	90.0	68.0 (51.2, 84.5)***

Indirect intervention groups	Yi (n=50)	14.0	74.0	60.0 (46.1, 73.9)***
	Tibetan (n=50)	18.0	80.0	62.0 (47.2, 76.8)***
	Han (n=50)	22.0	90.0	68.0 (51.2, 84.5)***
Comparison groups	Yi (n=50)	16.0	18.0	2.0 (-0.3, 4.3) n.s.
	Tibetan (n=50)	14.0	18.0	4.0 (-0.9, 8.9) n.s.
	Han (n=50)	24.0	22.0	- 2.0 (-4.4, 0.4) n.s.
Correct attitudes toward HIV-related information				
Direct training groups	Yi (n=50)	20.0	84.0	64.0 (48.3, 79.7)***
	Tibetan (n=50)	22.0	90.0	68.0 (51.2, 84.5)***
	Han (n=50)	24.0	94.0	70.0 (53.8, 86.2)***
Indirect intervention groups	Yi (n=50)	16.0	72.0	56.0 (42.9, 69.1)***
	Tibetan (n=50)	18.0	76.0	58.0 (43.7, 72.2)***
	Han (n=50)	26.0	86.0	60.0 (46.1, 73.9)***
Comparison groups	Yi (n=50)	14.0	16.0	2.0 (-0.3, 4.3) n.s.
	Tibetan (n=50)	22.0	20.0	- 2.0 (-4.4, 0.4) n.s.
	Han (n=50)	22.0	26.0	4.0 (-0.9, 8.9) n.s.
Condom use with casual sexual partner/s				
Direct training groups (n=145)	Yi (n=47)	2.1	36.1	34.0 (14.2, 53,8)***
	Tibetan (n=50)	2.0	38.0	36.0 (16.2, 55,8)***
	Han (n=48)	6.3	47.9	41.6 (19.3, 63.9)***
Indirect intervention groups (n=137)	Yi (n=43)	2.3	27.9	25.6 (11.6, 39.6)***
	Tibetan (n=46)	4.3	30.4	26.1 (12.2, 40.0)***
	Han (n=48)	6.2	39.6	33.4 (14.0, 52.8)***
Comparison groups (n=144)	Yi (n=46)	2.2	4.3	2.1 (-0.4, 4.6) n.s.
	Tibetan (n=48)	2.0	4.1	2.1 (-0.4, 4.6) n.s.
	Han (n=50)	6.0	4.0	- 2.0 (-4.4, 0.4) n.s.
Condom use with regular sexual partner/s				
Direct training groups (n=131)	Yi (n=40)	2.5	37.5	35.0 (15.4, 54,6)***
	Tibetan (n=44)	2.2	38.6	36.4 (16.2, 56,6)***
	Han (n=47)	19.1	59.5	40.4 (18.3, 62.5)***
Indirect intervention groups (n=133)	Yi (n=43)	6.9	30.2	23.3 (12.4, 34.2)**
	Tibetan (n=44)	2.3	27.2	24.9 (13.5, 36.3)**
	Han (n=46)	17.1	50.0	32.9 (14.7, 51.1)***
Comparison groups (*n*=130)	Yi (*n*=44)	4.5	11.3	6.8 (-2.2, 13.8) n.s.
	Tibetan (*n*=42)	4.7	7.1	2.4 (-0.4, 5.2) n.s.
	Han (*n*=44)	18.1	15.9	- 2.2 (-4.6, 0.2) n.s.
Numbers who reported having sex with more than one sexual partners				
Direct training groups (*n*=145)	Yi (*n*=47)	68.0	52.6	- 15.4 (-21.8, -9.0)*
	Tibetan (*n*=50)	74.5	64.3	- 10.2 (-16.5, -4.0)*
	Han (*n*=48)	40.0	18.2	- 21.8 (-30.7, -12.9)***

Indirect intervention groups (n=137)	Yi (n=43)	68.2	58.9	- 9.3 (-14.7, -3.5)*
	Tibetan (n=46)	74.6	68.8	- 5.8 (-10.6, -1.0) n.s.
	Han (n=48)	40.5	27.0	- 13.5 (-19.1, -7.5) **
Comparison groups (n=144)	Yi (n=46)	67.8	69.6	1.8 (-0.2, 3.8) n.s.
	Tibetan (n=48)	72.9	77.0	4.1 (-0.7, 8.9) n.s.
	Han (n=44)	43.2	47.7	4.5 (-0.9, 9.9) n.s.

CI = Confidence interval; n.s. = no significance
* p <.05; ** p <.01; *** p <.001

3.3 *Improvement in Safe Sex Knowledge*

It can be seen from Table 4 that the number of participants who reached the criterion of 88% correct knowledge on the pre-test at baseline was very low in all cultural groups, with no significant differences between the direct training, indirect intervention and comparison groups. The Han cultural group was the best performer in each condition, and there was little difference between the Yi and Tibetans. Changes toward improved safe sex knowledge were highly significant (p < .001) in both the direct training and indirect intervention groups in all three cultural groups. There were no significant changes in the comparison groups.

3.4 *Improved Attitudes Toward HIV-Related Information*

The results for improved attitudes toward HIV-related information were similar to those for improved knowledge. Table 4 shows that all participants in both the direct training and the indirect intervention groups changed from very low scores at baseline on the pre-test to very high scores at post-test, with highly significant (p < .001) differences. No similar change occurred in the comparison groups.

3.5 *Protected Intercourse With Casual Sexual Partners*

The number of participants who reported having sex with casual partners was high in all groups. These data refer to vaginal sex only. Percentages in Table 4 show very low levels of condom use with casual sexual partners at baseline, with highly significant (p < .001) increases in all intervention groups. The Han groups again showed higher scores than the Yi and Tibetans. There were no significant differences in any of the comparison groups.

3.6 Protected Intercourse With Regular Sexual Partners

The percentage of participants who reported using a condom every time or most of the time with regular sexual partners at pre-test was very low, with the Han showing a much higher level of condom use than any of the Yi and Tibetan groups. The data refer to vaginal sex only. All intervention groups showed highly significant increases on the post-test, although increases were not as great in the Yi and Tibetan indirect intervention group as they were for casual sexual partners. Again no significant increases were found in the comparison groups.

3.7 Changes in Numbers of Sexual Partners

The data in Table 4 show that at baseline all groups reported having sex with more than one sexual partner. The percentages were much higher in the Yi and Tibetan groups than in the Han. Significant decreases were reported after the intervention in all but the Tibetans in the indirect intervention group. The decreases were greater in the Han than in the Yi and Tibetans, the greatest being reported by the Han direct training group. No decreases were reported by the comparison groups where the only changes were non significant increases.

4. Discussion

Impact of rapid social and economic development to ethnic minorities in China presents a new frontier for STI and HIV prevention. Yet China's traditional anti-epidemic campaign is significant lack of ethnic and cultural perspective to reflect the diversified and culturally appropriate approaches in HIV prevention. The dissemination of officially-sanctioned printed materials from local CDC and BCC program from individualism perspective of independent cultures and developed countries targeting different ethnic cultural populations has been the strategy broadly adopted for most of China's HIV education programs. The work presented here is a challenge to current both 'official-led' health promotion and international BCC, IEC and BCI approaches for STI and HIV prevention in different tribal groups and ethnic communities in China from indigenous and cultural perspective.

Findings from the study clearly indicated that in all three cultural groups the intervention activities were successful in significantly increasing HIV-related knowledge, improving attitudes toward safe sex, and promoting condom use for sex with both casual and regular sexual partners. The greatest increase occurred in the direct training groups, but the indirect intervention groups also showed significant increases, whereas no similar changes were found in the comparison groups. An important finding was the decrease in the number of sexual partners reported by the intervention groups.

Several factors in the research contributed to the effectiveness of the program. A key factor was the empowerment of the participants to fulfil and practice cultural appropriate strategy from human right perspective. Those who volunteered to take part in the direct training not only learned safer sex behaviour for themselves but also took ethno-cultural value and responsibility for the diffusion of the messages into their communities. The peer-based diffusion was supported by cultural and faith-based leaders, and other stakeholders in village levels to adopt their own initiatives with advocating social and cultural equality in access to health message and services. Peers' activities in the program embody human right perspective on protecting, promoting, respecting their right in using culturally appropriate communication strategy reducing vulnerability to HIV. Volunteers in the program were therefore shown great concern to involve in their own activities. As they in their turn became volunteers the total number of persons contacted, as shown in Table 2, also increased. The improvement in knowledge about HIV/AIDS was dramatic in all the intervention groups. An important aspect of this strategy was that that the approach taken did not take a punitive moralistic stance, nor did it set out to criticise the norms of sexual behaviour in any of the three cultures, Yi, Tibetan or Han. Moreover, the approach of "friend to friend" ensured that the participants did not perceive the intervention as something imposed upon them by outsiders and so-called "foreign experts".

Whereas much research on HIV/AIDS prevention in Western countries has concentrated on individual behaviour change (for example Fishbein, 1995; Fishbein et al., 1991), the methods employed made use of China's collectivist cultural style which dominates both the Han majority and the ethnic minorities. The locations in which the messages were passed on to the indirect intervention participants were in all cases familiar venues they gathered in groups with their friends. Participants who were living and working more centrally in or close to the towns were more likely to spend their time in these peer-based activities. In the Shi-Mian Yi ethnic community popular locations were people's drinking places and street corners near the market, and for the Tibetans they were get-together location for young people in the town, while for the trishaw drivers in Yaan-Yunjin town the favoured locations were at tea houses along the river bank, on street corners near to cinemas and restaurants, and at street waiting places for trishaws adjoining bus stations. In other places, particularly in the smaller villages of the Yi and Tibetan ethnic communities, drinking places and tea houses and home yards of the participants were more open to everyone in the community and not so conducive to discussing personal issues of sexual health.

A third important factor contributing to the effectiveness of the intervention was the adoption of appropriate linguistic styles. Because proficiency in reading and/or speaking Chinese could not be anticipated, all the research materials were translated into the local tribal and ethnic languages. However, to make the messages more acceptable, the participants were encouraged to use colloquial language in their interviews and group discussions and the humorous Qing Gang Gushi style to tell the role-model stories.

The effectiveness of the oral story-telling method was clearly demonstrated. For all participants the content of the stories was easy to understand, easy to remember and easy to relate to their peers. It was apparent that the messages in the stories could be related to their own experiences and the traditional Qing Gang Gushi style was very effective. Some differences between the stories occurred. In story 2, dealing with attitudes toward safe sex, beliefs and perceived social behavioural norms, the percentage agreement rates were lower in the direct training groups than in the indirect intervention groups for both the Yi and the Tibetan respondents. This difference could possibly be attributed to a freer colloquial language style being used to communicate with their peers. In story 4, dealing with the ease of putting the message to always carry a condom for casual sex into practice, the percentage agreement rate was the lowest, particularly in the Yi and Tibetan groups. Respondents said that it was not feasible always to carry a condom outside; condoms were not in their tradition, and poverty made it difficult to purchase them. Clearly, there is a need to develop complementary strategies to support these people to find other ways to ensure that they consistently use condoms with casual partners.

In evaluating the effectiveness of the diffusion technique, Three factors need to be considered: first, the evidence of the direct training groups' superior performance; second, the economic feasibility of the program in situations of poverty and social disadvantage; and third, the indigenous cultural-contextual aspects of collectivist cultures in the delivery of the health messages. The direct training groups were volunteers, selected for their acceptance by their peers and willingness to become involved in the program. They had access to assistance from health professionals, they took an active part in the planning, they participated in group discussions and in the translation of the stories into acceptable language. All these activities led to a sense of responsibility and identification with the program. It was therefore a positive result of the diffusion technique that the indirect intervention groups performed as well as they did, showing significant improvements from pre-testing to post-testing after five months.

The second factor, economic feasibility, is of great practical significance for ethnic minorities such as the Yi and Tibetans and for other local communities which have widespread educational and economic disadvantage or where different languages are spoken. It would be difficult for central funding authorities, or indeed international non-government agencies, to justify the expenditure required to conduct similar direct training programs on a large scale. The figures in Table 3 show how far reaching such a program could become. It was apparent hat the diffusion actually reached a much larger population than the numbers included in the pre and post-test evaluation.

Third factor, the indigenous/cultural contextual aspects in message diffusion is a key determinate in understanding the collective practices in adopting health perspective. The biggest challenge for health campaigns from cultural backgrounds in all these countries is the difficulty of reaching various audiences in traditional rural societies and diverse ethnic communities with uncountable local, tribal, and ethnic languages. The only solution so far is community-based education with printed small media, repeated in every village, not just in pidgin, but in local languages. Risk-taking practices among these young populations in tribal and ethnic Tibet and Yi communities are constructed culturally and historically in their collective behaviour with a traditional life-style. The customs of single young women regular open to sex for single men from different communities in these activities from "Xianqing" (the ceremony of marriage and exequies) in ethnic Yi society and "Dagou" (young men seasonal sexual visit to young women in their neighbour communities) in some Tibet areas are embedded collectively in their cultures and histories. The effects in promoting health message communication need to be integrated with diffusing in their cultural-contextual activities, rather than individual leaning in education campaign with group or non-group styles. In the other words, finding in the study indicated that the ethnic cultural contexts of interdependent/collectivist in the delivery of the health messages and the effects of modernization on traditional communication styles in most tribal groups and ethnic communities have greatly challenged official campaign and the BCC, IEC and BCI projects which are as unidimensional and individualistic perspective of independent cultures and developed societies.

Despite these favourable outcomes some limitations of the study need to be considered.

Because the responses were all in interviews the possibility of response bias has to be considered. While this was addressed in the direct training program, with particular training in good interviewing techniques, there was no way in which the delivery of the role-model stories with their safe sex health messages could be monitored. The possibility of saving face in responses to some of the more personal questions must also be kept in mind.

Random sampling could not be used to obtain the participants; hence the data cannot be regarded as representative of the entire Yi and Tibetan populations of these regions. Nor can the trishaw drivers of Yaan be regarded as representing the entire population of that town. However, the selection of the members of the direct training groups did meet the necessary criteria of suitability for the task for which they were to be trained. No selection criteria other than being of the appropriate age and group membership were necessary for the indirect intervention groups. Table 2 shows that the three cultural groups were sufficiently similar in their demographic make-up.

It could be argued that the concentration on condom use ignored other ways of influencing sexual behaviour. The choice of condom use was guided by the intention to avoid the implication of being critical of the traditional lifestyles of the ethnic communities. Condom use was a non-threatening and practical objective to aim for, and had some spin-off in the reduction of the number of sexual partners.

To build an effective cultural response for HIV, project need to address gender issues. Adopting a gender perspective should not be interpreted simply as promoting the rights of women. The familiar expression that women hold up half the sky is significant because it acknowledges that status benefits both sexes. Apparently, a limited focus on men sexual health in this study much needed consideration of the role of women in health promotion and health care in further stage. In china, the role of gender analysis often viewed as the function of women's organisation such as women's Federation. All areas of the health promotion in using cultural strategy with responsibility for health care services need to have a gender perspective. However, a focus on numerical indicators, such as the gender ratio of trainees, limitation in current design in this study is a lack to address the subtle causes underlying gender inequality in access to health care, which has been due to challenges from China's traditional socio-economic, socio-cultural barriers to women in ethnic community to seeking prior support in health care study.

Overall, the findings suggest that further work would be possibly to other cultures where oral communication traditions are strong and collectivist traditions override individualistic interpretations of the impact of the HIV and AIDS epidemic. It would be valuable to extend the research into other ethnic groups both potential benefits greatly for gender perspective in HIV education cultural practice in China.

REFERENCES

Ajzen, I., & Fishbein, M. (1994), *Understanding Attitudes and Predicting Social Behaviour,* Englewood Cliffs, NJ: Prentice-Hall.

Bandura, A. (1994), Social cognitive theory and exercise of control over HIV infection, in R. J. DiClemante & J. L. Peterson (Eds.), *Preventing AIDS: Theories and Methods of Behaviour Interventions*, pp. 25-59, New York: Plenum Press.

Bond, M.H. (Eds.), (1986), *The Psychology of the Chinese People,*. Hong Kong: Oxford University Press.

Bond, M. H. (1991), *Beyond the Chinese Face: Insights From Psychology,* New York: Oxford University Press.

Corby, N.H., & Wolitski, R.J. (1997), *Community HIV Prevention: The Long Beach AIDS Community Demonstration Project*, Long Beach, CA: California State University, The University Press.

Fishbein, M. (1995), Developing effective behaviour change interventions: Some lessons learned from behaviour research, in T.E. Backer, S.L. David & G. Soucy (Eds.), *Reviewing the Behaviour Sciences Knowledge Base on Technology Transfer* [NIDA Research Monograph No. 155, NIH Pub. No. 95-4035] pp. 246-261. Rockville, MD: National Institute on Drug Abuse.

Fisher, J.D. & Fisher, W.A. (1992), Changing AIDS-risk behaviour, *Psychological Bulletin,* 111, pp. 455-474.

Fishbein, M., Middlestadt, S.E., & Hitchcock, P.J. (1991), Using information to change sexually transmitted disease-related behaviour: An analysis based on the theory of reasoned action, in J.N. Wasserheit, S.O. Aral, K.K. Holmes, & P.J. Hitchcock (Eds.), *Research Issues in Human Behaviour and Sexual Transmitted Diseases in the AIDS Era*, pp. 243-257, Washington, DC: American Society for Microbiology.

Fisher, J.D., & Misovich, S.J. (1990), Social influence and AIDS preventive behaviour, in J. Edwards, R.S. Tindall, L. Health, & E.J. Posavac (Eds.), *Social Influence Processes and Prevention*, 39-70, New York: Plenum Press.

Gao, Q. (2003), Promoting governmental actions against HIV/AIDS in China, A entrusted speech by Mr. Hu Jintao, President of the People's Republic of China, presented by Executive Vice Minister of Public Health, China, at the HIV/AIDS High-level Meeting of the UN General Assembly Special Session on HIV/AIDS, Geneva, 09/22/2003.

Gong, H., Cheng, K., Li, C., Jian, Y., Han, Y., & Feng, Z. (2003), An behavioural survey on drug users and HIV-related sexual behaviour among Yi ethnic group in Sichuan, *Journal of Preventive Medicine Information*, 19, supplement, 31-32.

Ho, D.Y., Spinks, J.A., & Yeung, C.S.H. (Eds.), (1989), *Chinese Patterns of Behaviour: A Sourcebook of Psychological and Psychiatric Studies*, New York: Praeger.

Keats, D. & Wang, S. (2002), A pilot report on development of a cross-cultural strategy for promoting AIDS prevention in different ethnic groups in China, Internal report for the John and Daphne Keats Endowment Research Funding University of Newcastle.

Liao, C. (2001), Difficulties in adopting homogeneous prevention approach to target different cultural and language group, Paper presented at the *Annual Conference of Sichuan Associate of Sociology, Sichuan University, Chengdu, 11-12 March*.

Liu, G., Wang, D. Qin, G., Mao, X., *et al*. (2003), Analysis of current situation and trend of HIV/AIDS in Sichuan Province, *Chinese Journal of AIDS & STD*, 2(9), 79-80 and 89.

Luo, B. (2001), Urgent need to develop culturally appropriate approach to promote STIs/HIV education and social study for ethnic minorities, *Collection of Annual Conference of Sichuan Associate of Sociology*, Printed by Sichuan Associate of Sociology, China.

Luo, L. & Wu, S. (1996), A cross-sectional situational survey on reproductive transmitted infections (RTIs) among female of Naxi and Dai ethnic groups in Sichuan and Yaan, *West China Journal of Medicine, 12* (4), 469-473.

Luo, L. Wu, S. & Chen, J. (1999), A study on genital tract Chlamydia trachomatis and gonococcal infection in Han and minority women in China's two provinces, *Chinese Journal of Obstetric & Gynaecologic Research, 25*(3), 221-230.

Mao, Q. (2006, April), 650,000 HIV/AIDS cases in China, but most cases have not been covered in the figures. Press conference on national HIV/AIDS epidemics, Ministry of Public Health, *Xi Hua Wan*, http://health.sohu.com/20060411/n242742253.shtml

Mao, Y., Re, Z., Zheng, X., Pan, C., Liu, W. & Wang, L. (2002), HIV prevalence and KABP survey among pregnant women in Yining, Xinjian, *Chinese Journal of AIDS & STD*, 2(8), 91-93.

McAlister, A. (1997), The diffusion Accelerator: Combining media and interpersonal communication in community-level health promotion campaigns, in N. H. Corby & R. J. Wolitski (Eds.) *Community HIV Prevention: The Long Beach AIDS Community Demonstration Project*, California State University, University Press.

Ministry of Public Health, (1999), *A Report on Situational Analysis of HIV/AIDS Prevention and Control in China*, Printed by UN Theme Group on HIV/AIDS of China and Ministry of Public Health. *UN in China Website* by May 1999: www.unchina.org/unaids/main.html

Nucifra, J., Gallois, C., & Kashima, Y. (1993), Influences on condom use among undergraduates: testing the theories of reasoned action and planned behaviour, in D. Terry, C. Galloies, & M. McCamish (Eds.), *The Theory of Reasoned Action: Its Applications to AIDS-Preventive Behaviour*, 47-64, New York: Pergamon.

Prochaska, J.O., & DiClemente, C.C. (1986), Toward a comprehensive model of change, in W. R. Miller & N. Heather (Eds.), *Treating Addictive Behaviour: Processes of Change*, pp. 3-27, New York: Plenum Press.

Sichuan Centre of Disease Control (2001), *A Epidemiological Report on HIV/AIDS in Sichuan Province of China*, printed by Department of Public Health of Sichuan and Sichuan Office of China-UK AIDS Prevention and Control Project. Presented in Professional Seminar on HIV/AIDS Prevention and Program Development, April, Chengdu.

UNAIDS/WHO, (2004), *China Epidemiological Fact Sheet: 2004 Update*, Geneva: UNAIDS/WHO Working Group on Global HIV/AIDS and STI Surveillance.

UNCHINA, (1999), *Current Status of HIV in China*. *UN in China Website* by Dec. 1999: http://www.unchina.org/unaids/ekey3right1.html

Wang, S. (1998), STD and AIDS-related risk-taking sexual behaviour within the dual socioeconomic system of China, Ph.D. Thesis.

Wang, S. (2001), *Situational analysis of sexual health (SASH) in Sichuan: A model on rapidly sociological assessment for sexual behaviour in*

Sichuan, printed by China-UK AIDS Prevention Project, Sichuan Project Office, and Chengdu. Reprinted by National Project Office of China-UK AIDS Prevention Project (2003), Beijing.

Wang, S. (2006), Situational analysis of HIV-related risk-taking practices in Tibet, An internal Report submitted to Tibet Health Sectors Support Program (2006), Lhasa.

Wang, S., Cheng, M., & Melissa, G. (1995), Cultural metaphor of AIDS: a case study of HIV-related unsafe sex in different sociocultural settings of PRC, in Department of Research Office (Ed.) *Proceedings: Social Science Fronts*, published by Sichuan Social Sciences.

Wang, S. & Keats, D. (1999), Promoting health and preventing HIV/AIDS in the dual social system in China, in M. MacLachlan (Ed.), *Cultivating Health: Cultural Perspectives on Promoting Health*, John Wiley & Sons.

Wang, S., & Van de Ven, P. (2003), Peer HIV/AIDS education with volunteer trishaw drivers in Yaan, People's Republic of China: Process evaluation, *AIDS Education and Prevention*, 15(4), 334-345,20.

Wang, S. & Zhao, J. (2002), Sociological behavioural survey in HIV research need to focuses on beyond current acknowledged high-risk groups: A critical literature review on STIs prevalence and HIV/STIs-related risky behaviour among both high and low risky groups, *China-Sichuan Journal of Social Science Research*, 99 (2) 2002 *Supplement*, 46-59.

Wang, S. & Zhao, J. (2000), The use of local slang, colloquialisms, and community languages with the developing Safe Sex Role-Model Stories to target group in Sichuan, Chengduan, and Yaan-Yunjin-Yunjin areas, in Cheng, C. & Liu, Y (Eds.), *Proceedings on Strategic Exploration of Culturally Sensitivity in Sociology*, printed by China-BaShu Association of Cultural Study.

Wubuli, H., A-li, Y., Ma, W., Hai. T. (2002), A data analysis on HIV positive among drug user of Viwur ethnic group, *Chinese Journal of AIDS & STD*, 2(8), 87.

Xing, S. & Zhang, H. (2002), An epidemiological study for the first HIV case in Qinhai province, *Chinese Journal of AIDS & STD*, 1(8), 41.

Zhang, J. (2001), Chinese minority groups, in G. H. Cheng & J. Liu (Eds.), *Dictionary of Chinese Culture* (pp. 236-272), Huna People's Publishing House Press.

5

ISSUES AND PERSPECTIVES OF HIV-AIDS AMONG TRIBAL PEOPLE IN THE KORAPUT DISTRICT OF ORISSA

DR. P.K. KAR, PUJASHREE MISHRA &
SOUBHAGYA RANJAN PADHI

Introduction

HIV./AIDS epidemic is a global crisis that demands urgent attention and sustained action by intermingle of individuals and civil society. It is imperative to bring a check on the overall epidemic and there by ensure a better lifestyle of each member of our society. In the 25 years since the first case was reported, AIDS has killed 25 million people, and infected 40 million more. In India the HIV./AIDS epidemic is more than 15 years old. Within this short period it has emerged not only the most serious public health problem but also as a major developmental issue. The national HIV. prevalence rate has raised from 0.1 per cent in 1986, to 0.8 per cent in 2001—an eight-fold increase in 15 years. Conservative estimates by the government say that perhaps as many as 4.5 million Indians are living with HIV./AIDS. According to UNAIDS there are 5.7 million people living with HIV. in India, majority of them are infected by unprotected sexual intercourse. In six states, more than one per cent of the population has HIV. positive. Given India's large population, each 0.1 per cent increase in the prevalence rate would increase the number of adults living with HIV./AIDS by over half a million people. As elsewhere in the world, it is poor and marginalized people, and especially women, who are most vulnerable. A social response of blame, denial, discrimination and stigmatization of HIV positive people has had to further exclusion of people who are already marginalized. Health services, even communities and their families often reject people with HIV.

Compelling Facts about HIV/AIDS

- Nearly one percent (about 4 million people) of adult population estimated to have HIV.
- In six states, more than one percent of the general population is HIV positive based on antenatal clinical surveys.
- Among 90 percent of the cases reported fall within the most economically productive age group of 15 to 44 and one in four cases of HIV in India is among women.
- Given India's large population, a mere 0.1 percent increase in prevalence rate would increase the number of adults living with HIV/AIDS by over half a million persons.
- HIV/AIDS is already affected India's children. By the end of 1999, UNAIDS estimated that approximately 160.000 children in India under the age 15 are with HIV/AIDS.
- Surveillance data shows that the virus has started to spread from high-risk population to the general population and is moving from urban to rural areas.

India occupies a unique position in the tribal map of the world. The tribal population forms a significant part of our country's population. It constitutes 8% of the total population of India. They occupy around 15% of the geographical area of India, which is the most inaccessible and underdeveloped area.

The highest number of tribes is represented by the state of Orissa. These tribal groups inhabit widely varying ecological and geo-climatic conditions in different concentration throughout the state and distinct biological isolates with characteristic cultural and socio-economic background. They are mostly homogeneous, culturally firm and have developed strong magico-religious health care system of their own. They live and survive in their own style.

Brief Background of the District and Problem

As per the scheduled Area Order 1977, Orissa is one of the scheduled areas. The order again specifies that Koraput district is one of the major scheduled areas of the state. Koraput was the largest district of Orissa till 1992 (undivided districts of Koraput), and was divided into four districts—Koraput, Nabarangpur, Rayagada and Malkangiri on 2nd October 1992. The tribal communities are living throughout the length and breadth of the district. 62 types of tribes inhabit the Koraput district. Majority of the people speak the local language of Kuvi, Gadaba, and Paraja. The major types of the primitive tribes are Paraja, Kondha, Soura, Gadaba, Halva, Bhumia, Koya, Kotia, Pentia, Santala and Bhatada. According to 2001 census the total tribal population of the district is 5, 85,830 which constitute almost 50% of the total population of the district. Among tribal population women constitutes 50.44%.

The health of tribals is probably one of the most inadequately researched areas in international public health. The health status of tribals is miserable and there is a lack of awareness towards HIV-AIDS among them. The deadly HIV/AIDS diseases are rapidly spreading among tribals due to their lack of awareness. According to UNAIDS programme, HIV estimate among tribal is 0.1 percent of the adult population, i.e. 70000-80000. The State AIDS Cell (SAC) observe that there are 4,193 HIV positive cases in Orissa. What is more alarming is that compared to their male counterparts, the afflictions among females in the 20-25 age group are more. The killer AIDS is slowly taking in its grip in the district of Koraput. According to Chief District Medical Officer (CDMO) more than 300 HIV positive cases had been identified in the district in the last three years. One can imagine that the unofficial and unreported HIV-AIDS must be much more than this. Even the surveys conducted by voluntary organizations reveal that the number is a lot more than what is mentioned in the government records.

Koraput district in Orissa is a centre for industries both large and small, and the heart of a highway network. Many young people migrate there from rural areas seeking jobs. The population is very mobile and there is a high demand for commercial sex. These conditions are risk factors for the spread of HIV/AIDS and other sexually transmitted infections (STIs). Knowledge of HIV/AIDS and of STIs among them is very low and the safe sex is not practiced. It is poor and illiterate tribal people; especially tribal women are most vulnerable to this hazardous epidemic.

In recent years, several international and national initiatives have begun to focus attention on the long-neglected area of HIV-AIDS among tribals. But still there are wide gaps in knowledge regarding the levels, determinants and consequences of HIV-AIDS on tribal's health problems in Koraput district, which is one of the most underdeveloped regions of our country. The health status of tribal in this district has never taken seriously. Though some intensive fieldwork has been taken by social scientists still most of them treated the problem of tribal health in peripheral and casual manner. For a meaningful understanding of the HIV-AIDS among the tribes, it is important to understand how under the existing social, economic and cultural setting this epidemic can be best prevented. The present paper addresses this neglected area at the societal, administrative and policy level with the following objectives.

Objective

At present there is little understanding of how HIV-AIDS affect tribal's lives. In this context information are collected on various levels, trends and determinants of HIV-AIDS and its consequences on tribal's health problems in Koraput district. The study also focuses on various socio-cultural and political contexts in which they experience many stigmas, which affect their physical and mental conditions.

Determinants of HIV/ AIDS

The health status of a community is closely linked to the way they perceive various health problems along with their accessibility to various health care facilities. Primitive tribal groups have specific health problems and genetic abnormalities like sickle cell anaemia, G-6-Pd red cell enzyme deficiency and STD. Unsanitary condition, ignorance, lack of health education are the main factors responsible for a majority of health problems.

With lower literacy rate among most of the tribal, the risk of HIV has increased. Most of tribals practice polygamous marriages, which often cause HIV-AIDS and STD infections. Moreover virginity was not very much cherished. Many of the tribal communities are slack towards pre marital and post marital sex relations. Along with the cultural practices there are some other factors, which also causes HIV among tribals. These are:

- Lack of knowledge about HIV-AIDS.
- Lack of access to contraceptive.
- Poverty intensified with unavailability of livelihood leading to migration of tribals to nearby states to work as labourers put them at higher risk for engaging in unsafe sexual practices.

- Cultural acceptance of commercial sex work among some tribal groups.
- Lack of modern health facility: The situation is worse when the hospital and the modern facilities to prevent the HIV-AIDS are less or not exist at all.
- Lack of supporting Agencies: Help providing agencies for the HIV-AIDS patients are not enough for these tribal populations.
- Social approval for the use of alcohol and few drugs as a part of tradition and sometime related to religious practices.
- Expense and prejudices associated with the preventive measure of HIV.

Reasons of Vulnerability to HIV/AIDS

- There is high rate of prostitute migration from Andhra Pradesh, which is said to be the high prevalence state on HIV/AIDS in the country. The high-risk people like the truck drivers, youth and migrant labours are the victim because of the un-safe sex practices with the female sex workers.
- Most of the patient who are detected HIV positive belonged to the labour class. They contracted the disease while working outside the state and then returned home to spread the virus. National Highway–43 in Koraput has connected three states i.e., Andhra Pradesh, Orissa and Chattishgarh. More than 500 trucks passes over every day through this Highway. There are about 34 major spots in between Koraput to Kotpad and from Boriguama to Nawrangapur District, where the truckers take food and refreshments. These truckers during their resting time seek to have sex with female sex workers that subsequently leave them vulnerable to AIDS.
- High incidence of TB & Malnutrition makes it easier for HIV progress rapidly.
- Poverty being one of the major causes making people prone to the HIV. Since people do not find other

alternate livelihood sources, they are forced to involve in the commercial sex and become susceptible to HIV/AIDS. Poverty also forces them to migrate outside their native place. Nobody can recognize them in a distant urban place and no family member usually stay there to scrutinize their day-to-day activities. Due to this, they don't have fear for doing illegal sex activities including attending sex workers and pay for it at later stage.

- Some of the tribal communities have traditional practices that can increase young women's vulnerability to HIV/AIDS. In Koraput district, the tribals have the festival, wherein girls and boys dance together and drink locally made country liquor. After the dance, the boy chooses a girl and they sleep together and have sex. At this time even outsiders and non-tribal join in and choose their sex partner. Because of this tribal girls often face sexual exploitation, violence and HIV/AIDS infection. There are also 'fairs' where adolescent boys and girls interact freely, also consume alcohol and have unsafe sex, on occasion, with more than one partner. In tribal society when a young girl attains puberty (become *jubatman*) she used to stay at a different house (*Dhangedy Basa* or *Basa Ghar*). There she can physically enjoy with many adolescent boys, involve with unsafe sex and invite HIV. Early marriage and pressure to have a child also increases the vulnerability of young girls to HIV/AIDS and other sexually infected diseases (*Sabaies*).
- The health care service is very poor in most tribal and rural parts of Orissa. Moreover, tribals have a lot of superstitions and beliefs that creates a social and cultural barrier in accessing health services. Anecdotal evidence suggests abortions for unmarried girls and STI presence amongst boys is not an uncommon occurrence. Both, rural and tribal communities, access untrained *Deisaries* (tribal priest or quacks) and traditional birth attendants for all their health problems, which cannot prevent but spread HIV/AIDS.

- Government health centres are also perceived to be providing low quality of service. Lack of basic infrastructural facilities, absence of qualified doctors and non-availability of essential instruments and lab-testing facilities are also responsible for the spread of HIV. No wonder that tribals like to access the services of quacks, Disari and on issues of confidentiality especially with regard to STIs.
- Both young boys/men and girls/women in the tribal family consume home-made liquor, on an almost daily basis. It is difficult to practice safer sex under its influence, even if one was aware of the issue. Lack of knowledge on basics facts of life and lack of knowledge of HIV/AIDS/STI prevention compounds the problem. The uses of condom among these communities are abysmally low. Besides that they do not consult the qualified doctors to get the treatment. The migration (from the district to outside district and from outside district to the district) is very high. All these factors contribute towards the vulnerability of the community to HIV/AIDS/STI.
- Various crude birth practices are found to exist in many tribal communities of Koraput. More than 90% of deliveries are conducted at home attended by elderly ladies of the household. No specific precautions are observed at the time of conducting deliveries, which resulted in an increased susceptibility to various infections. These practices also increase the risk of mother to child transmission of diseases like HIV/AIDS.
- Proper nutrition is best frontline drug for AIDS. However among tribals malnutrition is common and greatly affects the ability to resist infection, leading to chronic illness. A high incidence of malnutrition is found among the primitive tribal groups of Koraput, which is also responsible for the spread of HIV/AIDS.
- So far as the diagnosis of the disease is concerned, the tribal face great difficulty, particularly when they are confronted with any thing different from the

common diseases of every day occurrence. Due to this, many opportunistic infection like STI and STD are not reported as sometime tribal relate them with supernatural power, or with any mystic figure.

- In tribal societies social relations are fabricated by certain social values prescribed through the institution of marriage, youth dormitories, etc. The youth dormitories play a very important role in relation to the health of tribal. On one hand it gives sex related education and on other hand by allowing for free mixing of young boys and girls, it also bring a platform for the risk of STD. With the lower literacy rate among the most of the tribal, the risk of HIV has increased.
- Various marriage practices also increased the risk of HIV/AIDS and other opportunistic infections. There is a greater incidence of consanguineous marriages among some of the tribal groups. Consanguineous marriages often result in an increased probability of abortions, miscarriage, stillbirths, neonatal deaths, and increase susceptibility to infectious diseases etc. Many tribes practice polyandry and polygyny types of marriages. These marriage practices also set tribal population at the risk of HIV/AIDS and STD infections. Among tribals, age at marriage is very low. Furthermore virginity is not very much valued. Many of tribal societies are lax towards premarital sex relations, which are considered as training in the art of love and sex life and often ended in marriage. But these practices also put them at the risk of opportunistic infections. Child marriage as a part of cultural behaviour is still prevalent among tribal. These cultural practices contribute to a continuous and physically draining fatigue. The risk is also closely related to inappropriate care or poor hygiene in connection with child-birth, abortion etc.

Challenges

Government has not provided the Anti-retroviral Therapy (ART) facility for the AIDS infected people of the KBK region.

The only Art centre for southern Orissa is located at Berhampur but the centre is not easily accessible by the poor tribals as it is situated nearly 300 km from Koraput and other nearby tribal dominated districts. Though treatment is provided free of cost, most of the HIV positive and AIDS infected people of Koraput and previous undivided district of Koraput can not afford the transportation charges to Berhampur. An ART centre needs to be set up at the district headquarters, Koraput.

- Lack of awareness is the most crucial barrier for the prevention of aids. Most of the tribals are illiterates and they have no basic knowledge about the diseases. And for lack of awareness the diseases is spreading.
- Anti-retroviral (ARVs) significantly slow downs the progress from infection to disease. But it is provided by government only to states in which there is a high prevalence of HIV. Whatever drugs are there for the prevention of HIV-AIDS are only available at district headquarters. The key high-risk group i.e. mobile labourers are not showing their interest for travelling to district headquarters hospital to pick up these drugs. Because this means losing one day's wages, paying for the travel up and down and food. There is an urgent need of availability of these drugs at the block and village level.
- Living with HIV-AIDS is a costly business. HIV is evident as a devastatingly debilitating not merely in physical aspect but also it delivers an equally fatal blow on the financial well being of the infected person. The financial burden on people living with HIV-AIDS is enormous. Sustaining themselves and their families, which might include other HIV positive persons, is a difficult task. According to a recent study on the socio-economic impact of HIV on the Indian population done by the National Council of Applied Economics Research (NCAER) and supported by NACO and the United Nations Development Programme (UNDP)— "the negative impact of HIV is likely to have over the next decade on economic growth and livelihoods of people, particularly the poor, if current trends are not heeded" (*HINDU*, 1st December, 2006.)

- While states have been asked to ensure Medicare for persons with HIV, often facilities in government hospitals are insufficient. The NCAER study also showed that how, on average, the per capita medical expenses of HIV households are four times higher than those of non-HIV households. Majority of people living with this virus are unable to afford for their HIV treatment. Those who have developed resistance to the first line of ARV drugs provided free of cost by government requires to shift for second line drugs. But the second line drugs cost about 10 times that of the first line of drugs i.e. Rs. 8,000–Rs. 10,000. If these people will not access second line ARV drugs now, probably many of them would not survive for long. It is very distressing that India, a country that has a huge share in the production of generic AIDS drugs globally, is unable to supply ARVs to its own people.
- The other subsidiary expenses also causes economic burden for those people who live with HIV. A good nutritional diet like supplement of protein, iron, and other vitamins is very much essential for those patients who are on ARVs. So apart from their drug and regular living costs, funds have to be arranged to provide for good nutrition and hospitalization, if any. This adds more agony and brings unending stress in their life.
- The Voluntary Confidential Counselling Testing Centre (VCCTC) although exist at Koraput headquarters hospital, still that is not adequate enough for the treatment of HIV-AIDS patient. The infrastructure and facilities at this centre should increase for the better prevention of HIV-AIDS at this region. The state government should extend testing and treatment facilities at all the public Health centres.
- Often the district AIDS cell does not receive adequate funds to treat the HIV patients. Government should provide adequate funds for combating AIDS among the tribals.
- Most of the HIV affected patients and their family members are facing socio-economic stigmas in the

district. Sometimes the community members ostracize the family of HIV. affected people, denied them for their human rights. Due to the fear of social stigma like segregation from the community, ridicule, untouchability etc., many HIV. infected people do not report about their disease and ultimately die in silence.

Prevention of AIDS

In present scenario of HIV.-AIDS in Koraput, if we really want to restrict its spread we have to spread the awareness of HIV.-AIDS in all groups and areas and not among those who are infected. With specific reference to tribal community who are governed by their own traditions, it is not an easy task to teach them about HIV.-AIDS. We have to use their specific cultural patterns to combat this dangerous epidemic. This needs a very serious step and effort. With the help of target intervention we can restrict the spread of HIV.-AIDS among tribal group. Tribal social institutions especially Youth Dormitory can be used in a better way to control the spread of HIV. Nevertheless the following are the some of suggestions to restrict this deadly epidemic:

Coordination with Faith-Based Organizations

Coordination with faith-based organizations is one of the prime sources of strength in combating HIV.-AIDS. Hindus and Christian religious leaders, especially the *Disharies* of tribal communities must be taken into confidence and treated as partners to stop HIV. among tribals. Disharies should also adequately train through scientific medical education for a rational treatment of tribal HIV. positive people.

Awareness for the Entire Community

Only focusing on "high risk" groups may fail to address the risks to larger population groups, notably the wives of men who may have multiple sex partners. Therefore one had to work for reducing high-risk behaviour across all groups in both rural communities and in towns. In order to reach these wider groups both government as well as NGOs should use a vast range of methods, including AIDS prevention stalls at weekly markets, and theatre. Awareness for safe sex should spread to all the places of the district. Campaign for using condom during sex must shift to remote tribal villages.

Government should form various self-help groups (SHGs) in tribal villages, with the initial aim of helping villagers, mostly women and spread the awareness campaign against HIV-AIDS. These SHGs will definitely help to empower women and create a consciousness for HIV in their family and larger community. Various audio-visual presentations can have a strong impact on tribal communities, to prevent HIV-AIDS.

Social Marketing For Female Condoms

"Social marketing" of female condoms will definitely act as a protective gear not only against the dreaded HIV-AIDS but also against loutish husbands. These condoms will enable countless women, who are forced to have sex regularly with their AIDS infected husbands, to have an option not to become victims as well.

National AIDS Control Organization (NACO) has recently declared to distribute female condoms among women in eight states, where the number of HIV-AIDS case are very high. Orissa is not one of those states, so there is no provision of social marketing of female condoms here. However the authorities should also consider Orissa for such distribution as AIDS is rapidly increasing in Orissa in recent days.

Proper Scrutiny for Financial Support to AIDS Patient

NACO had introduced reimbursement of medical bills up to Rs. 2000 for each HIV infected persons in the district two years back. The funds meant for the purpose are placed with State AIDS cell. However not a single person has availed of the facility so far. (Indian Express). Most of the HIV affected persons are hail from Below Poverty Line (BPL) and are not aware of such schemes or cannot affords to avail it. Many complex bureaucratic procedures also sometimes create bottleneck for the ignorant and less aware tribal mass to avail this scheme. There is urgent need of distributing these funds among infected HIV persons for the prevention of this dreaded epidemic and NACO should provide these funds to the district administration for a better result.

Accountability

In a real sense every body should be accountable for the prevention of HIV./AIDS. Very recently on the eve of World AIDS day, the UN chief Mr. Kofi Annan has rightly made a vivacious appeal to the world community to show accountability for addressing the scourge of HIV./AIDS. In coming year accountability should be the theme of AIDS prevention programmes, which requires all political leaders in specific and the wider civil society in general to make a decision and declaration to stop this epidemic. Accountability is required not just for those who are in power but also for health workers, community leaders and religious institutions to protect the vulnerable groups from HIV./AIDS and to care the affected persons and their family members. All of us should spread the message that "Silence is death" in order to combat AIDS.

Use of Tribal Dialect

Most of the government personnel and even NGOs people do not have commanding knowledge about tribal dialect. They use Oriya language, which often treated as an alien language by most of the primitive people. Various technical concepts regarding HIV. should be communicated to them in their own dialect, so that they not only aware about this hazardous epidemic but also make aware to their new young generation about this diseases.

Looking AIDS beyond Safe Sex

So far most of the AIDS prevention campaign has been given importance to mere safe sex. But we have to focus on other important aspects like blood transformation and others.

Reducing Malnutrition

To restrict the spread of epidemic among the tribals, their nutritional level, hygienic condition and other health improving measures have to be undertaken besides reducing susceptibility of infection to malaria, TB, STD which can further increase the risk of HIV among the tribal population.

Training for Traditional Medicinal Practitioner

In many tribal areas, herbal therapies are widely in use by HIV positive people. Among the tribal where modern medicine system is not full-fledge, the people primarily take indigenous herbal medicine at the time of need. Cadres of traditional health practitioners, spiritualists, birth attendants and herbalists are found in every village of tribal areas. These traditional health providers have a high degree of credibility in tribal society. So the risk of infection on HIV/AIDS can be reduced by imparting awareness, knowledge and preventive measures through these traditional health practitioners, spiritualists, birth attendants, traditional midwives and herbalists as these are integral part of tribal's traditional culture.

Advocacy With Civil Society Organizations

HIV/AIDS is no longer a health issue but a developmental issue and hence needs supportive and cooperative action from all quarters of society. Civil society comprises the totality of voluntary civic and social organizations and institutions that form the basis of functioning a society. These are the element, which facilitates better awareness, build social capital, trust, shared values and thereby essential for creating wakefulness to curb HIV/AIDS.

So far the civil society organizations as a whole do have a little or no understanding on the STD/HIV/AIDS issue in the state. However in order to strengthen the capacity for the effective prevention of HIV, the interaction between government and civil society becomes imperative. The staffs of civil society organizations need to be sensitized on the subject. The organization belong to the community or work in very close co-ordination with the community need to understand the menace of HIV/AIDS in order to mainstream it into their current developmental programmes and activities.

Intervention in the Community

In the backdrop the current scenario there is a need for immediate intervention of various NGOs in the community for awareness and prevention of RTI/STD/ HIV/AIDS. Through this we can provide accessible, affordable, available and acceptable basic health care in the tribal communities. It will help to build capacity of the community and to develop resources within the community for fighting against this killer epidemic. By forming health committees within the community and with active participation of tribals, prevention of HIV will be more effective.

A. Prevention

IEC and BBC are the pivotal instruments, which play major role in the prevention of HIV/AIDS. As there is no cure of HIV/AIDS, prevention is the most effective strategy to control the pandemic. It is possible through mass awareness by providing information and education to the civil society and behaviour change communication to those having high-risk behaviour.

- IEC: Information, education and Communication (IEC) is a process that enlightens, encourages and facilitates people to adopt and maintain healthy practices and life skills. It empowers individuals and enables them to make correct decision about safer sex practices. IEC can creates a environment, which is conducive for the treatment of affected persons through number of activities viz. distributing leaflets and booklets, pasting poster in public places, wall writing and roadside hoardings, awareness generation meetings, street plays and video shows, school education programmes etc. However while implementing these IEC programmes one must be careful about certain things. IEC must be in local language or dialects, more pectoral than words and need based.
- BBC: Behaviour change communication (BBC) is the tool to change the risk behaviour of people affected by HIV/AIDS. It also develops the life skill of the individual to live a healthy life. The following are

A proposed Model of Intervention Components:

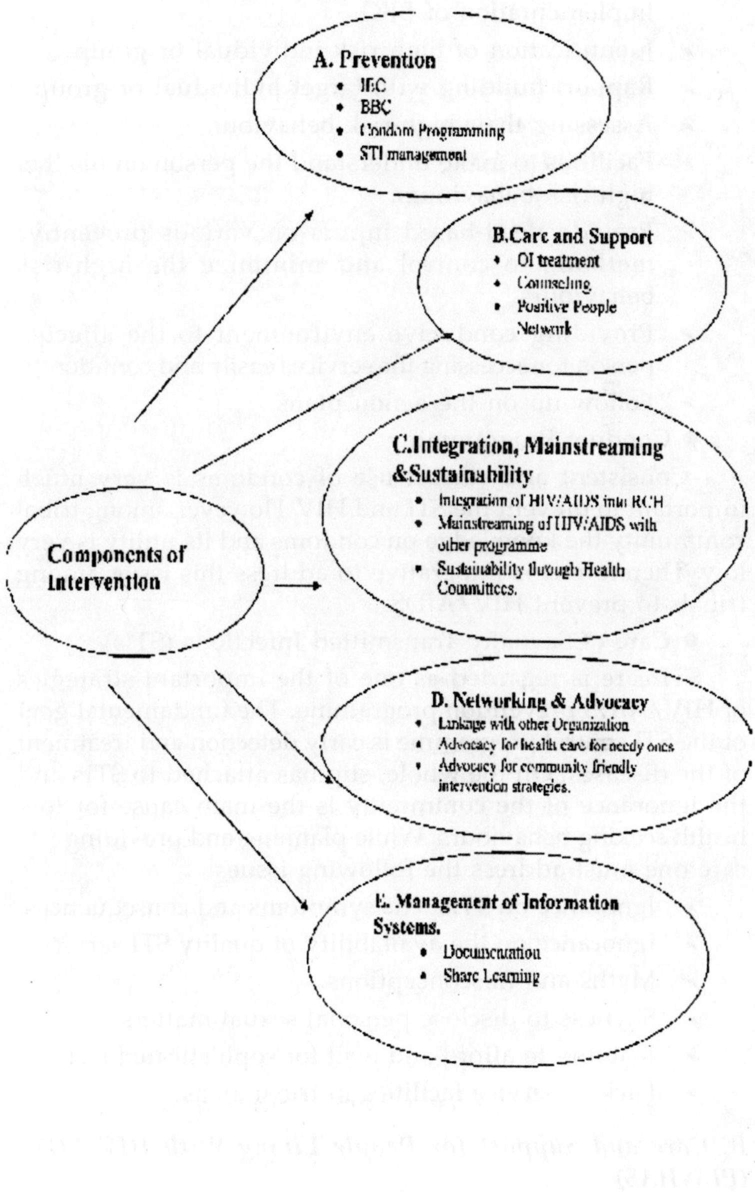

some of the significant steps for the proper implementation of BBC.

- ➢ Identification of high risk individual or group.
- ➢ Rapport building with target individual or group.
- ➢ Assessing their high-risk behaviour.
- ➢ Facilities to make understand the person on his/her high-risk behaviours.
- ➢ Provide need-based inputs on various preventive methods to control and minimize the high-risk behaviours.
- ➢ Providing conducive environment to the affected person for accessing the services easily and confidently.
- ➢ Follow-up on the action plans.

- Condom Programming

Consistent and correct use of condoms is very much important to prevent the STI and HIV. However among tribal community the knowledge on condoms and its utility is very low. Therefore it is imperative to address this issue among tribals to prevent HIV/AIDS.

- Care of Sexually Transmitted Infections (STIs)

STI care is regarded as one of the important strategies of HIV/AIDS prevention programme. The fundamental goal of the STI control programme is early detection and treatment of the diseases. On the whole, stigmas attached to STIs and the ignorance of the community is the main cause for low health seeking behaviours. While planning and providing STI care one must address the following issues.

- ➢ Ignorance on STIs – its symptoms and consequences.
- ➢ Ignorance on the availability of quality STI services.
- ➢ Myths and misconceptions.
- ➢ Shyness to disclose personal sexual matters.
- ➢ Inability to afford and wait for sophisticated testing.
- ➢ Lack of service facilities in tribal areas.

B. Care and Support for People Living With HIV-AIDS (PLWHAS)

People living with HIV/AIDS face much physical and

psychological tension for several reasons viz. Opportunistic infection, loss of income, fear of death, stigma in family and community etc. Therefore during this period they need special care and support to live an easy life. After identification of a person as PLWHA only subsequent to a positive status report from any one of the voluntary counselling and testing centre (V.CTC), various steps should be taken to give him support. However to provide care and support the following activities must be undertaken:

- Treatment of Opportunistic Infection (OI)

The PLWHA must be facilitated for treatment of opportunistic infections in collaboration with district health department and other institutions providing OI treatments.

- Counselling

Counselling to people through health education act as a catalyst for preventing HIV./AIDS. However during the counselling session the following issues should be addressed carefully—

- ➢ Developing the attitude to cope with his/her hazardous health conditions.
- ➢ Consumption of balanced diet.
- ➢ Early treatments of OIs, along with information on the range of HIV. care services available.
- ➢ Preventive measures to be taken to prevent other common diseases prevalent in the area, along with taking safe drinking water, using mosquito net, refrain from smoking, doing mild exercises etc.
- ➢ Motivating for living positively with HIV./AIDS.
- ➢ Counselling on family issues.

- Positive Peoples Network

The PLWHAs must be organized through SHGs, which can advocate for PLWHA—friendly policies apart from providing emotional support to each other. For a broader support and sustenance, they may be facilitated to establish linkages with state and national level positive peoples network.

C. Integration, Mainstreaming and Sustainability

- Integration of HIV/AIDS into RCH

There exist a significant relationship between HIV/AIDS and reproductive health care. The policies and programmes must be integrated to the broader RCH for the effective prevention of HIV/AIDS.

- Mainstreaming HIV/AIDS with other developmental activities

Envisaging the brisk growth of HIV/AIDS, there is an urgent need to prevent this treacherous disease at national level. Hence it is sine-qua-none to take HIV issue as a key issue in the entire development programme.

- Sustainability

Sustainability is a major component of all the policies and programmes for which the following activities need to be done:

- Identifying, developing and activating more and more peer educators in the community.
- Activating more Capacity building Organizations in the community.
- Encouraging condom use in the community.
- Promoting both govt. and non-govt. developing agents to work in the community.
- Sensitizing health care provider on STD care.

D. Networking and Advocacy

- Linkage with other Organizations of civil society for a better prevention work.
- Advocate for accessible, available and acceptable health care services for the infected and affected with RTI, STDs and HIV/AIDS.
- Advocate with government for use of 'community friendly' HIV/AIDS intervention strategies.

E. Management of Information System (MIS)

Documentation of the scenario, various practices and impacts along with share learning is very much essential for analyzing this issue. A proper MIS is required for monitoring and assessing the progress of various programmes as well as keeping in tract with its achievements, best practices and lesson learnt in the line with the programme objectives laid down.

Conclusion

We must stop the continued spread of HIV-AIDS, for which there is as yet no cure. Prevention of HIV-AIDS needs for a holistic approach. Instead of start on to act when people become sick, treatment and support should be provided right at the beginning. Social support systems including financial support and insurance must also be provided especially to those in pitiable conditions.

The prevention programmes has to be inclusive. It has to cater to the needs of the infected and the affected and strengthen the capacity and skills of whole communities. People living with HIV/AIDS need programmes that address human rights and legal issues, and also information and training for alternative livelihoods. Peer education is a key strategy for behaviour change. HIV/AIDS work needs to be integrated with reproductive health care to increases the coverage and impact. But for this to happen, the programme providers also have to work inclusively. That means government doctors, health workers and other authorities, NGOs and traditional providers have to work more closely together and reinforce each other's skills. This in turn also requires networking and advocacy with district legislators and other political stakeholders who can establish policies and resources from the top in order to create "friendly" services.

In the absence of cure, experience shows that the problem of HIV cannot be solved by medical solutions alone, but must involve all sectors of society. Prime minister Mr. Manmohan Singh has rightly made this clear at the National Youth Convention on HIV-AIDS when he said, "Non-governmental Organizations, civil society, the private sector, religious leaders ... must all play a prominent role ... leading a healthy and safe sexual life is one of the commitments we must all makes."

REFERENCES

Basu, S.K. (1993): *Tribal Health in India,* Manak Publishers, New Delhi.

Bose, A.B. (1970): "Problems of Education Development of Scheduled Tribes", *Man in India,* Vol. L (1).

Cook, R.J. (1994): *Women Health and Human Rights,* Switzerland: World Health Organization.

District Statistical Hand Book of Koraput (2001): *Directorate of Economics and Statistics,* Orissa, Bhubaneswar.

Government of Orissa (1991): *Tribal Sub-Plan 1992-97,* Bhubaneswar: H & TW Departments.

Mohapatra, P.C., Samal, J. and Pradhan, N.N. (2003): *Integrated Early Childhood Development Programme in Koraput District of Orissa,* Koraput: Council of Analytical Tribal Studies.

Pati, R.N and Das, J. (2002) *Tribal and Indigenous People of India: Problems and Prospectus,* New Delhi: A.P.H. Publishing Corporation.

United Nations Population Fund (UNEPA), 1999. "Integrated Population and Development Project Report".

Kalla, A.K and Joshi Ed. (2004), *Tribal Health and Medicine,* Concept Publishing Company, New Delhi.

News Paper – *The Hindu*

New Paper – *The Indian Express.*

Singhal, Arvin and Evert M. Rogers (2003): *Combating AIDS Communication Strategy in Action,* Sage Publication, New Delhi.

Roy, Debubrata (2001): *Community Action on HIV for Indian NGOs,* Voluntary Health Association of India, Published by VHAI Press.

6

SOCIAL ASSESSMENT OF HIV/AIDS AMONG AUTOCHTHONES OF RAJASTHAN

DR. DEVESH K. SAHU & MS. ANKITA ARYA

Background and Rationale

After Africa, India has the second largest concentration of tribal population in the world. Indian tribes constitute around 8.2 percent of nation's total population (Census 2001). Poverty and poor infrastructural development in tribal dominant areas have been the main reasons contributing to the inability of health programmes in reaching out to tribal populations, which includes the National AIDS Control Programme.

"The socio-cultural milieu of Rajasthan does not reveal one homogenous regional entity. Although Rajasthan is perceived in a holistic sense, it is in reality an assemblage of dispersed localized traditions. These have diverse traditional cultural and sub-cultural regions identified and recognized by people for their distinct characteristics. Accordingly, there are distinct variation in dialect, style of dress, food habits, customs, sacred belief systems, caste and ethnicity in different parts of the region. Both geography and historicity have had a deep influence on the lives of the people in Rajasthan making the process of social transformation difficult and challenging" (Singh 1998).

The assessment reaffirmed that illiteracy, migration and poor access to media makes the tribal population socially vulnerable. With regard to HIV vulnerability, tribal women are particularly vulnerable to HIV/AIDS since they commence sexual activity at an early age. Sexual practices varied widely, sexual relationships out of wedlock were reported to be a common phenomenon. Among tribal communities, girls and boys staying together before marriage is a socially acceptable norm. Couples are also at liberty to divorce and remarry. Males are involved in premarital or extra marital sex. Condoms are generally not used, as these are disliked.

The tribal communities are mostly unaware of STIs and HIV/AIDS. Awareness is much lower among women. In most of the tribal dominated districts the awareness regarding services for prevention, diagnosis, treatment and care for STIs and HIV/AIDS is considerably low amongst tribal people. Treatment seeking behaviour for most health problems including STIs, revealed initial resort to home remedies or self medication by buying medicines over the counter from grocery followed by visits to the traditional healers.

Many previous studies have also reported that due to stigma and shame associated with RTIs/STDs the tribal women suffering from RTI/STIs did not consult any physician unless the problem became very acute. Health facilities like the CHC/PHC were reported to be visited only when the problem became unbearable. Private health facilities were used, particularly when the location of public sector facilities was not convenient. Access to health care is yet a problem for tribal people because of scattered settlements and difficult terrain, inadequate accountability and monitoring of health service delivery to tribal people, unhelpful attitudes of health service personnel, non availability of manpower at health facilities etc.

Not much specific interventions had been started among tribals in the study areas by the government, private or public sector collaborators. Though in Rajasthan, a small proportion of these populations were covered under the interventions designed for the high-risk (CSW and migrants) and other groups. Very few NGOs, are reported to be working specifically with tribal people on HIV/AIDS. Although NGOs in some tribal areas of Rajasthan are synchronizing ideas of communication for their social development but there is a dearth of IEC material communicating in local dialect of tribal people to increase their level of knowledge and awareness about HIV/AIDS and other communicable diseases.

Thus a tool like social assessment is required to uncover the social causes and consequences of epidemic which in turn necessitates to explore the different tribal groups and to understand the social environment of these identified tribal communities which are vulnerable to HIV/AIDS due to such socio- economic and cultural factors. It is also important to assess their level of knowledge about STI/HIV/AIDS and also to assess their risk behaviours. Apart from that, it is pertinent to know about the institutions providing HIV/AIDS services to these groups and the policy environment around these groups. Identifying gaps with respect to the reach of the programme in the tribal communities and measures to be taken against it are among the other components of the present social assessment study.

Specific Objectives of the Social Assessment

The social assessment among tribal people has the following specific objectives:

1. To undertake a comprehensive social assessment that documents the prevalence and risk of HIV/AIDS among tribal people.
2. To assess their levels of awareness, knowledge, social, cultural and behavioural causes and consequences of HIV/AIDS.

Assessment Methodology

Social assessment is a qualitative research and the information is collected through:

A. Desk Based Research

Review of available relevant literature was made. The following policies and other documents have been examined and analyzed to understand vulnerability of the tribal people:

1. National HIV/AIDS Prevention and Control Policy

2. National Health Policy 2002
3. National Population Policy 2002
4. National Rural Health Mission-Vision Document
5. The National RCH and RNTCP Program Documents

B. Primary Assessment

The primary assessment was carried out among tribal people, Key informants and service providers are done. Qualitative methods like Focus Group Discussions, Key Informant Interviews and In-depth Interviews were used. The rationale behind selecting Rajasthan to conduct this social assessment is: firstly this state considered vulnerable due to influx and out flux of migrants, secondly it is one of the important tourist destination in India with considerable tribal population. As per the census 2001 Udaipur is the numerically tribal dominated district with different socio-cultural characteristics. The golden history of Mewar, makes Udaipur one of the most important tourist place in India, presence of industries and the location of this district makes it a most suitable area for the present study.

Block and villages with high concentration of tribal population (one falling on the National Highways and another from remote area) and where from large number of people particularly males migrate temporarily to neighbouring big cities were selected purposively. In each selected village, unmarried and married male and female (15-49 age group) were selected purposively for group discussion and one to one interviews.

Basic Information about Tribal People

The following are the salient findings regarding behavioural and other practices that are relevant to the programme planners:

1. Low level of awareness and knowledge regarding STI/ HIV/AIDS and misconceptions that exist exasperates this situation.
2. Widely varying sexual practices (high level of pre-marital and extra marital sexual practices) and contact

with external high risk population like truckers and other Non-tribal people increases their vulnerability.

3. Specific communication strategy designed to suit the needs and culture of the target group would be necessary. The choice of medium for communication preferably in local dialects would also be critical. Folk media, Inter Personal Communication and messages through peer groups could be main choices. The concept of community radio can also be introduced.
4. Non-availability and/or lack of access to health care facilities were one of the main factors discouraging health seeking. Trust in faith healers and non qualified private practitioners and easy accessibility made them rely on these sources for seeking treatments for illnesses. Role of such providers in referral needs to be reckoned in programme design.
5. Gender bias towards females for health care seeking needs to be addressed
6. High level of stigma associated with STI and HIV/AIDS is a challenge that needs to be addressed
7. Youth are emerging as a highly vulnerable group in these areas as they are mostly migrating to the big cities like Ahmedabad, Mumbai and Surat etc.

Socio-economic and Cultural Dimensions of HIV/AIDS

The finding of the present social assessment shows that HIV/AIDS is a disease that can only be fought with deep-routed changes in attitude, behaviour, values and practices. Larger social issues associated with HIV/AIDS includes man's and women's unsafe sexual behaviour, substance abuse, masculinity, sexual violence and associated factors like low level of literacy, poverty, child marriages, unemployment, and gender etc. The girl's early age of marriage makes them biologically more vulnerable. Poverty is one of the important factors which lead to a kind of risk behaviour or make people more vulnerable about HIV/AIDS. Poverty is directly related to nutritional status and health seeking behaviour. This is especially relevant with respect to STI.

Prostitution has become a lucrative business for women without social support; poverty is another contributing factor driving women into this trade. For many poor women, sex work is often the only means of earning a livelihood and maintaining the family. In these situations poor women become vulnerable to HIV/AIDS not only because they have multiple sex partners but also because they are unable to bargain for safe sex with their clients. Unscrupulous persons (mostly of non-tribal) are illegally luring, abducting, forcing and compelling young girls and women for their own benefits.

Due to consecutive droughts in the area makes most of the young men migrate to urban areas like Udaipur city, Ahmedabad, Surat and Mumbai in search of employment leaving their family behind very often. Deaths due to HIV and AIDS are also reported in the villages during discussion (some of the deaths seem to be diagnosed deaths whereas many other are based on perceived cause). Thus this circular migration has led to increase in the spread of HIV/AIDS. These young men generally work in poor working environment without negotiation power and in the absence of their wives, some of them often form partnership and relationship with other women in their place of migration. Unemployment may also lead to other types of risk behaviour like substance use.

Education is often viewed as a panacea of all social and economic problems affecting a country. It is used as one of the indicators of social development. In the present assessment study, it was found that years of schooling had a positive co-relation with knowledge about HIV/AIDS. It also prevents in indulging risky behaviours and helps in having proper health seeking behaviour.

One of the prerequisites for good health is access to health care. The finding of the present social assessment shows that availability, accessibility and affordability of health care services are still a big challenge among the tribal people. Quality of the health services, gender of the health care providers, and faith in traditional system of medicine are the major blocks in access to proper health care. The public health care institutions are either not available or of poor quality whereas private health care institutions are unaffordable. High level of poverty and low incomes are other important contributing factors which presumably restrict the demand for better health care.

With respect to gender, the assessment findings describes that woman has the least access to health care, due to her culture of silence and tolerance. The unavailability of health services in the vicinity, her status in the family, and the gender of the health care provider minimize women's access to health care. The problem is compounded, as women are accompanied by men to the doctor and she is not encouraged to communicate her health problem directly to the doctor. As a result she often resorts to self medication or traditional curative methods.

The findings of the assessment study further depicts that women are neither having access yu;c es nor have awareness and rights to have safe sex. The finding of discussion shows that they are afraid to ask their husband to use condom who lives outside the village during his visit to home which may often lead to domestic and sexual violence too. The low level of awareness and knowledge on care and prevention of STIs and also poor knowledge on STDs increases the risk of acquiring HIV/AIDS. The reasons for high incidence of RTIs and STIs include ignorance and unawareness about the causes and symptoms, treatment and diagnostic facilities.

The other social dimensions of HIV/AIDS includes the tribal's attitude to the disease, the social stigma attached to it, social responses of fear, anxiety, denial and stigma, discrimination by health care providers, disowning by the families and friends, have become literally nightmares for HIV positive cases and AIDS patients, not only among the tribal people in the area, but also in the rest of the state.

The cultural dimension of HIV/AIDS includes the traditional value system defines sex and sexuality in their traditional ways which has an implication as misconception on sex and sexuality. Sex is comparatively open and acceptable in the tribal societies but it is now not any more endogamous in the practice. Through sexual networking, migration has exposed these tribal communities in the risk of HIV/AIDS.

The young and other male members of the tribal communities who are migrating to the big cities contracting HIV infection and carrying other diseases through the contact with CSWs and other sexual partners whereas girls and wives especially of road site villages who are left behind at the home to take care about the elder members of the family and traditional occupation are being exposed through the sexual networking with the non-tribal people.

Similarly there are some cultural practices like *Nata Pratha*. The present study also revealed that engaging in *Nata* and having many sexual partners at a time is very common among tribal communities living in the study area. According to the *Nata* tradition, if a woman is not happy living with her husband then she can leave him and go for *Nata* with the person of her choice. Though it is a safety mechanism developed and sanctioned by the society to save her from the struggle and rights to live happy life but it also exposes her to many sexual partners. This socially sanctioned exposure of women and men to multiple sexual partners increases their susceptibility for opportunistic infections may result in HIV/AIDS.

Discussion and Conclusion

The tribal people of the study area have poor health generally due to their poverty and socio-cultural vulnerability. Tribal people are known to have sexual practices that differ from those of mainstream cultures, and prevalence of sexually transmitted infections. Their low level of awareness and knowledge makes them more vulnerable about the prevalence of STD/HIV/AIDS among them. Solution to these larger societal issues rests with political support, police and other enforcement authorities, citizens' pressure groups, NGOs and activists, social and women's welfare departments, school education, etc.

There are no specific policies that directly impinge or address the tribal issues but there is enough scope to derive from the various policies that there are areas that can be interpreted to be applicable to the Tribal people. This has been discussed in the interpretation section of each policy.

However, it is concluded that specific issues addressing the requirements of tribal people needs to be developed separately drawing from the different policies that are already in place. This exercise needs to be carried out on a priority basis.

Although few NGOs have started working among these tribal communities and started providing support to people living with HIV./AIDS through their community outreach programmes but these NGOs providing health services are mostly located in urban areas and covering small geographical pockets only. Though there are also few NGOs who have developed successful referral systems but they are very few in the number. Most of the awareness campaign happened in the study area was mainly in the Hindi and could not use the local language consequently looses much of its impact.

There is clear cut need of making efforts to ensure availability of culturally appropriate and quality health care services for the tribal people to decrease morbidity and mortality associated with HIV. infections and also use of information communication technology should be done to increase the level and awareness about RTIs/STIs and HIV./AIDS and minimize the socio-cultural and economic impact resulting from HIV./AIDS among the local tribal people. Also some efforts should be made for asset based community development through public-private partnership.

Recommendations

1. Multi-pronged approach may be adopted to reach out tribal people.
2. A policy decision regarding the necessity to intervene with this group needs to be taken.
3. A culturally appropriate integrate health package has to be developed and provided among the tribal communities
4. State should carry out a mapping exercise in order to identify high risk tribal belts and gather information on HIV./STI prevalence among tribal communities through the sentinel surveys.
5. There is a need to have a effective communication

strategy on stigma, discrimination, care and support more clearly.

6. There is a need to collaborate or co-ordinate with Department of Tourism, Women and Child Development and Tribal Development to introduce some short term skill development courses to provide them some alternative livelihood opportunities.

REFERENCES

1. DFID Policy Paper 2005: Reducing poverty by tackling social exclusion.
2. Annual report (200-01): Ministry of Tribal Affairs: http://tribal.nic.in/chapter1.html
3. AVERT (2006): HIV/AIDS in India: 1-2 (www.avert.org/aidsindia.htm)
4. Basu, S.K. (1993): Health Status of Tribal Women in India, NIHFW: 3-4
5. Bhasin, V. (2004), Sexual illnesses and under utilization of Biomedicine among Tribal Women of Rajasthan, *Anthropologist*, 6 (1): 1-12
6. Census of India. 1991 Part II B (i) PCA- General Population (Vol. I & II).
   http://www.education.nic.in/htmalweb/stat1.html.
7. Central TB Division, Directorate General of Health services, MoHFW (2005): Revised National Tuberculosis Control Programme, Tribal Action Plan (Proposed for the World Bank assisted RNTCP II Project)
   http://www.tbcindia.org/pdfs/RNTCP%20II%20Tribal%20Action%20Plan_10th%20May%2005.pdf
8. CMS Report (2006): Moving Ahead: An Assessment of Current Communication Efforts & Strategies for HIV/AIDS: 1-25
9. Department of Family Welfare, MoHFW, GOI (2004): Project Implementation Plan for Vulnerable Groups Under RCH II: 11
   http://mohfw.nic.in/VOLUNERABLE%20COMMUNITIES%20MODIFIEDpdf
10. DoH&FW (M) Govt. of Rajasthan (2003) :District Strategic Plan, Udaipur
    http://www.youandaids.org/Charca/Resources/DSP%20Udaipur.pdf
11. Gandotra, M.M. et. al (2001), Population Research Centre, MS.

University, Baroda: The Demography of tribal population in Western India;1 http://www.iussp.org/Brazil2001/s40/S48_P08_Gandotra.pdf

12. Institute of Health System (IHS), Hyderabad (2005): Institutional assessment of NACP, a NACO Supported study: 7-28
13. Integrated Disease Surveillance Project, Tribal Development Plan (2002):6 http://mohfw.nic.in/TDP.pdf
14. Integrated Disease Surveillance Project 2003: Tribal Development Plan. Downloaded from http://www.mohfw.nic.in/TDP.pdf.
15. Jejheebhoy, S., Sebastian, M. 2003. Actions that Protect: Promoting Sexual and Reproductive Health and Choice among Young People in India, Regional Working Papers No. 18, India: Population Council.
16. Mehta, M, The HIV/AIDS Crisis in India, South Asia Monitor CSIS No. 58 May 2003 www.csis.org
17. Mutatkar, R.K., 2004, Report on Health Issues in Nandurbar District: Maharashtra Human Development Action Research Study, The Maharashtra Association of Anthropological Sciences, Pune, India.
18. NACO (2001): Baseline Behavioural Surveillance Survey among General Population: 61-62.
19. NACO, 2001, Disaggregated data from National BSS: KAP of Young Adults (15-24 years)
20. NACO (2005): TOR for Social Assessment of NACP Arrangements
21. NACO Report (2005): Assessment of Extent of HIV/AIDS Prevalence among Central Police and Paramilitary Forces
22. Naik *et. al* (2005) Rural Indian tribal communities: an emerging high-risk group for HIV/AIDS in http://www.pubmedcentral.nih.gov/articlerender.fcgi?artid=554109
23. National Consultation on Human Rights and HIV/AIDS: Organised by National Human Rights Commission in Partnership with NACO, Lawyers Collective, UNICEF and UNAIDS, New Delhi, 24-25 Nov, 2000
24. National Family Health Survey-2 (1998-99), International Institute of Population Sciences; 1,48,230
25. Singh, K.S., People of India National Series, Volume III: *The Scheduled Tribes*, Anthropological Survey of India, Oxford University Press, New Delhi, 2003.

7

ENERGY AND NUTRIENT INTAKES AMONG WOMEN IN TOK MUDA VILLAGE, SELANGOR, MALAYSIA

DR. SNIGDHA MISHRA, SETI HAIREYAH,
DR. PRADIP KUMAR MISHRA, DR. ASBI BIN ALI &
DR. JUNAINAH ABDUL HAMID

Introduction

"Nutrition is a key element in any strategy to reduce the global burden of disease. Hunger, malnutrition, obesity and unsafe food all cause disease, and better nutrition will translate into large improvements in health among all of us, irrespective of our wealth and home country", (Brundtland, 2000). It emphasises the importance of the nutrition which is essential for all of us from the earliest weeks after conception until our death. (John and Lendal, 1989)

Generally, the nutrient requirements of women vary according to their different stages. Like pregnant women need more calories than non-pregnant women. Maternal nutrition is an important determinant of the course and outcome of pregnancy and seventy five per cent of foetal growth is related to maternal nutritional status (Pallavi *et al,* 2002 and Hassapidou and Papadopoulou, 2000).

Nutritional assessment of rural Malay women in Tok Muda, the study area which is located in Kapar, Klang has not been done yet. Most of the housing areas are within easy reach of the main road, while some houses situated further away are served by a network of footpaths. It is accessible by a country road about 10km from Kapar town, and another road about 20 km from Kuala Selangor.

Static community nurse clinic known as Klinik Kesihatan Desa Kampung Tok Muda, provided health facilities to this rural area. The dispensary was managed by a hospital assistant, but a medical and health officer were also available at the clinic. This clinic also provides maternal and child health services for this area. The nearest health clinic to this area is in Kapar town whereas the nearest government hospital is in Klang. Hence, the present study was undertaken to highlight the nutritional problems of the adult women of the village, Tok Muda with the following specific objectives.

Methodology

Tok Muda village is about 80km from Shah Alam. This village is located in the Kapar, which is in the Royal capital, Klang. This village (Kampung) has been marked as a squatter area in this State by Klang Municipal Council. The study was carried out among the adult Malay women living in Tok Muda village.

One hundred and eleven families were selected by simple random sampling from this village. A total of one hundred and eleven adult (aged 19 to 50 years) females survey were the subjects for the present study.

The questionnaire formulated was based on three aspects: socio-economic background, dietary survey and clinical assessment. A pilot study was done prior to the survey to select the area which was suitable for survey. Subjects were interviewed individually by house to house survey where the interviews took place in the house of the respondent. The interviews were conducted in the local Malay dialect directed to the subjects.

Dietary survey was conducted on the households with modified 24 hour dietary recall method. The amount of food consumed was estimated as accurately as possible using standardized household measurements such as bowls, cups, plates, glass and spoons. Macronutrients and micronutrients were calculated from the food they had consumed using

Nutrient Composition of Malaysian Foods Table (Tee *et.al.*, 1997) and then compared with The Recommend Nutrient Intakes for Malaysia 2005: Summary Table (Ministry of Health Malaysia).

To do the anthropometric measurements, height was measured to the nearest 0.1 cm using a microtoise and weight was measured to the nearest 0.5kg using Tanita, Japan beam balance. Body weight was measured in light clothing and without shoes. Bodyweight status was assessed based on Body Mass Index (BMI), determined by the following formula:

$$\text{Body Mass Index (BMI)} = \frac{\text{Weight (kg)}}{\text{Height (m)}^2}$$

Measured BMI was later compared with the BMI ready reckoner table (Shahar *et al*, 2002) to determine status of BMI such as underweight, pre-obese and obese.

A biochemical test for determination of haemoglobin level was done for the adult women who were willing to cooperate. Blood was collected by finger prick method from 100 adult women in their houses using disposable lancets with indirect Cyanmethemoglobin method, (Sari *et al*, 2001 and ISE *et al*, 2002).

The collected data was analyzed using the Statistical Package for the Social Sciences (SPSS ver.13.0) for windows. Values were expressed as percentage and mean ± SD.

Results and Discussions

Socio- Economic Background

A total of 111 houses, representing 100% of all houses in this study were visited and interviewed. The response and co-operation of the respondents were satisfactory. The results are presented in Figure 1.

The typical rural village house is very simple. The wood and tile houses were more common (59.5%) followed by brick and tile (25.2%). The houses with wood and the roof made of zinc accounted for 15.3%. They never wore slippers in the house and all the houses observed were always clean.

The context of monthly income was studied in this survey.

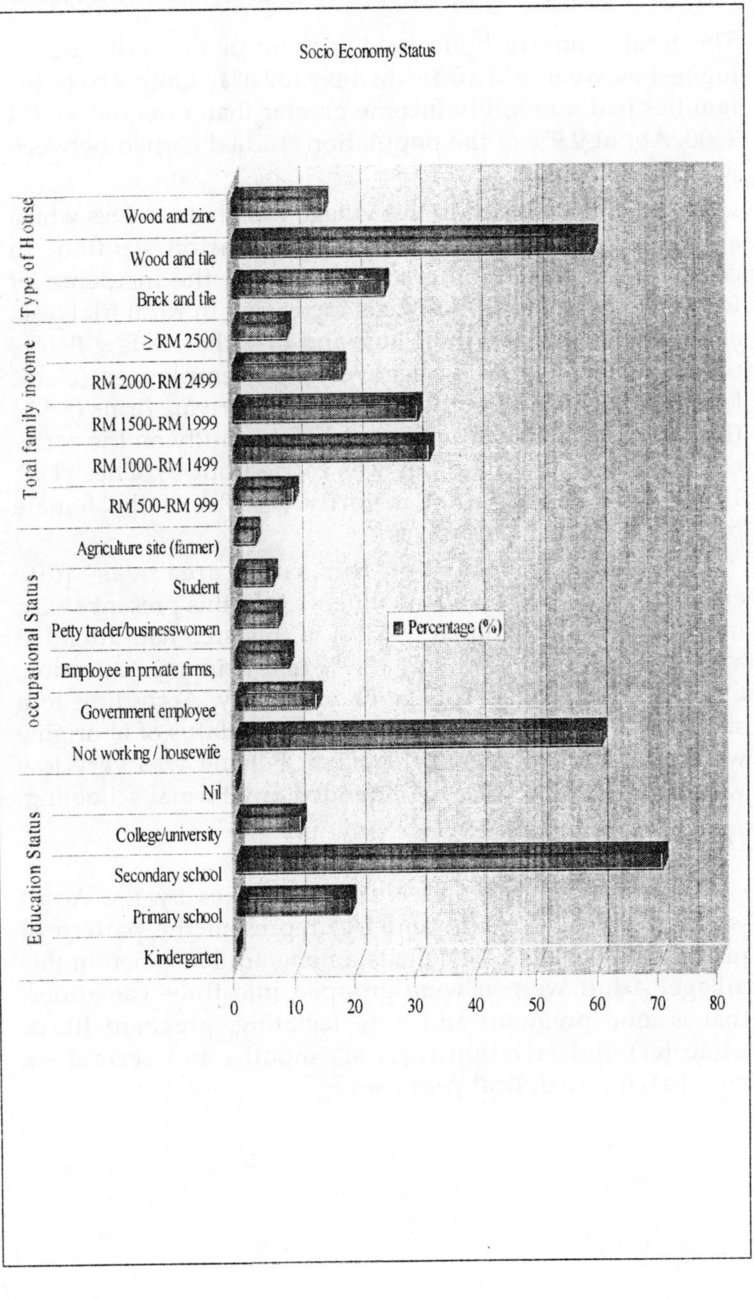
Socio Economy Status
Type of House
Wood and zinc
Wood and tile
Brick and tile
Total family income
≥ RM 2500
RM 2000-RM 2499
RM 1500-RM 1999
RM 1000-RM 1499
RM 500-RM 999
occupational Status
Agriculture site (farmer)
Student
Petty trader/businesswomen
Employee in private firms,
Government employee
Not working / housewife
Education Status
Nil
College/university
Secondary school
Primary school
Kindergarten
Percentage (%)
0 10 20 30 40 50 60 70 80

The total monthly household income of this village was highest between RM 1000-RM 1499 (32.4%). Only 9 % of the families had a monthly income greater than or equal to RM 2500. About 9.9% of the population studied earned between RM 500-RM999.

Most of the women in this village were housewives which accounts for 60.4% of the total population studied. In communities undergoing social changes, the incidence of women joining the workforce is increasing in rural Malaysia as they work to help their husband or father. A few (9.0%) of the women worked as government employees (clerk, labours, typist teacher) and employees in private firms (3.6%) (Factories, house construction). A similar study on the socio-economic profile of families was carried out by Chee *et.al.*, 1997 which showed that majority (74.3%) of the female population were housewives.

Educational status for this rural area was quite encouraging as there were no illiterates. In this present study, most of the adult women (70.3%) in this area had attended a secondary education, and 18.9% had primary education. Only 10.8% attended college or university. According to a study done by Lim *et.al.* 1998 educational status of aborigine women in two villages in Kuantan, Pahang was very low with 41.2% not ever having attended any formal schooling.

Dietary Survey

Deficit of Energy and Nutrient Intakes by the Adult women Tables 1(a), 1(b) and 1(c) represent the pattern of nutrient intakes and its deficits among adult women in this village. Adult women were grouped into three categories, that is, non pregnant and non- lactating, pregnant (three trimester) and lactation (first six months and second six months), for analytical purposes.

Table 1(a): Energy and Nutrient Intakes of Non-Pregnant and Non-Lactating Women

	GROUPS OF WOMEN (non-pregnant and non lactating)					
	19-29 years			*30-50 years*		
Nutrition	*Actual intake (mean ± SD)*	**RNI*	*Percentage of deficit(%)*	*Actual intake (mean ± SD)*	**RNI*	*Percentage of deficit(%)*
Energy (Kcal)	1352.1± 354.2	2000	32.4	1295.5 ± 360.4	2180	40.6
Protein (g)	43.7 ± 7.9	55	20.5	42.9 ± 7.1	55	22.0
Calcium (mg)	448.1 ± 85.2	800	44.0	454.5 ± 96.4	800	43.2
Ferum (mg)	9.0 ± 4.0	29	69.0	9.3 ± 4.1	29	67.9
Thiamin (mg)	0.5 ± 0.2	1.1	54.5	0.5 ± 0.2	1.1	54.5
Riboflavin (mg)	0.6 ± 0.2	1.1	45.5	0.6 ± 0.2	1.1	45.5
Vitamin A (μg RE)	397.6 ± 53.5	500	20.5	399.5 ± 50.9	500	20.1
Vitamin C (mg)	37.9 ± 9.2	70	45.9	38.7 ± 9.2	70	44.7

* *Source:* Recommended Nutrient Index (RNI) for Malaysia 2005: Ministry of Health, Malaysia.

Table 1(c): Energy and Nutrient Intakes of Lactating Women

	GROUPS OF WOMEN					
	Lactating 1st 6 months			*Lactating 2nd 6 months*		
Nutrition	*Actual intake (mean ± SD)*	**RNI*	*Percentage of deficit(%)*	*Actual intake (mean ± SD)*	**RNI*	*Percentage of deficit(%)*
Energy (Kcal)	1711.3 ± 339.3	2500	31.5	1593 ± 400.2	b	b
Protein (g)	51.0 ± 12.6	75	32.0	49.8 ± 4.3	70	28.9
Calcium (mg)	605.0 ± 58.1	1000	39.5	674.0 ± 70.7	1000	32.6
Ferum (mg)	8.0 ± 5.0	15	46.7	11.9 ± 1.8	32	62.8
Thiamin (mg)	0.8 ± 0.1	1.5	46.7	0.9 ± 0.1	1.5	40.0
Riboflavin (mg)	0.6 ± 0.4	1.6	62.5	0.7 ± 0.2	1.6	56.3
Vitamin A (μg RE)	584.0 ±7 0.4	850	31.3	547.0 ± 1.4	850	35.6
Vitamin C (mg)	58.7 ± 28.1	95	38.2	54.4 ± 6.4	95	42.7

**Source:* Recommended Nutrient Index (RNI) for Malaysia 2005: Ministry of Health, Malaysia.

b: No recommendations. Energy requirements depend on amount of breastmilk produced.

Table 1(b): Energy and Nutrient Intakes of Pregnant Women

	GROUPS OF WOMEN								
	Pregnant (1st Trimester)			*Pregnant (2nd Trimester)*			*Pregnant (3rd Trimester)*		
	Actual intake (mean ± SD)	**RNI*	*Percentage deficit (%)*	*Actual intake (mean ± SD)*	**RNI*	*Percentage deficit (%)*	*Actual intake (mean ± SD)*	**RNI*	*Percentage of deficit (%)*
Energy (Kcal)	1089.8 ±158.6	2000	45.5	1597.5 ± 355.7	2360	32.3	1293.0 ± 73.5	2470	47.7
Protein (g)	45.5 ± 8.1	62.5	27.2	46.4 ± 11.3	62.5	25.8	51.2 ± 7.9	62.5	18.1
Calcium (mg)	590.8 ± 91.5	1000	40.9	697.0 ± 69.3	1000	30.3	701.5 ± 79.9	1000	29.9
Ferum (mg)	10.7 ± 3.6	29	63.1	8.0 ± 1.1	a	a	8.5 ± 3.8	a	a
Thiamin (mg)	0.7 ± 0.2	1.4	50.0	0.8 ± 0.1	1.4	42.9	0.9 ± 0.1	1.4	35.7
Riboflavin (mg)	0.6 ± 0.4	1.4	57.1	0.6 ± 0.4	1.4	57.1	0.8 ± 0.1	1.4	42.9
Vitamin A (μgRE)	548.0 ± 98.7	800	31.5	486.0 ± 84.9	800	39.3	618.0 ± 70.7	800	22.8
Vitamin C (mg)	57.7 ± 3.9	80	27.9	53.8 ± 1.4	80	32.8	40.1 ± 5.2	80	49.9

**Source:* Recommended Nutrient Index (RNI) for Malaysia 2005: Ministry of Health Malaysia

a: Iron supplements in tablet form was recommended for all pregnant women. In the non-anaemic pregnant women, daily supplements of 100mg iron given during second half of pregnancy are adequate. In anaemic women, higher doses are usually required.

The nutrient intakes were calculated based on the consumption of food, recorded by a 24-hours dietary recall survey. Mean intake of energy and other nutrients of the all groups of adult women was found to be lower than the Malaysian Recommended Nutrient Intake.

Results in this study for energy intake was similar to the study conducted in two villages in Kuantan, Pahang (Lim *et.al.*, 1998) among aborigine women, where the levels of energy are 40%-50% short of meeting the required levels. In the present study also similar figures (31.5%-47.7%) were obtained. This may be due to large proportion of sample being housewives who do not engage with heavy work outside which requires more energy. It maybe attributed to the faulty food intake pattern and lack of dietary knowledge.

Intake of protein seemed to be very close to the requirements where the percentages of deficit for RNI vary from 18.1% to 32.0% (table 1a, 1b and 1c). Fish was daily taken by the adult women due to its low cost and availability; hence it was the main source of protein. As a result of frequent intake of vegetables and fruits the mean level of Vitamin A also seems to be very close to recommendations for these three groups. Zhao, 1994 suggest that high protein intake may enhance the risk of chronic degenerative diseases, especially coronary heart disease and osteoporosis.

Iron (ferum) intakes were the lowest among the non-pregnant, non-lactating and early pregnancy where the percentage of deficit for required levels of RNI were 69.0% (19-29 years), 67.9% (30-50%) and 63.1% (1st trimester) respectively. These required levels were slightly high in lactating women where the percentage of deficit for required levels decreased to 46.7% and 62.8% lactating first six months and lactating second six months respectively.

For pregnant women in 2nd and 3rd trimester, iron supplements in the form of tablet are recommended. Most of the pregnant women went for check-up in the nearest health care centre, Klinik Desa Kampung Tok Muda.

A study reported by Geok *et.al.* 2003 among underweight/ overweight and normal weight mothers, iron intake was similar to present study where intake was the lowest among the nutrients, with 57.2%-62.5% of deficit for required levels of RNI. Riboflavin and thiamine intakes were also lower in pregnant (42.9-57.1% and 56.3-62.5% respectively) and the non-pregnant, non- lactating women (45.5% and 54.5%) than the lactating women (35.7-50% and 40.0-46.7%).

Methods of Cooking

Table 2 gives the preferable methods of cooking by the adult women. Methods that were used for cooking by the adult women in this village were recorded in the questionnaire. There were two methods that were most common among the adult women in rural area. Those were frying (98.2%) and others such as gravy (76.6%). Most of the respondents were using these methods nearly everyday in their cooking.

Table 2: Preferable Methods of Cooking

Method of Cooking	*Number*	*Percentage (%)*
Boiling	30	27.0
Frying	109	98.2
Roasting	14	12.6
Others(gulai, curry)	85	76.6

Frying their main choice of method because it requires only a short time to prepare. Frying and gravy method seems to be easier and most wanted by the other family members because it was tastier than other method. Only a small amount of people used other technique such as boiling (27%) and roasting (12.6%).

A study done by Gregorio, 1992 on some effects of deep frying on the dietary fat intake also stated that the greatest proportion of method used in thermal culinary processes mainly frying, although many other processes are also used both industrially and in the home, such as canning and stewing in oil. He also stated that, fried food has been thought to be difficult to digest, and there were even some hints at toxicity.

Another study by Saibaba *et.al.* 2005 on nutritional status of adolescent girls of urban slums, Andhra Pradesh and their nutritional knowledge and practices, suggest that subjects need more exposure with respect to certain cooking habits which will minimize the nutritional loss in food items such as discarding excess water after cooking dal/vegetables.

Food Prohibitions During Some Special Conditions

Table 3 presents the food prohibitions during some special conditions. Food beliefs and prohibitions play a strong role during special condition where the beliefs related to food are strictly followed by adult women. These practices have been practiced from generation to generation even though some practices are beginning to fade.

Pregnancy

From the above table, the list of foods that are avoided during pregnancy has been showed. Most of women practiced these restrictions because of the fear that anything may happen to their baby or may lead to miscarriages. Quite a large number (28.6%) of women avoided chicken which was classified as hot foods.

Confinement

The first 44 days after childbirth is known as *tempoh berpantang* (period of restriction). Most of the mothers followed the food prohibitions during this period because they believed this was the time their bodies are most vulnerable to foods and good food helps in the healing of the womb faster. Most of the foods that were avoided were cold foods (34.9%), sour and acidic foods (23.8%) and poison foods (22.2%). Ginger and spices were allowed in this period as there were known as 'warm foods' and give warmth and helped to heal the womb beside body massage (*mengurut*).

Another cultural practise is 'bertungku' where the women wrap a piece of cloth on her stomach to flatten the stomach. The cloth was previously underlined by certain leaves *(lengkuas)* and stone near to fire. Women also consumed 'jamu', the traditional pills to overall wellness and energy. These newly mothers advised to eat liver and spleen to replace the blood loss in childbirth.

	Hot foods	Durian, chicken, chillies	cause headache	18	28.6
	Foods causing wind	Bananas, vegetables: kangkung, peanuts	cause indigestion, stomach upset	14	22.2
	Cold foods	Cucumber, watermelon, beans (kacang panjang)	generally unwell, can fall in sick	11	17.5
Confinement	Cold foods	Vegetables, cucumber, ice -water, coconut, watermelon, pumpkin	poor blood circulation	22	34.9
	Sour /acidic fruits	Mangoes, limes, pineapples, asam jawa (tamarind)	heavy bleeding	15	23.8
	Poison foods and Itchy foods	Certain fishes e.g. kembong, keli (catfish), stingray, prawn, egg	vomiting, stomach upset	14	22.2
	Others	Certain vegetables, fruits, gravy, drinks	prevent rapid healing	12	19.1
Lactation	Itchy foods	Sea-foods e.g., keli (catfish), prawns, cockles	cause rashes in baby	25	39.7
	Cold foods	Bananas, cucumber, cabbage	stomach upset to baby	13	20.6
	Windy foods	Jackfruit, tapioca	baby gets colic pain	14	22.2
	Others	Pineapples, mangoes, ginger, spices, herbs	cause diarrhoea in baby	11	17.5
Illness	Cold foods	Ice-water, water-melon	generally unwell, sickness become severe	92	82.9

Lactation

During the lactation period, itchy foods (39.7%), cold foods (20.6%) and windy foods (22.2%) were given top priority for food avoidance. Whereas other foods (17.5%) such as pineapple and some herbs were avoided because of the fear of causing diarrhoea in the baby. Many mothers avoided such foods that are listed because they believed such foods carry harmful substances that affect their baby through breast feeding. A study done among Kamba women in Kenya by Ginneken and Muller, 1984 report that there are no particular foods was omitted from the habitual diet during pregnancy and lactation.

Illness

About 82.9% of the women agreed that cold foods were avoided during illness as it could worsen the condition. Only a few (17.1%) women did not give much importance on the food prohibitions as they thought that symptoms like fever and cough were quite common and also depended on various environmental factors.

Body Mass Index (BMI) Status

Figure 2 shows the Body Mass Index (BMI) for the adult women in this village.

Majority (50.5%) of the adult women had a normal BMI. From the above table, it can be seen that 23.4% were underweight. In a study by Ismail, 1995 which the results compiled from earlier reports, shows that among adult females in rural areas , underweight prevalence were higher (30.9%) with an interestingly low incidence (20.1%) of overweight.

Overweight problems had a remark with pre-obese stage, obese stage 1 and obese stage-2 with 17.1%, 7.2% and 1.8% respectively. Most of the subjects do not exercise and have a sedentary lifestyle. Dullo, 1996 noted that the management of obesity has a long and disappointing history where in the majority of cases, the result is a transient phase of weight loss, followed by a return to the obese condition within a few years.

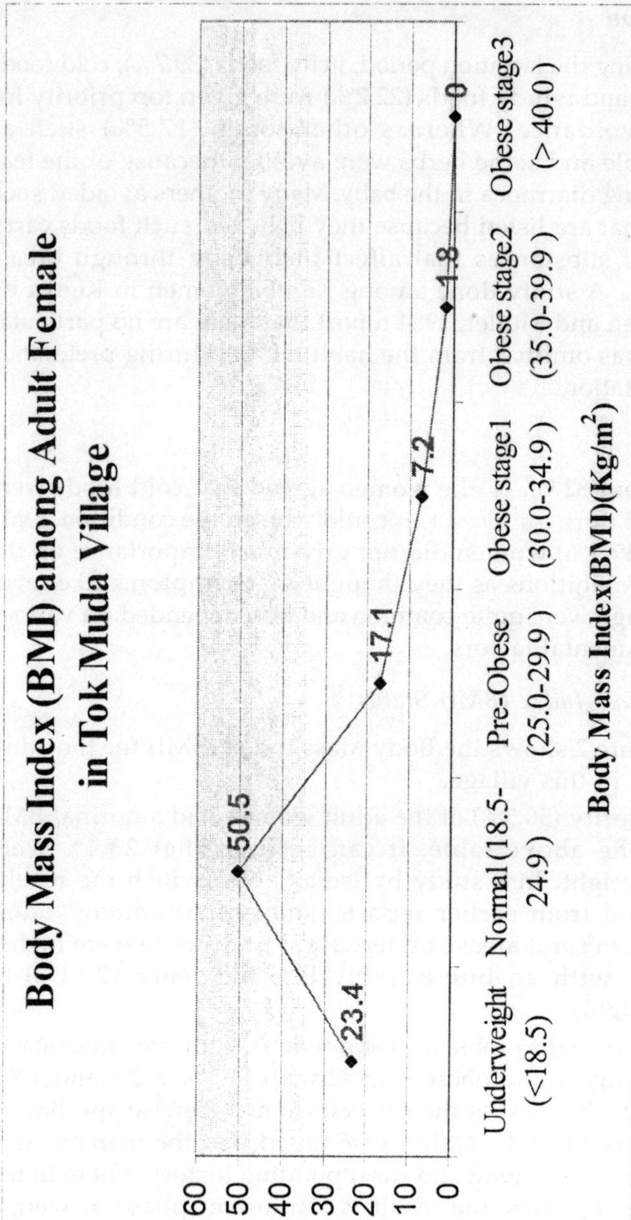

Figure 2: Body Mass Index (BMI) among Adult Female

Mean ± SD: 22.4 ± 4.4

Biochemical Analysis

In order to obtain a more comprehensive picture of the extent of anaemia in the village, haemoglobin levels were determined in almost all subjects studied. The blood sample was collected after the respondents gave their concern. Only 100 of them were willing for the haemoglobin test. The following cut-off values for haemoglobin were used to diagnose anaemia.

Table 4: The Haemoglobin Values (g/dl) of the Adult Women

Age groups	* *Hb level*
Non-pregnant women	< 12g/dl
Pregnant women	< 11 g/dl

*The cut-off values for haemoglobin levels to diagnose anaemia (WHO, 1997)

Figure 3 Shows the haemoglobin values (g/dl) among adult women.

About 86.0% of the respondents had normal haemoglobin values whereas 10% of normal women had less than 12 g/dl. In a similar study carried out by Tee *et.al.* 1998, it was found that the prevalence of anaemia was more severe (25%) among the adult females. About 4% of the pregnant mothers had less than 11 g/dL. Even though the percentage seems to be small, it reveals them likely to be anaemic. Normally, the iron supplementation was prescribed during pregnancy. This likely anaemic condition in pregnant women maybe due to poor compliance.

There are 246 patients (at national level) and 16 patients (in Selangor State) between 20-54 years reported had discharged from hospital in 2003 due to iron deficiency anaemia (Ministry of Health, 2004). A study (Ahmad *et.al.*, 1997) done on the anaemia status during pregnancy in rural Kelantan shows that inadequate child spacing is one of the reason for insufficient iron stores. They have little time to build up their iron levels between pregnancies.

This study was based on a small voluntary sample, and thus did not represent the general nutrition profile of rural adult women in Malaysia. However, this study is able to provide an overview of nutritional conditions in this particular area. Hence, the nutritional status in this rural area was found to be at risk for some major nutritional deficiencies. Therefore,

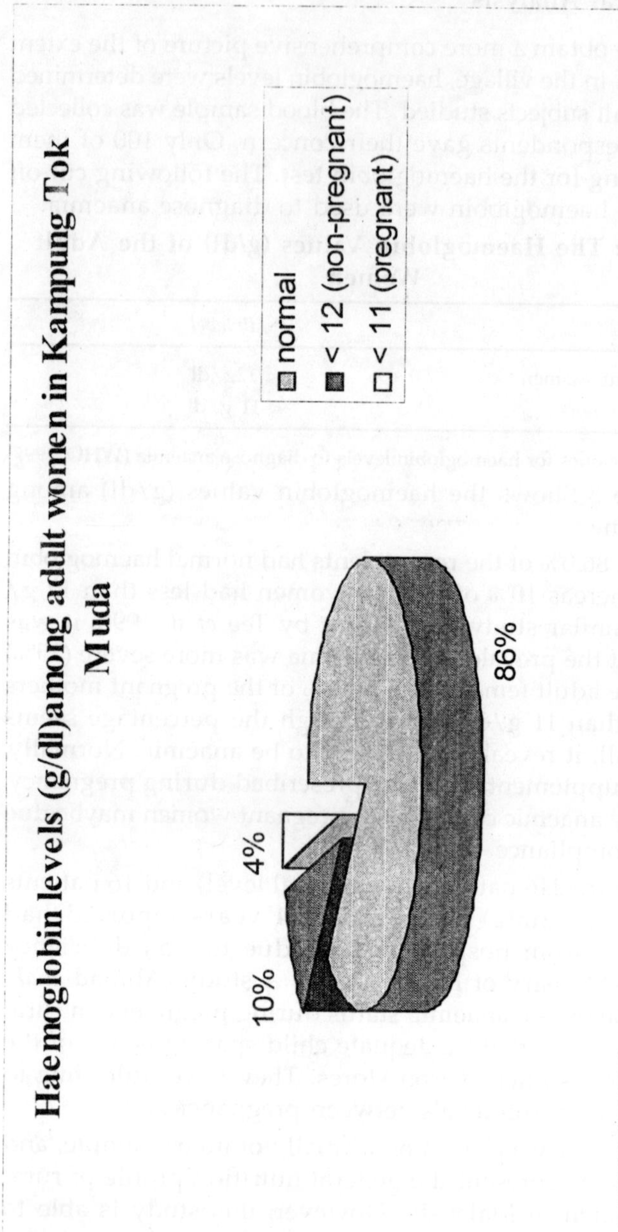

Figure 3: The Haemoglobin Values (g/dl) of the Adult Women
Mean ± SD: 13.1 ± 1.1

it is suggested that further research focusing on specific nutrients is necessary to address the factors contributing to the nutrient deficiencies. There is a need to undertake similar studies in order to eradicate malnutrition.

Acknowledgements

We wish to express our sincere gratitude to KUTPM, for giving us permission to conduct this study. We are also grateful to the Penghulu (head of village) for the permission and the Nursery Teacher, Doctor and Nurses at Klinik Desa Kampung Tok Muda, Klang Municipal Council, Family Health Development Division and IDS (Information Distribution System) Department of Ministry of Health Malaysia and Institute for Medical Research. The guideline and help from the dietitians at the Department of Dietetics, University Malaya Medical Centre and laboratory staff in College is also acknowledged. This paper would not have been possible without the participation of the one hundred and eleven adult women from Kampung Tok Muda. A big 'Thank you', to all our respondents who gave their valuable time and information for the successful completion of this project.

REFERENCES

1. A.G. Dullo, Hurdles and Hopes in the Management of Human Obesity, *Malaysian Journal of Nutrition* 2, 87-111 (1996).
2. Chee Heng Leng, Khor Geok Lin and Tee E Siong, Nutritional Assessment of Rural Villages and Estates in Peninsular Malaysia: I. Socio-Economic Profile of Households, *Malaysian Journal of Nutrition* 3, 1-19 (1997).
3. Lim Hwei Mian and Chee Heng Leng, Nutritional Status and Reproductive Health of Orang Asli Women in Two Villages in Kuantan, Pahang, *Malaysian Journal of Nutrition* 4, 31-34 (1998).
4. Ismail, M.N., Zawiah, H., Chee, S.S. and Ng, K.K., Prevalence of Obesity and Chronic Energy Deficiency (CED) in Adult Malaysians, *Malaysian Journal of Nutrition* 1, 1-9 (1995).
5. Tee E Siong, Khor Geok Lin and Tony Ng Kock War; Nutritional Assessment of Rural Villages and Estates in Peninsular Malaysia III. Prevalence of Anaemia, *Malaysia Journal of Nutrition* 4, 1-29 (1998).

6. Zulkifli Ahmad, Rogayah Jaafar, M. Hashim Mohd Hassan, Mohd Shukri Othman and Azmi Hashim, Anaemia During Pregnancy in Rural Kelantan, *Malaysia Journal of Nutrition* 3,83-90 (1997).
7. A. Saibaba, M. Mohan Ram, G.V. Ramana Rao, Uma Devi, T.S. Syamala, Nutritional Status of Adolescent Girls of Urban Slums and the Impact of IEC On Their Nutritional Knowledge and Practices, *Indian Journal of Community Medicine*, Vol. 27, No. 4, 1-9 (2005).
8. Pallavi, P. Kharade and Usha Anthony, Nutritional Status and Outcome of Pregnancy in Young and Older Mothers in Mumbai, *The Indian Journal of Nutrition Dietetics* 39, 26-30(2002).
9. Dr Geok Lin Khor and Dr Zalilah Mohd Sharif, Dual Forms of Malnutrition in The Same Households in Malaysia—A Case Study Among Malay Rural Households, *Asia Pacific Journal of Clinical Nutrition* 12(4), 427-436 (2003).
10. Zhao Xi-he, Dietary Protein, Amino Acids and their Relation to Health, *Asia Pacific Journal of Clinical Nutrition* 3, 131-134 (1994).
11. M.Hassapidou and Natali Papadopoulou, Assessment of the Dietary Intakes of Healthy Adult Pregnant Women in Cyprus, *Nutrition and Food Science*30, MCB University Press, 111-115 (2000).
12. Gregorio Varela and Baltasar Ruiz-Roso, Some Effects of Deep Frying on the Dietary Fat Intake, *Nutrition reviews*, Vol. 33, No.9,256-262 (1992)
13. Mayang Sari, Saskia de Pee and Elviyanti Martini, Estimating the Prevalence of Anaemia: A comparison of three methods, *Bulletin of the World Health Organization*, World Health Organization, 506-511 (2001).
14. Dr. Suzana Shahar , Rafidah Ghazali and Dr. Noor Aini , BMI Ready Reckoner Table, Atlas of food Exchanges and Portion Sizes, MDC publishers Printers SDN.BHD, 61 (2002).
15. J.K. Van Ginneken and A.S. Muller, *Maternal and Child Health in Rural Kenya: An Epidemiological Study*, Croom Helm Ltd., 127-140(1984).
16. John B. Knight and Lendal H. Kotschevar, *Quantity Food Production, Planning, and Management*, Second edition, Van Nostrand Reinhold, New York, 15-22 (1989).
17. Tee E Siong, Mohd. Ismail Noor, Mohd. Nasir Azudin and Khathijah Idris, *Nutrient Composition of Malaysian Foods*, 4th Edition, IMR, 1-187 (1997).
18. Dr Gro Harlem Brundtland, Director, WHO, World Economic Forum (2000).

19. ISEC, PRC, and Bangalore, Rapid Household Survey (District Level House Hold Survey) in Idduki district of Kerala State, Reproductive and Child Health (RCH), International Institute for Population Sciences 85-93 (2002).
20. Inpatient Morbidity and Mortality List, Untuk Tahun 2003, Peringkat Nasional, Sistem Maklumat Pengurusan Kesihatan, KKM, LPD 206, Ver.3.34 (2004).
21. Census, Klang Municipal Council, Local Government Printing (2000).
22. The Recommend Nutrient Intakes for Malaysia 2005: Summary Table, Ministry of Health, Government Printing (2005).

8

PRACTICE OF ETHNO-MEDICINE AMONG THE TRIBALS

BIBEKANANDA NAYAK

Introduction

The natural environment plays an important role in formation of tribal culture. It flourishes in the specific ecological conditions. The traditional knowledge of treatment of various diseases is a part of tribal holistic culture. Hence, the socio-cultural anthropologists take keen interest in studying interaction between man, society and culture in general and ethno-medicine and tribal in particular. The tribals mainly depend on their forest environment from where they collect the medicinal herbs, plants, roots, tubers, fruits, flowers, leaves etc., to treat the aïlments. After the trail and error method of application of the herbs available in the forests, the knowledge of the same is passed on from generation to generation. This constitutes a vital aspect of folk medication.

Tribal medicinal practices have also been mixed with magic and witchcraft. Spiritual and herbal treatment has played an important role in influencing the physical and psychological condition among the tribals. It has been providing an alternative in the absence of allopathic medication.

Chaudhri (1986) stated that that among the tribal's the diseases are commonly related to the belief in different deities and spirits. But Mahapatra states that among the tribal communities diseases are usually thought to occur due two reasons: *(a)* due to belief in supernatural forces—any negative act against such forces may cause harm to the self as well as the community *(b)* due to physical factors like living in unsanitary conditions; though this is not so commonly accepted.

According to Swami (1994:15) the supernatural causes of sickness as perceived by the tribals can be classified as the following: 1. soul loss, 2. breach of taboo, 3. sorcery, 4. ghosts of ancestors, 5. ancestral spirits and supernatural power, 6. evil eye, evil mouth, 7. mana, and 8. fetish.

Generally the tribals believed in the curse of devil or some other kinds of spirits bringing about deadly diseases. This was not only considered to harm only a particular individual but also the whole village or tribal community. The cure of disease was thought in terms of worshipping the spirit, thereby making sacrifices and keeping the surroundings clean. The later approach to some extent can be considered to be scientific. Moreover, the tribal medication also relies on various herbs available in the forests. The same practice is also seen among Ayurvedia, Unani, Sidha, Homeopathy, and Yoga in the modern world. Therefore, to reject the tribal medicine to be unscientific should be dealt with care, so as to not ignore another aspect of medical treatment.

The Ethnomedical Model: It's Significance to Health and Medicinal Practice

It is not a realistic assumption that western medical practice is pre-dominant form of medical system. Inspite of it, various other systems also exist side by side. Traditional and indigenous medicines are very unlikely to spread if they are not effectively promoted by the policy makers. Generally the bureaucrats, political leaders, NGOs can play an influential role in such a scenario. At the same time, the prospect of indigenous medicines would be low, if they are not widely accepted by the community members.

Leslie (1980) observes that even though biomedicine is almost always less scientific than it appears, health professionals throughout the world tend to translate proposals for cooperation with practitioners of alternative therapies as advocating the legitimization of quackery (Imperato, 1977). They contend such collaboration would require acceptance of procedures whose efficacy is at best difficult to evaluate according to conventional scientific criteria. These external, superficial interpretations of unfamiliar therapies (which may lead to conclusions of "quackery") and assumptions about their efficacy tend to screen out significant behaviour and health care. At the same time, the difficulties of differentiating between genuine healers and those who have few skills apart from extracting their client's money must not be underestimated (International Development Research Center 1980).

In all societies, medical systems function as social systems that attach meaning to and structure the experience of sickness (Fabrega 1977; Leslie 1980). Medical anthropologists and most other social and behavioural scientist now recognize the analytical and practical value of distinguishing between disease and illness as two elements of *sickness*. *Disease* connotes the impairment of biological and/or psychological processes, whereas *illness* can be described as "the psychosocial experience and meaning of perceived disease" (Kleinman 1980: 72).

Most of the modern medical practitioners do not differentiate between disease and illness while prescribing medication. They should consider the culture and the nature of disease to be same, whether it may be psychosocial or biological. However, medicine should be given in the context of the culture of the societies and their environment.

The work of Kleinman (1980), Lesile (1980), and others suggests that the purposes of biomedicine, insofar as these are directed toward individual and community health can be advanced by integrating the principles of the "ethnomedical" model into biomedical practice. Building upon recent developments in semantics anthropology, ethnomethodology, and comparative medical studies, the *ethnomedical approach* places particular emphasis on the "meaning contexts of sickness," and join different systems of medical knowledge. Health, disease, and illness are interpreted in the light of the many ways these terms are perceived by patients, families, practitioners, and communities.

In practice, the "ethnomedical analyst," whether medical practitioner or a social scientist, recognizes that people adopt sick roles when they do not have diseases, and experience diseases without being ill or taking on sick roles (Leslie 1980). As already noted, the biological and psychosocial realities, while interdependent, are not the same thing; and their relationship is culturally defined and structured.

There are socio-cultural differences between different communities and regions in respect to their way of living, food habits, environments etc. Therefore the way of treatment varies from one place to another. Some diseases may be common in a particular place but may be rarely in other. So, the medical practitioner needs to be aware of the pattern of diseases and the climatic condition. For example, Malaria is the common disease in the tribal area but rarely found in cities. So, ethnomedical knowledge of that locality is considered to be important.

Contemporary American popular culture also illustrates the relevance of the ethnomedical approach. It contains a rich but largely unsurveyed variety of culturally constructed patterns of symptoms perception, labelling, communication, and behavioural responses. For example, terms such as "nervous breakdown", "male menopause", "professional burnout", "shell-shock", "rape", "lump in the breast", "upset stomach", and even "cancer" have profound personal, cultural, and social meanings that are crucial to establishing a basic for the provision of psychologically and culturally appropriate clinical care. They also reflect changing beliefs about the cause and severity of illness; yet there are few systematic accounts of popular American or other EMs and "networks" in the literature of social and medicine (Good 1987: 19).

In contrast, ethnomedical analysis employs an interdisciplinary and interpretive methodology. It rejects the truncated, compartmentalized, and pre-selective approach to sickness in favour of examining a broad range of cultural specific and transcultural experiences in both clinical transactions and in the extraclinical domain of healing. Analysis is focused on the actual illness experiences of people and examines how they are perceived, labelled, communicated, and managed in interactions with family, social network, and therapist. In terms of this framework the social *geography* of therapy systems assumes much greater complexity, dynamism, and spatial range through the redefinition of "relevant" actors and through assessment of their locational behaviour (Good 1987: 20).

Medical professionals, social scientists, health planners and the local people should keep in mind the availability of natural resources like plants, shrubs, herbs and their utilization should be taken into consideration while forming the policies. Both biology and environment can help in determining the health and well being of an individual.

There are at least three other factors that should finally convince social scientists (and biomedical professionals) of the usefulness of the ethnomedical approach. First, its applications are not restricted to traditional and "non-Western" medical systems. It is also appropriate to the analysis of both lay and professional health behaviour in societies where biomedicine is dominant, co-dominant, or only a variant. Second, it serves to demystify and make more interpretable the otherwise exotic and perplexing aura (especially for Westerners) that typically surrounds the practices of both traditional and popular healers and their clientele (Rappoport 1980). Finally, it should directly lead to more psychosocially and biomedically sophisticated models of health problems and therapeutic alternatives, and to more effective utilization of health services (Klenman 1978a).

The Relevance of Ethnomedical System

The total medical resources available to and utilized by a community or society, including popular, traditional biomedical forms of therapy, can be said to constitute its *ethnomedical system*. An ethnomedical system evolves from a people's world view. It incorporates theories of illness and patterns of illness behaviour that reflect socially constructed systems of meaning, values, norms, and interpersonal relations. Ethnomedical systems are maintained by an array of supporting social institutions and therapy specialists, including (in the technologically less-developed countries) newer roles such as medical assistants, nurses, and university-trained physicians.

The spatial arrangement and interplay of resources and places where various phases and elements of disease, illness, and therapy are identified, acted out, studied, and administered. As conceived here, an ethnomedical system encompasses all of the acquired systematic knowledge, resources, organizational patterns, behaviours, and strategies (traditional, indigenous, scientific, imported) that are utilized by a community to promote the individual and collective well-being of its members" (Good 1987: 22).

Ethnomedical systems are socially accepted designs for labelling and managing illness that are both adjustable and adaptable to changes occurring in other social and economic subsystems. They are flexible wholes that can selectively accommodate and borrow from exotic medical traditions without losing their underlying conceptual coherence and integrity (Janzen 1978). This idea may be compared with Press's (1980: 47) definition of a medical system, which he interprets as "a patterned, interrelated body of values and deliberate practices governed by a single paradigm of the meaning, identification, prevention and treatment of sickness".

An ethnomedical system also includes the *full complement* of health care strategies acceptable to some or all members of a community, including biomedicine as well as self-treatment and traditional practitioners. This model is compatible and nearly coincident with Kleinman's (1980: 50) model of health care, which he defines as *"a local cultural system composed of three overlapping parts: the popular, professional, and folk sectors"*. The *popular* sphere of health care, which centres on self-treatment by the individual and family, is generally the first therapeutics choice for most people in most cultures. It is thus the largest, but also the least examined and poorly understood, part of any health care system. The popular sphere contains several levels, including individual, family, social networks, and community beliefs and activities. It is "the lay, non-professional, non-specialist, popular culture arena in which illness is first defined and health care activities initiated" (Kleinman 1980: 50).

In the technologically less-developed countries, traditionally based indigenous beliefs and practices generally serve as the "core" reference points in the ethnomedical systems for most of the population, although competition, complementarity and interdependence of different systems are typical wherever biomedicine is also available (Good 1987: 23).

Tribal Medical Practitioners

Due to the belief in supernatural and religion in matters concerning health; the tribals are almost invariably found to repose faith in diviners or the traditional medicine men, sorcerers, and shamans. The role of the priests as seen in non-tribal communities for praying to the high gods in rarely seen in the tribal communities (usually who have not been converted to Christianity) for the treatment of diseases. Usually the lesser important and inferior deities, spirits, ghosts are appeased and the shamans are employed for this. Anthropologists have occasionally viewed shamans as 'holistic' healers who function as alternative model for healing to the mechanistic allopathic physician or surgeon who is seen constrained by Cartesan assumptions about the separation of mind and body (Pandian: 1991). It is realized that the shamans play a very crucial role in the society, particularly in carrying on the traditions of the past and in maintaining the carrying on the traditions of the past and in maintaining the social order. Philip Sagant (1996: 361-65) writes, "by encouraging people to maker peace with past, the shaman in his own way takes up where political institutions leave off. He has the same goals: to consolidate alliances, to remove obstacles to the creation of the network of social relations and accept them... The shaman has a monopoly on the transmission of myths. It is well known that society reproduces itself through this transmission; identical from one generation to the next....Illness is born of a breakdown in social order. The shaman guarantees social order" (Burmun 2003:10).

Levi-Strauss placed the role of the shaman in the upkeep of social order very cogently, "whereas a psychoanalytic cure is based upon the patient's recovery of his individual myth, constructed with elements from his past, the cure in shamanism is predicted on the patient's receiving the social myth from his collective tradition. The collective myth used by the shaman does not correspond to the patient's personal state but reintegrates his alienating experience of sickness within a meaningful whole (Kakar: 1982).

In the recent times, according to Pandian (1991), a few anthropologist and other scholars have invented the shamans as having 'social moral' functions, an association that, seldom exists in non-urban cultures. Members of the 'counter-culture' movements often reject explicitly or implicitly, what they perceive to be western cosmological and social systems and strive to promote a shamanistic world-view. Ethnographic data or shamanism is occasionally used by those disenchanted with 'conventional morality' of the West, and in recent times the shaman and shamanism have become significant symbols of various counter-culture, human-potential, self-actualizations, and psychotherapeutic movements as well as among certain celebrities" (Burmun 2003:11).

Therapeutic Practices

There appears to be different opinions among the scholars about the ways of treatment among the tribals. Basu, Jindal and Kshatriya (1994) believe that the tribals by and large are averse to medical treatment as they have firm faith in their traditional system of treatment which is based on superstition, belief in supernatural power hostile spirits. Their treatment ends with appeasement and controlling these powers (Burmun 2003:12).

Swami, however, suggests that treatment of diseases among the tribes may not resemble the modern scientific method as prevalent in western medicine, but it will be wrong to assume that it has no science. It rather moves in a way which covers not only a scientific principle, but also involves the society at large to overcome the catastrophe. Swain (1994:17) writes, "Treatment, naturally would be influenced by cause of sickness perceived by the group. It has been observed that however primitive a group is, it has some scientific knowledge, which it is gathered/learnt through traditional experience. The tribal people do have some scientific knowledge which they have learnt through trial and error method. But this knowledge does not exist in isolation, rather is part of their entire socio-cultural-religious system. Besides, magic is a part of tribal religion". Swami is rather more emphatic about the collective approach to the system of aetiology. He cites the example of Mikirs in this regard, "the Mikirs of Assam believe that leprosy is transmitted by blood, touch and contamination of water. It is also due to violation of existing social norms and customs. According to them when one member is affected the entire family is believed to be affected by evil spirits" (Burmun 2003:12).

Touch and heal forms an important part of tribal medical practice. This is also intertwined with the significance of faith. However, the same practice can also be said to be effective in an allopathic treatment. In other words it can be said that rapport with the patients, helps the physician for efficient medical practice. Therefore, both tribal and allopathic medicine can be said to involve some psychological therapeutic practices.

Basu et al (1994), Inspite of stressing on the psychological dimension of primitive medicine, suggest that the tribals very strong faith in herbal medicine as well. They write, "there is enough evidence to suggest that the tribals have very strong faith in herbal medicines as well. The tribal population groups do use the indigenous herbal concoctions to avoid pregnancies, treatment of fertility and some common ailments". They have also observed that some of the tribals of Bastar region in Madhya Pradesh make use of Ayurvedic medicine along with traditional indigenous medicines. They also mention that at present many of the tribes take advantage of allopathy, but their attitude towards modern medical care is not encouraging. Sachidananda (1994) elaborates a bit more than this, "in most societies besides recourse to supernatural remedies, we find caterization, surgery, fracture treatment to trephining, inoculation against smallpox and snake bite, and enormous pharmacopoeia including opium, quinine, digitalis and many other useful drugs. It must be remembered; however, that such a treatment is not done in a rationale sense (of ours) but is rapt in spells, prayers, manual rites and dances. All these add up to the psycho-therapeutic qualities of tribal methods of healing. The primitive psychotherapist's strength comes from the interpersonal ties between doctor and patient but also from the effect of the frequent participation of the entire community in his treatment" (Burmun 2003: 13).

Chaudhuri (1990) stresses on the ramifications of the society at large in the treatment of diseases, "Health and treatment also reflect the social solidarity of a community. In a tribal community, for example, illness and the consequent treatment is not always an individual or familial affair, as the decision about the nature of treatment may be taken at a community level. In case of some specific diseases, not only the diseased person or his/her family, but the total village community is affected. All the other families are expected to observe certain taboos of norm of food habits. The non-observation of such practices often calls for action by the village council. One cannot deny the impact of the psychological support in the context of treatment and cure which is very common in tribal communities." He further states that the reassurance which the traditional tribal medicinal system offers to the patients, the modern physician does not offer this. Neuman and Lauro (1982) also think similarly and stress that destroying the traditional medical system is equivalent to destroying a vital element of culture (Burmun 2003: 13).

Pandian (1991) states that often divinatory-healing and witch-craft-sorcery beliefs and rituals indirectly support or affirm the social structure and dramatize the importance of equal distribution of wealth, homogeneity of culture, channel anxiety and promote social control. Mathur (1951-52) on the other hand states that the phenomenon of which has important social control mechanism, "the witches are conceived to be anti-social in motives and they employ their art for the evil purposes such as destruction of an enemy, the promotion of quarrels and the like. They are dreaded and hated by the people; usually they are widows or barren women" (Burmun 2003: 14).

The tribal mainly dependent on their following forest produce for treatment of the diseases.

Treatment of Diseases

Diseases	*Medicinal herbs used by kondh tribe of Orissa*
Eye disorder	Amla
Respiratory disorder	Ankarant
Dysentery	Ashok
Heart diseases	Brahmi
Skin diseases	Neem
Toothache	Basanga
Amnesia	Harida
Mental disorder	Bahada
Acne problem	Dudura
Stomachache, worms	Palash tree
loose motion	Chatiana
pneumonia	Indramaris
Blood pressure	Sarpagandha
Arthritis	Kaulikhia
Obesity	Purugi
Night blindness	Swetapurushi
Con/mole	Chighakuti
Cough and cold	Tulshi
Fever	Karam tree

Medical Pluralism

Coexistence of various traditional medical systems, such as Yoruba, Unani-Tibbi, Ayurvedic, or classical Chinese, with each other and with biomedicine is a well-documented phenomenon in many parts of Africa, Asia and Latin America. Together these different modes of interpreting and responding to sickness from what Charles Leslie describes (in Janzen 1978: 14) as "more or less pluralistic, more or less integrated, and more or less syncretistic regional systems" (Good 1987: 8).

International awareness of the role and contributions of traditional therapy systems in African societies is primarily a postcolonial development. This emerging consciousness coincides with a growing realization that the kind of biomedical delivery system introduced by colonial administration s and subsequently inherited by independent African governments does not and cannot meet many of their societies' most pressing health care requirements. Rooted in the old colonial system, the western-inspired blueprint for medical care is inefficiently designed, dependent on expensively trained personnel working in budget-absorbing hospitals, and too often grossly overwhelmed by the unrealistic expectations and demands placed upon it. In many ways it is inappropriate and of limited relevance to the conditions of life of people in developing countries (Dorozynski 1975). It renders insufficient care even in central urban areas, and practically no care in large rural present, prevailing social and cultural values and actual attendance patterns indicate that biomedicine is not preferred for many illness, nor for common events such as child birth (Good 1987: 9).

Ahemed and Kolker (1979) identify seven general functions, both psychological and sociological, that traditional indigenous medical systems performed independently of the local presence or adequacy of biomedicine. These are: *(1)* relief of stress and anxiety created by the uncertainties of illness; *(2)* low cost (a questionable assertion addressed later) and convenience; *(3)* reinforcement of the patient through primary groups involvement in diagnosis and treatment; *(4)* control of deviance; *(5)* minimization of the trauma of cultural change *(6)* alleviation of personal stress in the urban areas caused by social dislocation, uprooting, and anomie; and *(7)* promotion of ethnic identity. Nchinda (1976) has argued that traditional African medical systems survive because they satisfy the following four basis users' requirements (each of which has an important locational dimension): accessibility, availability, acceptability, and dependability (Good 1987:11).

At urging of the W.H.O., biomedical opinion has recently begun to shift toward a more open stance regarding the validity and potential efficiency of elements of the traditionally-based medical systems (Akerele 1984). Although heated controversy continues and opposition by biomedical practitioners is widespread, there is increasing interest in the potential benefits to be obtained from simulating cooperative theraperative activities between biomedically oriented and traditional-style healers (Neumann& Lauro 1982).

Despite their individual and collective strengths, probably no single therapy system, or combination of systems, is today adequately meeting even the most basic health care needs in the Third World. Separately or together, all fall short (Good *et al* 1979). In their quest for health, people attempt to compensate for these deficiencies by utilizing both traditional and biomedical services. Such joint use is made concurrently or sequentially for the same or different aspects of the same illness. In this sense the pluralistic medical services. Such joint use is made concurrently or sequentially for the same or different aspects of the same illness. In this sense the pluralistic medical systems are informally but rather haphazardly integrated. In the great majority of cases, however, the traditionally based therapies and practitioners continue to be ignored by their country's ministry of health and thus by its Western-trained medical and health planning establishment (Good 1987:11).

Summing up

It can be concluded with the saying that both allopathic and tribal medicines have their importance within their own contexts. Demeaning or devaluing any of them would be harmful for the whole arena of medical research. The basic thrust lies in adopting the positive impact from each of them thereby repealing the negative. This can only be made possible by the efficient administration of the politicians, bureaucrats, researchers, NGOs. Interventions should be taken for promoting both preventive and curative health care by taking the help of various plural therapeutic procedures.

REFERENCES

Ahmed, P.I. & Kolker, A. (1979). The role of indigenous medicine in W.H.O.'s definition of health. In P.I. Ahmed & G.V. Coelho (Eds.) *Toward a New Definition of Health*. Plenum Press, New York.

Basu, S.(1994) *Tribal Health*. National Institute of Health & Family Welfare. New Delhi.

Bhowmick, P.K.(1989). *The Chenchus of the Forests and Plateaus:A Hunting-Gathering Tribe in Transition*. Institute of Social Research and Applied Anthropology,Calcutta.

Burman, J.J. Roy (2003). *Tribal Medicine: Traditional Practices and Changes in Sikkim*, Mittal Publications, New Delhi.

Chaudhuri, B.(1986). Medical Anthropology in India with Special Reference to Tribal Population. In B.Chaudhuri.Edt.*Tribal Health:Socio Cultural Dimensions*. Inter-India Pub, New Delhi.

Fabrega, H. (1977) The scope of ethnomedical science. *Cultre, Medicine and Psychiatry*, 1, 9-23.

Good, B. (1977) The heart of what's the matter: the semantics of illness in Iran. *Culture, Medicine, Psychiatry*, 1, 25-58.

Good, C.M., Hunter, J.M., Katz, S.H., & Katz, S.S. (1979).The interface of dual systems of health care in developing world; toward health policy initiatives in Africa. *Social Science and Medicine*, 13D, 141-154.

Haimendorf, C.V. Furer, (1943) *The Chenchus: Jungle Folk of The Deccan*, Mcmillan & Co. Ltd., London.

Hand, W.D. (Ed.)(1976) *American Folk Medicine: A Symposium*. University of California Press, Berkeley.

Janzen, J.M. (1978) *The Quest for Therapy in Lower Zaire*. University of California Press. Berkeley.

Kleinman, A. (1978a). Concepts and a model for comparison of medical systems as cultural systems. *Social Science and Medicine*, 12, 85-93.

Kleinman,A. (1980) *Patients and Healers in the Context of Culture*. University of California Press, Berkeley.

Leslie, C. (1980). Medical pluralism in world perspective. *Social science and Medicine*, 14B, 191-195.

Mahapatra, L.K. (1986) Concept of health Among the Tribal population Groups of india and its Socio-Economic Correlates.

Mahapatra, L.K. (1994) Concept of health Among the Tribal population Groups of india and its Socio-Economic Correlates. In S. Basu (Ed). *Tribal Health in India*, Manak Publications, Delhi.

Nchinda, T.C. (1976) Traditional and western medicine in Africa:Collaboration or confrontation? *Tropical Doctor*, July, 133-135.

Neumann, A.K. & Lauuro, P. (1982) Ethnomedicine and biomedicine linking. *Social Science and Medicine*, 16, 1817-1824.

Pfifferling, J.H. (1975). Some issues in the consideration of non-Western and Western folk practices as epidemiological data. *Social science and medicine*, 9, 655-658.

Rappoport, H. (1980) The integration of scientific and traditional healing: The problem of demystification. In P.R. Ulin & M.H. Segal (Eds.) *Traditional Health Care Delivery in Contemporary Africa*, Africa Series, No. 35, Maxwell School of Citizenship and Public Affairs, Syracuse University, Syracuse, NY.

Sachidananda (1994) Socio-cultural dimentions of tribal health. In S. Basu (Ed.) *Tribal Health in India*, Manak Publications, Delhi.

Sarkar, A. and Dasgupta, S. (2000) *Ethno-ecology of Indian Tribes: Diversity in Cultural Adaptation*, Rawat Publications, New Delhi.

SECTION II: TRIBAL WELFARE

9

ROLE OF GOVERNMENT AGENCIES IN THE WELFARE OF THE TRIBES OF ORISSA: A CASE STUDY OF SCHEDULED CASTE AND SCHEDULED TRIBE RESEARCH AND TRAINING INSTITUTE

N. PANIGRAHI

Introduction

Perhaps a unique feature of India as a nation State of the world is that it has established through Constitutional as well as non-Constitutional measures an elaborate system of preferential arrangements and institutions for the multitude of ethnic minorities in general and tribal communities in particular. While understanding the historical reasons for the backwardness of such tribal groups, the country has made Constitutional provisions, various special plans and programmes for their welfare and development, and has been allocating substantial funds for this purpose.

The paper is divided into four parts. First, it gives an account of the Scheduled Areas and presents a socio-cultural profile of the tribal communities living therein. Secondly, it provides an account on the origin, objectives and growth of the Scheduled Castes and Scheduled Tribes Research and Training Institute (thus known as SC&ST R&TI). Thirdly, it describes various activities performed by SC&ST R&TI from 1980 to 2000 in the state of Orissa. Fourthly the paper critically analyses the overall functioning of SC&ST R&TI. It also identifies the vital opportunities available to the institute to expedite its performance.

Provision of special protective measures for the development of tribal communities was felt necessary since late 19th century and were reflected at different points of time in the form of the Scheduled District Act of 1874, the Indian Education Commission of 1882, Government of India Act of 1919 and 1935 which paid some attention to special treatment of the tribal communities. During the post-independent period Thakkar Bapa, Jaipal Singh, and few others played a major role in reshaping the Tribal Welfare programmes and Protective measures. As a result, series of Constitutional provisions in the form of Articles and Schedules have been incorporated in the Constitution of India for the welfare and development of the tribal people.

The Constitutional commitments for the welfare of the Scheduled Tribes include the Fundamental Rights in Part III; Directive Principles of State Policy in Part IV; Scheduled and Tribal Areas in Part X; Finance and Property affairs in Part XII; special provisions relating to certain classes in Part XVI; and lastly, the Fifth and Sixth Schedules. Besides these, there are certain special provisions for the tribals which are also contained in the Articles of 14, 15(4), 16(4), 17, 19(5), 23, 24, 29, 38, 39, 39(A), 41, 43, 46, 47, 48, 48(A), 164, 330, 332, 334, 335 and 338, 339(1), 342 and 371(A, B, C) of the Constitution of India. Article 244 of the Constitution of India provides various provisions under Fifth Schedule for the administration and control of Scheduled Areas and Scheduled Tribes in States other than Assam, Nagaland, Manipur, Meghalaya, Tripura and Mizoram. Similarly, Article 244(2) deals with the provisions of the Sixth Schedule applied to the North-Eastern States of India for similar purposes. The Governor of the State under Para 5 of the Fifth Schedule of the Indian Constitution, can frame rules for peaceful and good governance of Scheduled Areas can make rules.

Indeed the State of Orissa during both pre-and-post-independent era has taken many legislative measures for the welfare of the tribal people. Apart from the legislative measures, there are different agencies directly and/or indirectly engaged in matters of protection, welfare and development of the Scheduled Tribes and Scheduled Areas of the state. The Tribes Advisory Council (TAC), National Commission for Scheduled Castes and Scheduled Tribes (NCSC&ST), and Scheduled Castes and Scheduled Tribes Research and Training Institute (SC&ST R&TI) are some of the agencies which operate from the state headquarters, and contribute towards informing policy decisions. The Orissa Forest Development Corporation Ltd (OFDC), Tribal Development Co-operative Corporation Ltd. (TDCC), Orissa Scheduled Caste and Scheduled Tribe Development Finance Co-operative Corporation Limited (OSFDC Ltd) and Panchayati Raj Institutions (PRI) are some of the institutions that are directly engaged in the implementation of tribal development programmes in the state.

Release of Funds from Government of India

The paper tries to find out the extent of fund support provided by Government of India during the period 1990-91 to 1997-98 to different TRIs of India. The objective is to know what principle Government of India follows when allocate funds to these centres. The ST population in Orissa shares 21.06 per cent, is little less than Madhya Pradesh (Old) (23.27%), Manipur (34.41%), and Tripura (30.95%), who have also TRIs (1991 Census Report). Similarly, the literacy status of the STs in Orissa was 22.31 per cent was the third lowest among the States who have TRIs (Andhra Pradesh had 17.16%, Rajasthan had 19.44%). These two indicators sufficiently establish that the State of Orissa has a substantial tribal population who are much below the average development indices. This situation when compared with other States having TRIs at one level demands the flow of more funds from GOI to Orissa.

The data indicate that the States like Assam, Andhra Pradesh, Bihar, Kerala, Maharashtra, Rajasthan, Tamil Nadu, and West Bengal, who have less tribal population and higher literacy status, have received more funds than Orissa (Table 1). This low level of fund flow to Orissa may be due to multiple reasons. It may be that the State is unable to highlight tribal problems of the State, may be due to poor leadership projection both at bureaucratic and political levels. Is it that

Government of India while allocating funds discriminates among the states and does not follow a realistic approach? The fact remains that the State of Orissa with higher tribal concentration is backward in many respects and has received less funds compared to many other states. This has grossly affected the functioning of TRI of the State of Orissa.

I

I.0 Scheduled Areas in Orissa

In Orissa the Scheduled Areas have been amended three times, in 1950, 1975 and 1977. In fact Para Fifth and Sixth of the Fifth Schedule do not contemplate any agency area or track to be Scheduled suo-moto. It is the Governor who, while administering the Scheduled Areas, may propose any agency area either as wholly or partly to be Scheduled and the Government makes necessary laws and put them under the administration of the Scheduled Area. The Constitutional guidelines indicate that the areas included in Scheduled Area should have concentration of tribal population at least fifty per cent or more, and is considered to be backward which needs special attention. Almost 44.21 per cent of the total land area of the State has been constitutionally declared as Scheduled Area, which covers most of the districts except the coastal districts and few in-land areas. The districts declared as Scheduled Area with heavy density of Scheduled Tribes include Malkangiri (58.51%), Mayurbhanja (57.87%), Nawarangpur (55.26%), Rayagada (54.99%), Sundargarh (50.74%), Koraput (50.67%), Kondhamal (50.13%), Keonjhar (44.62%), Gajapati (47.88%), and Jharsuguda (33.31%) (Government of Orissa, 1995-96).

I.1 Tribal Communities of Orissa

Next to Maharashtra and Chhattisgarh, Orissa has the third largest concentration of tribal population in the country. Out of 427 Scheduled Tribes of the country, Orissa has 62 tribal communities, who constitute 27.08 per cent of State's population. The tribal communities living in the State range from small communities like *Chenchu, Bonda, Juanga, Didayi* to large communities like *Munda, Santals, Kondh, Oraon, Saora and Bhuyan.* The tribal communities of the State can be categorised as hunter-gatherer-nomads, hunter-gatherer and shifting cultivators, simple artisans, settled agriculturists, industrial and urban unskilled and semi-skilled workers (Behura, 1990).

In Orissa out of 62 Scheduled Tribes, 11 groups have been declared as Primitive Tribal Groups. They are: *Bonda Paraja, Chuktia Bunion, Didayi, Dongaria Kondha, Hill Kharia, Juanga, Kutia Kondh, Lanjia Saora, Lodha, Mankiridia, Birhor,* and, *Paudi Bhuiyan,* and *Saora.* These tribal communities have differences with each other, which are reflected in their political, economic and socio-cultural life. However, they have similarities as regards their dependency on the nature for livelihood and in adherence to nature-spirit complexes. Few of these vulnerable communities like *Birhor, Kondh and Paudi Bhuyan* are also found beyond the State boundaries and are distributed in the States of Jharkhand, Chhatishgarh, Assam and West Bengal. Almost all these communities are divided into certain sub groups who reside on hill-tops and hill slopes. Their economic life pre-eminently centres on collection of various forest produces, practice of shifting cultivation, hunting and gathering. Some of them over the time have adopted terraced cultivation and settled agriculture; however, more or less they still adhere to the collection of minor forest produces. Many of these communities have successfully adopted rope making, basket making, wage labour, horticulture etc.

The tribal communities of Orissa are patrilineal, partilocal, patriarchal by nature and posses both nuclear and extended form of family. For them marriage by negotiation is always considered as socially approved and most prestigious. They adhere to their culture, traditional practices and have bounded worldview. Clans or similar organizations like *Birinda* (among the Saoras) basically regulate their social organizations and marriages (Panigrahi, 1998). Breach of customary practices by the members results in social excommunication and imposition of fines. The secular and sacerdotal village functionaries known differently among different communities perform the role of village head, priest, shaman etc. who look after their political and religious functions. The ethnic identities of these communities by and large are reflected in their dress pattern, housing structure, ornaments, gods, goddesses and spirits, both benevolent and malevolent.

II

II.0 Origin and growth of SC&ST R&TI

Government of India in order to carry out research, organize training programme, seminars and discussions on various subjects relevant for tribal welfare provides financial assistance under three components, namely, *(i)* grants to the state Governments for the TRIs on mutual sharing basis that is 50:50; *(ii)* award of Doctoral and Post-Doctoral fellowships to the students who are registered in Universities on 100 percent basis; *(iii)* financial assistance to Government and non-Government institutions/Organizations for conducting research and evaluation studies. The states having a sizeable proportion of tribal population have set up their own Tribal Research Institutes as required under the Constitution. Presently there are 14 Tribal Research Institutes in the country. They are Andhra Pradesh, Assam, Bihar, Gujrat, Kerala, Madhya Pradesh, Maharashtra, Manipur, Orissa, Rajasthan, Tamil Nadu, Tripura, Uttar Pradesh, West Bengal, Himachal Pradesh*, Arunachal Pradesh and Karnataka. The State TRIs are engaged in conduct research and evaluation, seminar and workshops on various aspects relevant for the tribal communities. They also provide training and orientation to the state Government employees engaged in tribal welfare administration and prepares Tribal Sub-Plans. Some of TRIs also have museums to exhibit the tribal artifacts.

II.1 Origin of SC&ST R&TI in Orissa

Scheduled Castes and Scheduled Tribes Research and Training Institute is one of the State level agencies working for tribal development in the state. This institute started as a semi-official organisation during 1952 and at that time was known as Tribal Research Bureau. The objective of this Bureau was to collect, and process basic data on various aspects of the cultural processes of scheduled groups in the state of Orissa, and render advisory services to both Government of Orissa and Government of India on matters of their socio-economic development. During 1967 an Orientation Training Institute was set up by Govt. of Orissa at Machakund (presently in Malkangiri district). The objective behind this was to impart training to different categories of government officials working in tribal regions of Orissa.

Government of Orissa in 1972 finally merged both Research Bureau and the Orientation Training Institute and formed a new State level called Tribal and Harijan Research-cum-Training Institute (T.H.R.T.I.) under the administrative control of Secretary, T. and R.W. Department of the Government of Orissa. With the rise of a controversy over the issue of the term "Harijan" during 1980 (GOI, Home Ministry, 1980), Government of Orissa again redesigned this institute as Scheduled Castes and Scheduled Tribes Research and Training Institute (SC&ST&RTI) on dt. 31.12.1994.

II.2 Objectives of SC&ST, R&TI

The prime objectives of the institute are multiple by nature. Firstly, it formulates action plans for the development of SCs and STs; undertakes ethnographic and monographic studies on different SC and ST communities of Orissa. It evaluates the development programmes meant for the Scheduled groups of Orissa and organises training programme for those who are working in Scheduled Areas on tribal related issues; and finally, the institute documents various aspects of socio-cultural and politico-economic life of the tribal and caste people of Orissa.

An Advisory Board is constituted for a period of 3 years, with the Chief Minister of the State as Chairman and Minister, ST and SC Development Department as Vice-Chairman, which is supposed to meet twice a year. The Advisory Board advises the Institute on various policy matters relating to the development of SCs and STs of Orissa.

III

III.0 Functioning of SC&ST R&TI

The functioning of the SC&ST R&TI has been assessed based on the data collected from various sources and of official records. However, an attempt has been made to trace back its performance at least to the last ten to fifteen years. The performance of the Institute has been presented as per different activities, like research, evaluation, determination of caste status and organising training programmes.

III.1 Research and Evaluation

Undertaking of research and evaluation studies are the major focus of SC &ST R&TI. Various research and evaluation studies which have been carried out by the Institute are basically decided and entrusted by three different expert and policy bodies. They are viz. SC and ST R&TI. Advisory Board; SC and ST Development Department of Government of Orissa; and the Director, SC and ST R&TI. Apart from special studies on tribal communities, the Institute has also assigned research work from other Departments of both Government of India and the State Government.

The Institute carries out research on Scheduled Castes and Scheduled Tribes on various aspects of their life way processes, and this, is one of its important functions. While scanning the records available during the period of 1977-2002, it has been observed that there were 105 research studies enlisted which have been undertaken by SC&ST R&TI on various issues like ethnographic and monographic studies, welfare activities, ethno-linguistics, health and nutrition and land problems. A few other studies have also been carried out by the institute on ethnicity, education, migration, forest, and the problem of shifting cultivation (Table 2). The achievements with regard to the research studies carried out by the Institute reflect that around 30.47 per cent of the studies are basically of ethnographic nature. The Institute is trailing behind to complete monographs on 62 tribal communities of Orissa. Even all the Primitive Tribal Groups of the State have not been covered for monographic studies. Around 9.52 per cent of the total research studies have focussed on the study of tribal language dialect and 10.47 per cent of the studies have focussed on health and nutrition issues of the tribal people. The Institute has conducted very few studies on core issues of the tribal people like displacement (0.95%), indebtedness (0.95), bonded labour (0.95), shifting cultivation (2.85%), outward migration (2.85%), etc. A substantial number of studies on these issues would have contributed much to the State for framing policies and implementing schemes.

Especially with reference to the provisions of Fifth Schedule of the Constitution of India, it is observed that the Institute has not undertaken adequate studies among different tribal communities. An attempt has been made to find out the district-wise distribution of different research studies so far undertaken by SC&ST R&TI. The review brings out that the majority of research studies have been carried out in the districts of Koraput, Rayagada, Kondhmal, Mayurbhanj, Sundargarh, Keonjhar, Nawarangpur, Malkangiri, Gajapati, Bouda, Kalahandi, Angul and Jharsuguda (Table 3). More than thirty reports on different project areas of ITDAs and ITDPs have been prepared out of the data collected during the Universal Benchmark Survey which was conducted by the Institute in Scheduled Areas of Orissa during in 1978-80. Similarly, 17 individual documents have been prepared out of the Base line Survey and Need Assessments carried out for 10th Five Year Action Plan Period (2002-2007) covering all the 17 special micro project areas which have been implemented for the development of the primitive tribal groups (2001).

III.2 Determination of Caste Status

Determination of caste status of various tribal and non-tribal communities has been carried out by SC&ST R&TI. Studies on such caste categories for determination of status has been referred to either by the field level government functionaries or has been recommended by the Welfare Department. The data show that various communities belonging to Scheduled Tribes and Scheduled Castes have been recommended by Tribes

Advisory Council to Govt. of Orissa for inclusion and/or exclusion at different points of time, namely, 1978, 1981, 1985 and 1989. During 1978, as regards the determination of ethnic status, the institute has recommended almost 77 tribal subgroups for merger with existing 16 tribal communities. Out of that only one tribal community was identified for inclusion in the list of Scheduled Tribes of the State. Again during the year 1981 about 116 tribal subgroups have been recommended for merger with 22 existing Scheduled Tribal groups, whereas, only one community has been recommended for new entry in each Scheduled Tribe and in Scheduled Caste list of the State. Similarly, during 1985 a total of 22 tribal subgroups have been recommended for merger by the institute with seven Scheduled Tribal communities. Apart from that, four new tribal communities and one caste group have also been recommended for new entry in the scheduled list.

Data on the determination of caste status collected from 1990 to 1994 have also been analyzed. Almost 26.00 per cent and 20.00 per cent of proposed sub-communities have been finally recommended for their merger in Scheduled Tribe and Scheduled Caste categories respectively, whereas, almost 18.00 per cent STs and 28.00 per cent SCs are not found included in any of the list. Only 2 per cent from each scheduled category have been found to be suitable for inclusion in scheduled groups who are already in the list. Another analysis relating to the determination of caste status shows that more number of representations claiming independent scheduled status have come from existing tribal communities like *Saora* and *Savar, Khond, Bondo Paraja, Paraja, Kharia, Bagata, Gadaba, Luhara, Koya, Bhattoda/Dhatoda* etc. who have already been listed as Scheduled Tribe during 1950. This, at a certain level, indicates that there are various sub-sections of tribal communities who are still claiming for independent recognition in the Scheduled List of the State. However, they do not fit in as per the criteria adopted by the State to classify them as independent Scheduled categories.

As regards determination of caste status it is observed that while the minimum time period taken by the institute to complete a study of a community was 3 months, the maximum time taken to complete a study for this purpose was 10 years. The reasons for delay to complete such studies, as informed, are beyond the control of SC&ST R&TI. However, adoption of a time-bound planning may help SC&ST R&TI to complete such studies within the stipulated time period. In this regard, some TAC members of the State expressed their dissatisfaction saying that SC&ST R&TI while undertaking the studies for the determination of caste status is unable to complete them within the stipulated time period. They suggested that any assignment entrusted by TAC to SC&ST R&TI should be completed in time. This will help TAC to take policy decisions on various issues within a time frame.

III.3 Socio-Economic Survey

The socio-economic benchmark survey, which was undertaken during 1978 in the entire Scheduled Areas, is one of the major research activities of the institute. So far the data generated out of such a massive survey provides a good database for preparation of various schemes. A second mega baseline survey and need assessment was carried out in all the special micro projects covered all households. This need assessment was prepared for the 10th Five Year Action Plan period (2002-2007) for different primitive tribal communities. The institute has prepared 17 individual reports for 17 special micro projects. A total of 374 listed titles of different reports completed upto 2002 have been taken into consideration for analysis. While looking at the total number of socio-economic surveys so far carried out by the institute in various districts of Orissa, it is observed that socio-economic survey as a component in the entire research work is 12.03 per cent. Especially in connection with the provisions enshrined in the Fifth Schedule of the Constitution as regards land alienation, allotment of land among Scheduled Tribes and regulation of money-lending by private creditors, few studies have been conducted by the Institute. A study on indebtedness carried out among the Scheduled Tribes of Paralakhemundi Sub-Division seems to have contributed substantially to the understanding of the mechanisms of money lending going on in tribal areas. However, many socio-economic Bench-Mark Surveys have covered the issues relating to land alienation and indebtedness among the tribal people of Orissa.

The SC&ST R&TI is also assuming an active role in the preparation of Tribal Sub-Plan (TSP) document, project reports, action plans for Integrated Tribal Development Agencies (ITDAs). Several studies have been undertaken on identification of MADA, Cluster Pockets and Primitive Tribal Groups (PTGs). The institute has played an important role as support organization to the State as regards development of the weaker sections.

III.4 Training

III.4.1 Sources of Fund Support

Organization of Training programmes as one of the major activities of the institute aim at catering to the needs of Government Departments, Universities, and NGOs. Various Departments of Government of Orissa and Government of India provide fund for these training programmes. The 'Training Division of the Department of Personnel and Training', New Delhi; Ministry of Environment Forest and Wild Life; Ministry of Social Justice and Women Empowerment, and Ministry of Welfare of Government of India have financially supported SC& ST R&TI to organise various training programmes and workshops. These training programmes are organised by the Training Division of the Institute.

The training programmes sponsored by the Government of Orissa and Government of India during last 15 years (i.e. the period from 1983-84 to 1997-98) have been analyzed for the present purpose. The analysis is made according to the sources of funding; age, education and ethnic background of the participants; their distribution according to various departments they represent, the positions they held; various training issues covered, and the background of the resource persons.

III.4.2 Frequency of Training Programme

As regards the total number of training programmes organized and total training days covered during last 15 years under both the State and National level sponsored training programmes, the data reveal that, a total of 82 of State level training programmes have been carried out from 1983-84 to 1997-98. These training programmers have covered a total of 623 training days. The average training days per each programme is 7.89 days. There are 251 (19.57%) female and 1031 (80.42%) male trainees who participated in the training programmes. Almost 55 (67.07%) training programmes are meant for male participants and, 17(20.93%) number of programmes meant for female participants, whereas 10 (12.19%) number of programmes were meant for both male and female participants. Similarly, when one looks at the programmes sponsored by Government of India, it is reported that only 36 programmes have been organized by SC&ST R&TI during the above mentioned period (1983-84 to 1997-98). These programmes have covered a total of 474 training days, and an average of 13.16 man-days covered per each training programme. Out of a total of 891 trainee participants, 393 (44.10%) have been invited from outside the State, whereas, 498 (55.89%) participants are from within the State.

III.4.3 Major Areas of Training, Course Contents and Supply of Reading Materials

The major issues covered in State sponsored training programmes and their frequency has been described in Table -4. The data reflect that issues like the 'Constitutional Protective Measures' and 'Development Programmes'; 'Tribe, Society, Culture and Development'; 'Scheduled Caste and Tribal Welfare'; 'ORV Act and Rules' are some of the programmes which have been covered by SC&ST R&TI. Similarly, there are almost 7 different issues, which have been covered under 36 no. of training programmes sponsored by various Ministries of Govt. of India. This has covered issues like Development Planning, Monitoring and Evaluation Methodologies etc. The details of such issues so far covered are given in Table 5.

As regards the course contents and supply of reading materials to the trainees participants in various training programmes an attempt has been made here to analyse them. For example, the reading materials supplied during a national training programme on 'Environment Management and Tribal

Development' organised from 11.12.1995 to 18.12. 1995 show that it is of high standard, more academic and research oriented. The materials are informative and written by experienced authors. However, the reading materials could have also included various modern methodological practices like Participatory Rural Appraisal (PRA), Rapid Rural Appraisal (RRA), Strength-Weakness Opportunity and Threat (SWOT) analysis etc. for environmental management which are largely used by bi-lateral implementing agencies, NGOs and funding agencies like World Bank, SIDA, DANIDA, ODA etc. The reading materials provided during training programme are useful for the trainees.

Different Ministries of Govt. of India sponsor training programmes. It is difficult to find out the priority of the institute to select the issues. Certain training programmes like Tribal Development Administration, Health and Culture etc. though do not focus specific dimensions; nonetheless it is felt that these issues are appropriate since the tribal societies are backward.

III.4.4 Resource Persons

As regards the participation of Resource Persons in both national and State level training programmes are concerned, one observes that the resource persons called for providing training are belonging to two categories. They are in-house trainers, and outside or external trainers. The in-house resource persons who have provided training are Director, Ex-Director, Research Officers, Research Assistants, and Officer on Special Duty (OSD). Similarly, the resource persons who came from outside are either academicians (Basically Anthropologists) and/or administrators. Attempt has been made to distribute the number of training classes taken by different resource persons from 1983-84 to 1997-98. Data reflect that out of total 1448 classes, resource persons from outside have undertaken 49.72 per cent in which academicians have covered 19.61 per cent and administrators have covered 30.11 per cent of classes. The data reflect that the Director who is by position an Anthropologist has covered 8.63 per cent of the classes; Deputy Directors who belong to social science faculties have covered 7.52 per cent of the classes. The Research Officers, Research

Assistants and Officer on Special Duty (who is also an Anthropologist) have covered 15.74, 11.09, and 3.03 per cent of classes respectively. At certain level SC&ST R&TI have tried to bring a balance while identifying resource persons, however, anthropologists have played a major role in providing training in SC&ST R&TI. While discussing with the staff of Training Unit it is confirmed that training need and resource persons' expertise are taken into account while identifying resource persons for different training programmes.

III.4.5 Trainees' Official Position

Other dimensions of trainees, which have been looked at for our analysis are their official positions and disciplines to which they belonged. This at one level throws light on the importance of training inputs relevant for Government employees posted in tribal areas. In State level training programmes more number of officers from Welfare Department, such as, DWO, ADWO, WEO, S.O, CDPO, have participated (35.72%). The participation of Panchayati Raj functionaries (7.72%), Scheduled Caste and Scheduled Tribe Youths (7.33%), Ashram School Teachers (16.14%), OAS Officers (5.38%) is satisfactory. Data regarding the Departments of the trainee participants (as shown in Table 6) explain that, out of the total participants, almost 58.59 per cent were from the Welfare Department, and 10.45 per cent are from Panchayati Raj Department.

III.4.6 Trainees' Ethnic Background

The ethnic composition of the trainees and their participation is very important. The institute is meant for undertaking training programmes on SCs and STs on priority basis and also to train both tribals and non-tribals on various development issues. The data regarding ethnic composition of the trainees reflect that out of 1282 participants covered under the State level training programmes, almost 150 (11.70%), 314 (24.49%) and 818 (63.80%) belonged to Scheduled Castes, Scheduled Tribes and Other Caste groups respectively. The ethnic composition of the trainees in the National level training programmes indicate that participants belonging to Scheduled Castes (6.60%) and Scheduled Tribes (8.15%) are less compared to State level training programmes. This at certain level proves that SC&ST R&TI has not taken much care to include SC and ST participants in the training programmes proportionately. In order to encourage their participation, more number of special training programmes could have been organized for the STs and SCs.

III.4.7 Gender Composition

As regards the sex composition of the participants, one finds that the share of female participants in the State level training programmes is less (16.23%) compared to the national level training programmes. There was only one national level training programme specially meant for women, whereas, 12 (33.33%) training programmes were organized only for male and rest 23 training programmes were kept open for both male and female participants. At a certain level this perhaps suggests that the institute has not given adequate attention to include more number of women participants in their training programmes. The institute could have proposed and organized more number of training programmes especially for the women participants. This could have justified the gender component of the training to a great extent.

III.4.8 Trainees' Age

The age factor of the trainees is important. If the trainees are younger in age, the knowledge gained through training is more useful for a longer period; and if the trainees are senior persons, who are about to retire, then the knowledge gained out of training may be less useful. The State level training programmes reflect that around 35.91 per cent trainees are below 30 years of age, whereas, 22.46 per cent and 25.50 per cent are within the age group of 31 to 40 years and 41 to 50 years respectively. Similarly, in national level training programmes around 17.58 per cent trainees are below the age of 30 years, whereas, 34.71 per cent and 26.65 per cent of trainees are within the age group of 31 to 40 and 41 to 50 years respectively. This clearly indicates that the institute while selecting the trainees has purposefully laid emphasis on up gradation of the training skill of those with long year of experience.

Conclusion

The institute has contributed fairly in the field of research on tribal society, culture and has provided training to the personnel engaged in tribal development. But one hardly finds more than one or two studies/evaluation/training programme on any of the issues of land alienation, indebtedness and prohibition. Moreover no study has been undertaken on the functioning of Tribes Advisory Council (TAC) in the State of Orissa. Such a study would have helped reminding TAC members about their role and responsibilities and helped in streamlining the functioning of TAC in Orissa. The Institute could not establish organic linkages with different agencies who are working for the development of SCs and STs in the State. Because of this, the findings reported by the Institute through different studies have hardly taken into account by the related agencies. It wouldn't be inappropriate to say that the Institute could not maintain its consistency in projecting the problems of SCs and STs as it was doing during 1970s and partly in 1980's. This has partially affected the fund flow from Government of India to different Micro Projects meant for the development of Primitive tribal groups of the State. The analysis of fund flow to Micro Projects (Table 1) during the period 1990 to 1997 justifies its decline. When discussed with some senior professionals of SC&ST & RTI, it transpired that the assignment in respect of research, training, evaluation etc. are normally decided at higher level, namely by the Administrative Department and Advisory Board of SC&ST & RTI. The fact is that sufficient attention is needed to work on the core issues of the SC&ST communities of the State. Since the Government has established SC&ST & RTI for looking into the interest of these deprived ethic/minority groups (SCs & STs), it is expected that the State and the researchers of SC & ST & RTI have to play a strong, dynamic and vibrant role in days to come. The Institute is a part of Government machinery. It should be given certain autonomy to carry out research activities. Government control will curtail its efficiency.

Table 1

Release of Funds from Govt. of India to Different Tribal Research Institutes in India

Sl. No.	States having TRI	ST population 1991*	ST literacy 1991	Release of Funds (in lakhs) 90-91	91-92	92-93	93-94	94-95	95-96	96-97	97-98	Total
1	Andhra Pradesh	6.31	17.16	11.50	5.00	4.81	5.66	15.98	25.54	25.00	20.47	113.96
2	Assam	12.82	49.16	14.76	16.00	10.70	12.10	12.55	17.77	13.01	22.40	119.29
3	Bihar	7.66	26.78	—	9.25	9.82	12.71	10.63	14.73	0.00	—	57.14
4	Gujrat	14.92	36.45	1.18	2.25	2.19	0.55	6.15	0.14	0.00	8.90	21.18
5	Kerala	1.10	57.22	10.00	12.00	8.00	7.85	10.00	11.25	13.50	20.00	92.60
6	Madhya Pradesh	23.27	21.54	13.80	13.20	28.28	23.35	13.09	22.21	22.02	47.74	182.90
7	Maharashtra	9.27	36.79	4.34	5.80	11.27	23.75	24.30	0.00	22.70	49.45	141.61
8	Manipur	34.41	53.63	9.00	10.00	6.60	3.50	2.00	0.49	10.35	9.00	50.94
9	Orissa	22.21	22.31	1.60	2.60	3.22	3.73	8.59	12.90	6.70	5.85	45.19
10	Rajasthan	12.44	19.44	1.00	5.00	4.58	5.57	6.14	7.93	5.66	12.82	47.70
11	Tamil Nadu	1.03	27.89	25.00	11.54	9.44	7.39	7.12	16.54	9.30	30.50	116.83
12	Tripura	30.95	40.37	—	—	0.69	6.80	10.41	8.27	11.21	10.95	48.24
13	U.P.	0.21	35.70	10.00	5.00	3.46	4.98	0.00	1.12	4.27	—	28.83
14	West Bengal	5.59	27.78	—	5.48	1.03	0.93	1.19	10.83	6.06	21.80	47.32
15	Himachal Pradesh	4.22	47.09	—	—	0.31	0.27	0.21	0.28	0.22	—	1.29
16	Arunachal Pradesh		34.45	—	—	0.00	0.57	0.00	0.00	0.00	—	0.57
17	Karnataka		36.01	—	—	0.00	0.29	0.63	0.00	0.00	—	0.92

*Per cent to the total population of the state.

Source- Annual Report 1997-98, 98-99, Ministry of Social Justice and Empowerment, Government of India, New Delhi.

Table 2
Distribution of Research Studies According to the Issues Covered by SC&ST R&TI During 1977 to 1998

Sl. No.	*Major Study Issues*	*No. of Studies*
1	Ethnographic Studies	32
2	Studies on Welfare Schemes	16
3	Tribal Language Dialect	10
4	Health and Nutrition	11
5	Land Problems	5
6	Living Conditions of Tribals	5
7	Educational Problems	5
8	Forest Issues	6
9	Shifting Cultivation	3
10	Migration	2
11	Employment	2
12	Gender Issues	2
13	Natural Calamity	2
14	Indebtedness	1
15	Displacement	1
16	Bonded Labour	1
	Total	105

Source: SC&ST & RTI, Govt. of Orissa, Bhubaneswar.

Table 3
Distribution of Various Research Programmes Undertaken by SC&ST R&TI in Districts of Orissa (From 1974 to 2002)

Sl. No.	*Districts*	*No. of Socio-economic surveys*	*Preparation of Action Plan*	*Evaluation and Impact assessment*	*Research studies*	*Report in Ubms*	*Total*
	SCHEDULED AREA						
1	Koraput	2	6	3	12	2	25
2	Rayagada	6	6	4	6	2	24
3	Malkanagiri	2	6	2	3	2	6
4	Nawarangapur	2	1	1	0	1	5
5	Kandhamal	3	8	2	12	3	28
6	Gajapati	5	7	3	3	2	20

7	Mayurbhanja	4	11	5	11	6	37
8	Keonjhar	3	7	7	3	3	23
9	Sundargarh	4	5	2	5	2	18
10	Kalahandi	3	4	4	3	0	14
11	Balasore	2	2	2	1	2	9
12	Sambalpur	0	6	1	1	0	8
13	Ganjam	1	3	0	2	0	6
	Total	37	72	36	63	25	267
	% Of Total	13.85	26.96	13.48	23.59	9.36	100.00
	NON-SCHEDULED AREA						
1	Nayagarh	2	1	1	1	0	5
2	Puri	0	6	1	0	0	7
3	Khurda	0	2	1	1	0	4
4	Cuttack	0	4	0	0	0	4
5	Jajpur	0	0	1	1	0	2
6	Jagatsingpur	0	0	0	1	0	1
7	Kendrapada	0	1	0	0	0	1
8	Bhadrakh	0	1	0	0	0	1
9	Nuapada	0	10	1	2	0	13
10	Deogarh	1	4	2	1	2	10
11	Bargarh	0	1	0	0	0	1
12	Balangir(old)	0	1	0	1	0	2
13	Dhenkanal	0	3	0	1	0	4
14	Anugul	0	2	1	0	0	3
15	Jharsuguda	0	2	0	2	0	4
16	Boudh	2	2	2	2	0	8
17	Orissa General	3	1	3	30	0	37
	Total	8	41	13	43	2	7
	% Of Total	7.47	38.01	12.14	40.18	1.86	100.00
	Grand Total	45	113	49	105	27	374
	% Of Grand Total	12.03	30.21	13.10	28.07	7.21	100.00

Source: SC&ST R&TI, Govt. of Orissa, Bhubaneswar.

Table 4
Distribution of Major Issues Covered Under State Level Training Programs Organised by SC&ST R&TI During 1983-1984 to 1997-98

Sl. No.	*Major Issues*	*No. of Times Organised*	*Percentage*
1.	Constitutional Protective Measures and Development Program	22	26.51
2.	Tribal Society, Culture and Development	16	19.28
3.	Scheduled Caste Welfare	8	9.64
4.	ORV Act and Rules	6	7.23
5.	Training of Trainers of Beneficiary at ITDA levels	5	6.02
6.	Environment Management on Tribal Development	5	6.02
7.	Tribal Development Programs in Orissa	5	6.02
8.	Primitive Tribes and Development	5	6.02
9.	Reservation Act in Orissa	5	6.02
10.	Tribal Development Administration, Monitoring and Evaluation	3	3.61
11.	Role of Tribal Women in Tribal Welfare	3	3.61
	Total	83	100.00

Source: Training Registration Records SC ST R&TI. Govt. of Orissa, Bhubaneswar.

Table 5
Distribution of Major Issues Covered Under Central Govt. Training Programmes Organised by SC&ST R&TI During 1983–84 to 1997–98

Sl. No.	*Major Issues Covered*	*Frequency*	*Percentage*
1.	Planning, Monitoring, and Evaluations of Tribal Development Programs	9	25.00
2.	Tribal Women and Development	7	19.44

3.	Tribal Development Administration, Health and Culture	6	16.67
4.	Forest and Tribal Development	5	13.89
5.	Implementation of Tribal Development Programs	4	11.11
6.	Environmental Management and Tribal Development	3	8.33
7.	Society, Culture, Education and Development	2	5.56
	Total	36	100.00

Source: Training Registration Record, SC ST R&TI, Govt. of Orissa, Bhubaneswar.

Table 6

Distribution of Departments Representing in Various State Level Training Programmes Conducted by SC&ST R&TI From 1983-84 to 1997-98

Sl. No.	*Name of the Department*	*No. of Participants*	
		Nos.	*Percent*
1.	S.C and S.T. Development Department	755	58.89
2.	Panchayati Raj	134	10.45
3.	Industries	67	5.22
4.	General Administration	61	4.75
5.	Agriculture-Soil Conservation-Horticulture	60	4.63
6.	Women and Child Development	54	4.21
7.	Forest & Environment	47	3.66
8.	Revenue and Excise	46	3.58
9.	Rural Development	27	2.10
10.	Tourism and Culture	15	1.17
11.	Co-operation	15	1.17
12.	Fisheries and Animal Resource Development F & ARD	1	0.07
	Total	1282	100.00

Source: Training Registration Records, SC&ST R&TI, Govt. of Orissa, Bhubaneswar.

REFERENCES

Behura, N. K. 1990. The Tribal Development: A Critical review, *Jo Manav*, vol-3 Pp-22-32

Behura, N. K. and Panigrahi, N. 2001. Functioning of the Fifth Schedule of the Constitution of India in the State of Orissa, Report submitted to ICSSR, New Delhi, N.K.C. Centre for Development Studies, Bhubaneswar.

——— 2006. *Indian Constitution and the Tribals: Functioning of Fifth Schedule in the State of Orissa*, Rawat Publication, New Delhi.

Government of India 1997-98 and 1998-99. Annual Reports. Social Justice and Empowerment, New Delhi: Government of India.

Government of Orissa 1995-96, 99-2000. Report on the Annual Administration of Scheduled Areas in Orissa, ST and SC Development Department, Govt of Orissa.

Panigrahi, N. et al. 1998. Changes in Agriculture Pattern among the Lanjia Saora, *The Eastern Anthropologist*, vol. 51, No. 1, Jan-Mar-1998.

10

AN EVALUATION OF DEVELOPMENT PARADIGMS AND SUSTAINABLE DEVELOPMENT OF TRIBAL CHILDREN IN ORISSA

DR. S. N. TRIPATHY

India has undoubtedly made considerable progress in the last two decades in promoting child survival and basic education. Along with a supportive policy framework, including the recent legislation to make elementary education a fundamental right, there have been in existence some major initiatives for children. More prominently, these are in the form of centrally sponsored schemes such as the Reproductive Child Health Scheme (RCH) of the Department of Health and Family Welfare. The Integrated Child Development Services (ICDS) of the Department of Women and Child Development and several primary education schemes, including the District Primary Education Program (DPEP) and the government's flagship program, the Sarva Shiksha Abhiyan (SSA). As a result, noticeable progress has been made over the last fifty years, as seen in the rapid expansion of the ICDS and primary education delivery network across the country.

Programs can be effective under the right conditions, and these tend to be related to fundamental causes of malnutrition, such as social exclusion and women's status. Policy decisions and implementation may affect these conditions. In the process of negotiating investment from international financial institutions in nutritional improvement, the basic requirements underpinning programs may prove feasible issues for modification. At the same time, the simple but crucial decisions to actually commit resources and implement the programs themselves must be taken. Beyond context, the coexistence of key programs must be fostered.

Poverty alleviation facilitates nutrition improvements in two ways. First, the programs themselves provide household resources for improving nutrition. Second, poverty alleviation program organization can provide for the structure, outreach, and individual contact that nutrition activities can build on. The poverty alleviation organizations provide the best prospect of extending and supporting local programs. The direct effects of improvements such as in education, particularly for women, and in water and sanitation, have far-reaching effects on nutrition.

A number of issues that affect all potential programs remain to be resolved. Most involve research that should be undertaken at an early stage, and represent sensible investment in terms of program effectiveness in the future. Some of the salient issues are outlined here.

An issue which has concerned us is defining the contextual factors as well as how these can be changed through policy measures in order to improve program success. These issues can be researched and guidance provided for program design. More specifically, knowledge of the relative roles and cost-effectiveness of different community-based and facility-based activities is not yet well laid out. This could be improved from compilation and synthesis of current knowledge. Such research, although of general application, would be most useful in advance of detailed program planning. The relative effects of using resources for supplementary feeding, compared with using the same resources for behavioural change, could also be worked out as a generic issue. Population growth in India is in the cities and towns.

As a result, the malnourished are increasingly in urban areas. Yet most planning for improving nutrition refers to villages and rural communities. Research is needed on the most effective means of improving nutrition in urban areas, and where these have common features and problems, this research can be generic. We need to focus on nutrition-relevant programs in cities and their evaluations, as well as understand better the parallels with rural programs, especially regarding the appropriate forms of local organization. This review leads to extensive proposals for finance, and even more for recruiting and training millions of people. Better nutrition and development for children is a powerful outcome objective, with implications for society and development overall. In particular, problems of social exclusion, and discrimination by class and gender, would have some counteracting forces.

For individuals, specific nutritional problems would be well on the way to solution. Micronutrient deficiencies would be becoming a thing of the past, with goitre and iodine deficiency vanishing, and vitamin A deficiency no longer visible and sub-clinically much reduced. Anaemia would likely be in retreat, with successful fortification. Pregnant women in particular, others too, would be getting regular multiple micronutrient supplements. Low birth weight and early childhood growth failure, and associated sickness and death, would be much reduced—the next generation would be larger, healthier, benefit more from education, and be more productive.

Among the poorest segments of the population, increasing their income, their preference towards consuming calorie-intensive foods and the future changes in the relative price of the cereals can only reduce calorie malnutrition. Calorie income elasticity is nearly 0.5 implying that a one percent change in per capita income increases calorie consumption by half of one percent. It may take several years for the poorest population experiencing a deficit of calories to reach the required level of calorie consumption. Simultaneously, marginally and non-deficient income groups may also increase their consumption and reach levels that can be substantially higher than requirements. Hence, malnutrition in the poorest groups may coexist with a calorie surplus. Thus, regular income growth in the poorest population and accelerated food production are unfeasible solutions. The solution may be that reshuffle food availability from the groups with calorie surplus to those in deficit. Malnutrition may be more concentrated in the poorest segment and may be more children specific given the family size and income. Malnutrition is widely prevalent in children due to the fact that calorie-income elasticity for children is lower. Secondly, due to urbanization women's participation in the labour force has increased resulting in the deterioration of breast-feeding.

Additional food purchased for the infant, out of the additional earnings of the female participating in the labour force, does not compensate for the losses in breast milk consumption; the net effect is deterioration in the infant's nutritional status.

Other factors may also adversely affect the children. Other competing expenditures like transportation, clothing, housing etc. become more important in urban areas, affecting the share of income spent on food. Relative prices of food tend to rise. New commodities become available, such as entertainment and fashion, to be consumed basically by the adults. The result is that the share of income spent on food for children can decline because expenditures other than food become necessary and new commodities, relevant basically to adults, become available.

Calorie malnutrition in young children results from the fact that the family as a whole is malnourished. Secondly, calorie-wise children are discriminated relative to adults. Thirdly, discrimination among children according to some characteristics like intelligence, sex, birth order, feeding practices etc. In case, the entire family is malnourished, increase the household overall purchasing power of food—either by increasing their disposable income or lowering the relative price of calorie intensive food. Where there is discrimination among children, preferences of adults in allocation food to particular children can be influenced by emphasizing that it is an investment good. The rate of return to investment in education is a function of the initial level of nutrition.

The Tribal Scenario

In our country tribes constitute more than 8% of the total population, are languishing in the midst of poverty and backwardness. The tribals reside in forests and inaccessible hill areas and maintained their survival oriented culture. The agents of the new order represented by traders, moneylenders, and contractors entered to the tribal regions and exploited them. They provided money lending and took away their fertile lands as a result of which, the tribal proceeded to interior parts of forest. Tribal peoples being illiterate and unskilled are mostly belonging to the labouring community as they eke out their living through manual labour and wage earning. They are the exploited, indebted, and marginalized communities.

Devoid of life supporting system, the tribals have to (more than 90 percent) cultivate the poor quality of land paucity of land, work as agricultural labourers to eke out a living. These tribal labourers are the victims of myriad forms of exploitation by the highly inter-locking non-tribals axis of power that dominates the land, credit and input markets. As a result, the tribes migrate as construction workers, which require unskilled manual labour. They live in an inhuman condition devoid of all the human rights.

The backwardness of the tribal regions, widespread poverty of the tribals and problems of integrating them with the mainstream of civilization etc., are the stumbling blocks in the path of tribal development. Thus, the tribals in India continued to remain socially, economically and educationally backward and are languishing at the bottom of the socio-economic ladder. For generation together they are residing in inaccessible forest and hilly areas. Their geographical isolation and impoverished economy have made them object of exploitative economic and trade practices of non-tribal living or entering areas. The powerful exogenous forces of moneylenders, contractors, officials having their link with political personnel and police could exert dominant control and gratify the selfish greed of exploiting the tribals. The poverty stricken, illiterate, innocent, simple tribals fail to withstand the countervailing exogenous forces and becoming prey to all types of exploitation (Tripathy, 2007).

The extreme poverty compelled many tribals to sell or mortgage their lands to the people of the plains. As a result of which, the tribes of the region were driven to inaccessible forests and hill areas where they maintained their survival-oriented culture. The agents of the 'new order' represented by traders, moneylenders and contractors didn't leave them there either. The outcome of this oppressive 'new order' was that the 'tribal poor' have found themselves exceedingly indebted and alienated from most of their land except for a few pieces of eroded land strips (Tripathy, 1991, pp. 35-36).

Thus, the tribals from time to time deprived of their fertile lands and were subjected to ruthless exploitation by the invading people which have resulted in the hill men's flying in greater and greater wilderness. The infiltration of people from the plains continues resulting in depriving the hill men of the good lands they reclaimed (Tripathy, 1998, p. 232).

The effect of migration on health and education outcomes for poor tribes, particularly children, is an important dimension to evaluating the costs and benefits of migration. Most accounts of the effects of migration on health either assume that migration helps to spread disease, and places migrants in unhealthy working or living environments, or alternatively emphasizes the undoubted negative effects that the loss of skilled medical personnel has on the finance and functioning of the health services in sending countries. Similarly, many accounts of the effects of migration on education stress the risk that migration leads to children being taken out of school.

The resultant marginalization of millions of people threatens the fabric upon which our democracy has been founded. Apparently, people reposing their faith elect the representative who is supposed to protect their interest and safeguard their livelihoods. But the irony is that we behold a different scene when we find the tribal pockets, as the delicate foundation is shaken as their voice is not heeded.

Poverty Alleviation and Employment Generation Programmes

Poverty reduction has been an important goal of development

policy since the inception of planning in India. Various antipoverty, employment generation and basic services programmes have been in operation for decades in India. The ongoing reforms attach great importance to removal of poverty, and addressing specifically the wide variations across States and the rural-urban divide. Anti-poverty strategy has three broad components: promotion of economic growth; promotion of human development; and targeted programmes of poverty alleviation to address multi-dimensional nature of poverty. The various programmes targeted at the poor have been streamlined and strengthened in recent years, including through the NREGS.

The Food and Agriculture Organization (FAO) advocate per capita per day availability of food-intake is a robust indicator to measure food insecurity. But in recent years, the anthropometric indicators are increasingly being used to measure the incidence of food-insecurity. Institutions like WHO and UNICEF are largely in favour of anthropometric indicators to measure Food insecurity.

Meeting Program Needs

Implementing programs, when resources are committed will take a number of practical steps. Gaps in capacity must be filled. The needs will be:

(i) *Organization:* programs depend on local organization and decentralization of resources and decision-making; including fostering community level organizations, by assigning budgets, legislation, and other means;

(ii) *Training:* the effort envisaged for training village level workers, and their support, is extensive, and will require multilevel structures for training, materials, incentives, and supervision;

(iii) *Advocacy and social mobilization;* information; education; training; and support for service delivery as defined by UNICEF; and

(iv) *Mobilization of resources:* direct financial inputs will be required, especially for the large numbers of village workers and their facilitators who will need incentives and remuneration, likely beyond the capacity of communities and governments; for external finance, negotiations as to type and level will be needed, in conjunction with reallocation of governmental resources.

Issues for Program Design

A number of issues that affect all potential programs remain to be resolved. Most involve research that should be undertaken at an early stage, and represent sensible investment in terms of program effectiveness in the future. Some of the salient issues are outlined here.

Resources should be applied to a problem in such a way that the population can respond and the problem is alleviated. In nutritional terms, this means identifying accurately which population groups can respond to which type of intervention. For example, behavioural change (child feeding practices, for instance) may not be possible by some methods for some groups, and this needs to be better defined or ineffective programs will be designed.

A similar issue which has concerned us is defining the contextual factors as well as how these can be changed through policy measures in order to improve program success. These issues can be researched and guidance provided for program design. More specifically, knowledge of the relative roles and cost-effectiveness of different community-based and facility-based activities is not yet well laid out. This could be improved from compilation and synthesis of current knowledge. Such research, although of general application, would be most useful in advance of detailed program planning. The relative effects of using resources for supplementary feeding, compared with using the same resources for behavioural change, could also be worked out as a generic issue. Population growth in India is in the cities and towns.

As a result, the malnourished are increasingly in urban areas. Yet most planning for improving nutrition refers to villages and rural communities. Research is needed on the most effective means of improving nutrition in urban areas, and where these have common features and problems, this research can be generic. We need to focus on nutrition-relevant programs in cities and their evaluations, as well as understand better the parallels with rural programs, especially regarding the appropriate forms of local organization. The relationship of level of effort (for various activities) to impact needs to be better understood. This is likely to be nonlinear, which is crucial as it means that applying too low a level of resources is very wasteful. It does not mean that the problem will simply be solved more slowly; it means that it will not be solved at all until the level of effort is sufficient to cause change. This has enormous implications for planning investments, and needs to be researched. Finally, a number of technical issues need research, of which the clearest concern fortification, most urgently iron fortification of staple foods.

Economics of Intervention

Increasing their income, their preference towards consuming calorie-intensive foods and the future changes in the relative price of the cereals can only reduce calorie malnutrition in the poorest segments of the population. Calorie income elasticity is nearly 0.5 implying that a one percent change in per capita income increases calorie consumption by half of one percent. It may take several years for the poorest population experiencing a deficit of calories to reach the required level of calorie consumption. Simultaneously, marginally and non-deficient income groups may also increase their consumption and reach levels that can be substantially higher than requirements. Hence, malnutrition in the poorest groups may coexist with a calorie surplus. Thus, regular income growth in the poorest population and accelerated food production are unfeasible solutions. The solution may be that reshuffle food availability from the groups with calorie surplus to those in deficit. Malnutrition may be more concentrated in the poorest segment and may be more children specific given the family size and income.

Malnutrition is widely prevalent in children due to the fact that calorie-income elasticity for children is lower. Secondly, due to urbanization women's participation in the labour force has increased resulting in the deterioration of breast-feeding.

Additional food purchased for the infant, out of the additional earnings of the female participating in the labour force, does not compensate for the losses in breast milk consumption; the net effect is deterioration in the infant's nutritional status.

Other factors may also adversely affect the children. Other competing expenditures like transportation, clothing, housing etc. become more important in urban areas, affecting the share of income spent on food. Relative prices of food tend to rise. New commodities become available, such as entertainment and fashion, to be consumed basically by the adults. The result is that the share of income spent on food for children can decline because expenditures other than food become necessary and new commodities, relevant basically to adults, become available.

Economic Points of Intervention

Calorie malnutrition in young children results from the fact that the family as a whole is malnourished. Secondly, calorie-wise children are discriminated relative to adults. Thirdly, discrimination among children according to some characteristics like intelligence, sex, birth order, feeding practices etc. In case, the entire family is malnourished, increase the household overall purchasing power of food-either by increasing their disposable income or lowering the relative price of calorie intensive food. Where children are discriminated, specific food programmes that have an effect on children's consumption more than an equivalent income transfer to the household. Where there is discrimination among children, preferences of adults in allocation food to particular children can be influenced by emphasizing that it is an investment good. The rate of return to investment in education is a function of the initial level of nutrition.

Education & Health

School sector in Orissa is pathetic in rural and tribal areas. High incidence of inequality in the location of schools between the underdeveloped and developed districts is reported in the state. About 12,869 villages mostly located in southern and northern regions do not have school in 2002-03. In more than 12,000 schools there is only one teacher and in more than 22,000 schools, there is no room for each class. This situation led to high dropout and low enrolment in many rural schools. However, urban and developed coastal areas enjoy a better school infrastructure.

While allocation of funds on primary education was very low (2.11% of NSDP) during 1990s, the progress of some popular programme like mid-day meal and DPEP has been dismal in many tribal districts. This has reflected in the form of low literacy rate, especially female literacy at district level. Orissa Human Development Report (2004) gives a detailed analysis of disparities on a range of indicators, showing a decline in the gender disparity index, with emphasis that regional disparities in female literacy are larger than men's.

For well-being and nutrition security of rural community and tribal labour there is a need to enhance the productivity of their resources like land, livestock and fishponds. Secondly, there is also a need to enhance the economic value of their time and labour of the tribal labourers through a paradigm shift from unskilled to skilled work. They will have to be enabled to take to skilled non-farm employment through market driven micro- enterprises supported by micro-credit. Self-Help group (SHGs) of assetless tribal labourers will have to be sustainable through backward linkages to credit and technology and forward linkage with markets. We should reorient our social safety nets to create more employment in rural and tribal regions, help strengthen the human resource base through education, nutrition, and employment of women in backward tribal regions.

Health sector, particularly in southern and northern districts is grossly neglected. There is concentration of health institutions in coastal and other developed districts in comparison with tribal districts. While one medical institution was present per 92 sq km at state level, in tribal area it available per 123 sq km in 2002. With poor connectivity, tribal areas are worse affected in basic medical facilities including doctors and para-medical personals.

Regional variation in health sector is well documented in terms of variation in IMR. Southern and Western tribal districts like Koraput (110), Balangir (119), Kalahandi (107) and Phulbani (112).have much higher IMR in comparison with the coastal and other districts as well as the state average (87) during 2002. The high IMR has been persisting in many of these districts over a long period. High variation in rural (94) urban (61) and male (90) female (93) IMR also reported in the state.

On the other hand government spending on healthcare is one of the lowest in Orissa and is no remarkable change in recent years. Public expenditure on health was 3.61% of total budget during the year 1990-91 which declined to 2.54% during 2001-02. It may be noted that capital expenditure in health sector (expenditure such as equipment, medicines etc.) constitutes very low portion of total health expenditure and the rest is spent on salary and establishment. Capital expenditure in health sector was about 40 percent in 1996-97 which declined to 10 percent in 2001-02. The impact of the cut of expenditure on health and education sector is clearly discernable in poor human development in the state and the impacts are perhaps reflected in terms worsening human development, poverty and overall growth in rural areas. The quantum and pattern of expenditure and the rural urban differences in health and education sector seem pronouncing lopsided development in the state.

Special Problems of the State

The state is characterized by highly calamity prone with unpredictable characters, which erodes the existing use of resources. It also drains out substantial amount of resources (both of state as well as of households) to cope with the situation. While cumulative impact of calamities like drought is relatively high in Orissa, the state govt. has no long-term drought measures.

Ethnic composition of Orissa is different from other states. About 40 percent of people in the state are from backward castes and most of them live in rural areas. Most of the tribal population have uncertain property rights on land and have no physical and financial source to support their survival. Given minimal development of human capital among, they are excluded from the development process. State intervention to improve their resource base and income generating avenues has met with marginal success. Rather, the process of industrialization and development strategies followed over period has affected these communities. In large extent these factors are responsible for no remarkable social and economic change in rural areas.

The SC/ST groups are generally excluded from availing opportunities in a various spheres. Despite government reservations, few are able to participate in the development programme which are important in providing them income and other opportunities.

Role of governance is another key factor for low level of social and economic transformation of rural areas. The state is characterized by highly fragmented nature of polity and society and it is unable to articulate and involves in focusing the goal of the state. In such a situation the political process in articulating the development goal for rural areas is weak. In such a situation the broad social change of the state is ushered by the bureaucratic approaches whose goal is to fulfill the target. But in the process neither the target is achieved nor there effective monitoring mechanism in ensuring the process of rural development.

The effectiveness of different rural development programmes initiated by different organizations including state, NGOs etc. is low due to problem of governance and institutional problems. There is hardly any coordination among different institutions involved in the entire process. Many marginal groups belonging to SC/ST and others are unable to derive benefits from many development programmes under existing political process and bureaucratic set up due to their low bargaining power. Implicit collusion among the elites may be obstacles in having effective decentralization in the decision-making and programme implementation.

Basically, there are three types of problems that rural areas confront with within the state. First, there exists wide gap in income poverty between coastal region and hinterland Orissa and southern region.

Second, there are high differences in terms of capability enhancing infrastructure such as health, education and information between rural and urban areas.

Third, there is gender disparity in terms of access to employment, education and health care and across the rural areas and the situation is more pronounced among social groups.

Conclusion and Policy Implications

In spite of rapid industrialization and urbanization in the country, rural areas predominate and there is no remarkable diversification of rural economy with desirable level of social and economic changes in a backward state like Orissa. The dynamics of rural development in the state have hardly changed the quality of life among marginal groups and mainly the tribes, over period. This is clearly evident from the pattern and trend of growth, employment, poverty, agriculture and infrastructure and social sector development in the state. Of late, other backward states having more or less similar constraints have been able to improve rural life. Therefore, appropriate policy action with special focus on the areas and social groups is suggested to tackle this existing alarming situation. The issue of rural development is more complex and deep rooted and needs specific policy action may be beyond the conventional rural development programmes.

The backward districts in southern and northern regions of the state are caught in a vicious circle of multiple deprivation, social exclusion and poor human development. Improvement of social and economic infrastructure in backward regions could be one of top priority to encourage further investment and progress and enhance the capability of the rural poor.

Despite the fact that Orissa, confronts with several problems but the state has the potential to achieve a respectable level of development and to undermine the existing pattern of unequal social and economic pattern among different groups and areas.

The key areas for policy actions are correcting structural problems of the economy, accelerating agricultural growth, improving land distribution, investment in infrastructure and human development, good governance, strengthening rural institutions and civil society etc.

Stating that the arming of tribals to fight exploitation and policing their protests have been responsible for their growing sense of alienation and isolation, the government has come out with a draft policy to uplift this marginalized section of the population

The Indian government has released a draft national policy on tribals to address the issue of developing this section of the population in "an integrated and holistic manner". For the first time since the formation of the Indian republic, 60 years ago, the Ministry of Tribal Affairs released the draft document whose aim is to "uplift the tribals who have been facing acute poverty, alienation from land and lack of livelihood opportunities," in many parts of India. The document was released in New Delhi on July 21, 2006.

The policy will address issues such as the enhancement of human development indicators among scheduled tribes (STs) to bring them on a par with the general population, improvement of infrastructure in tribal areas, tribal control over the natural resource base, displacement and resettlement, and the equitable distribution of wealth and opportunities among tribals.

The policy also provides for regulatory protection, socio-economic and political empowerment, increased livelihood opportunities, improved governance and administration, preservation of tribal cultural and traditional rights and knowledge, and protection of tribal traditional knowledge in the intellectual property rights regime.

Steps will be taken to ensure that the benefits granted to ST communities are evenly spread among all ST communities, and, if so warranted, those populations that have caught up with the general population be de-scheduled. A time-bound programme will be initiated to identify the needs of nomadic tribes and their development.

The National Tribal Policy, 2006 outlines several new and continuing initiatives for accelerating the pace of welfare and development of tribal areas in the country. An institutionalized monitoring mechanism will be put in place at both the national and state level. Powers will be given to local communities to monitor and oversee the programme's planning and implementation.

The policy itself will be updated periodically. To make it a living document, the Cabinet Committee on Tribal Affairs (CCTA) will be asked to review the policy every three years and redefine its objectives and guiding principles, if necessary, and accordingly recast the strategy to address any new challenges that may emerge (*The Indian Express*, July 22, 2006, www.indiawnews.com, July 21, 2006)

The core principle of sustainable development is to improve human well-being over time, with the goal that children's lives be as good as, or better than, their parents'. A sustainable society has the capacity to deal with routine social, economic and environmental risks, including minor disasters, the loss of key persons, business cycles and the like. It has well-articulated productive knowledge and assets. Its members support, claim ownership in, and enhance their social and political institutions. They have the capacity for mutual self-help. A sustainable society nurtures and constructs its cultural identities.

In conclusion, we can very well remark that after the great depression of 1930's, the Keynesian ideas revolutionized the earlier perception and it was asserted that governmental intervention was a must for solving the problems of unemployment, which had afflicted the capitalistic societies by threatening their democratic fabric. The invisible hands of price mechanism was inoperative to make its free play inconsideration of the welfare state as the overwhelming evidence of market failure with regard to ecological issues were crystal clear.

Thus, it is concluded that the market forces by themselves can not guarantee equitable or sustainable development. Enlightened actions by the state are necessary if the lives of the poor, the pauperized labourers are to be protected as well as the ecological balance is to be maintained.

The mismatch between aggregate growth and disparity in the distributive justice has been an intricate component in the globalized Indian economy. In other words, the concentration of wealth in the hands of a few, their lust for production–maximization in one hand and the interest of the large segment of labourers for social good come in to a conflicting situation.

As such the state has to ensure guarantee with regard to nutritional food and health care to the weaker sections of the society and mainly the tribals through various intervention programmes. Stringent punishment must be inflicted on the delinquent officials and dishonest officers who indulge in corrupt practices and disallow the delivery mechanism to function as it ought to be.

REFERENCES

Tripathy, S.N. (1998): "Shifting Cultivation in tribal Orissa", in self-edited *Tribals in India: The Changing Scenario*, Discovery Publishing House, New Delhi.

Tripathy, S.N. (2000): *Glimpses on Tribal Development*, Discovery Publishing House, New Delhi.

Tripathy, S.N. (2007): *Tribal Development: Issues and Policy Options*, Anmol Publications, New Delhi.

11

SECONDARY EDUCATION: QUALITY PERSPECTIVE AND ISSUES IN TRIBAL REGION OF ORISSA

DR. DIBAKAR SARANGI

Concerns on quality education have been an important agenda in all discourses pertaining to human development. The vision document "India Vision 2020" considers and affirms that Education as an essential prerequisite for citizens of the post modern globalized societies. Also the document "Vision 2020: An agenda for school & Mass Education (Report of the Task Force, Depts. of SME, Govt. of Orissa, 2003)" envisions providing a "world Class education system in the state of Orissa". The rapid take over of Globalization, the growing emphasis on human rights and the constitutional declaration to make elementary education a Fundamental right of the citizens (the 93rd Constitutional Amendment) strengthened the quality perspectives as a matter of serious and urgent attention. On the very context, the present paper attempts to review the quality perspective of Secondary education in the K.B.K. region of Orissa.

Quality Perception & Quality Indicators

Quality in education is perceived in three ways:-

(i) As customer's satisfaction & expectations,

(ii) As a process to be continuously cultured, and

(iii) As a wholistic phenomena covering all aspects of educational inputs, process and the product.

To describe the present state of the quality concerns and affairs we hold an integrative view of quality. So far, indicators of quality education concerns the discussion is based on both "within system indicators" as well as "the indicators in the system's environment". Under "within system indicators" we have taken the references to the following aspects:

- Secondary Educational opportunities and access,
- Infrastructure: acquisition and use,
- Facilities/provisions,
- Human resources.
- Curriculum transactional process.
- Assessment of pupils' learning,
- Monitoring, supervision & system feedback.

Under the indicators in the System's Environment three aspects have been examined:

- Public & stake holders participation in education,
- Institutional interface & collaboration,
- Pupil productivity & interest in Secondary Education.

A) THE WITHIN-SYSTEM INDICATORS

1) Secondary Education: Opportunities, Access and Enrolment

The state strives to provide a high school to every panchayat. In comparison to the percentage of un-served habitations in the coastal regions (4 %) the K.B.K. percentage is much higher (more than 50% in Rayagada, Koraput, Nabarangpur and Malkangiri districts) (Vide Annexure No.1 & 2). Extremely thin population in Panchayats and the cost-benefit issues troubles raising schools in such habitations in K.B.K. districts. In the rural areas children especially the girls can not have access to the distant schools. Enrolment and retention till Secondary School completion is not satisfactory in the region (See Annexure-3). Unlike the Primary Education, the Secondary Education does not operate through alternative schooling system. Moreover, Private N.G.O.s and the community efforts although are trying to extend the opportunities and access to Secondary Education, the state patronage are feeble and shrinking. The special K.B.K. schemes does not appear to focus much on this aspects.

2) *Infrastructure Acquisition and Use*

Barring about 10% of the existing schools most schools of the K.B.K. region are lack in adequate infrastructure—School building, laboratories, play grounds, furniture, power supply, compound wall etc. Further, appropriate optimal utilization of the acquired infrastructure is a rare occurrence. Most of the schools do not possess the basic teaching-learning materials and the minimum library resources. Management of physical resources displays a very unfortunate scene. Supporting infrastructure like staff quarters, hostels are seriously dearth forcing the teachers to go for unethical practices like not staying in the headquarters, commuting from a distance etc. It has been observed that where ever residential provisions are available and utilized properly students' learning is better (Vide Annexure-4).

3) *Facilities and Provisions*

Special facilities for the S.C., S.T. and weaker sections in the form of stipends, accommodation and boarding provisions have been made. Wherever residential facilities are available for students and teachers inside the campus, the performance of the school are satisfactory. Free provision of study materials and text books would be instrumental towards quality secondary education for the native students of the region.

4) *Human Resources in K.B.K. Schools*

Large vacancies in the sanctioned posts are a frequent phenomenon. (See Annexure- 5). Even regular heads of the schools are available only in a limited Government schools. Limited number of teachers can not bring fair and justice to the school transaction in view of shifting role-relation of teacher and pupils. A virtual shortage of trained hands can be seen from the profiles of teachers appointed in recognized Un-aided schools and schools run by the missionaries and religious organizations in these areas. In many recognized un-aided schools teachers are only appointed in pen and paper.

Teachers' content resourcefulness, pedagogical skills and professional ethics points to a mixed scenario not only in the

South and Western part of the state but also in other regions. In respect of entry qualification for teachers into Upper Primary and Secondary stages through pre-service training, learners are left with Matric C.T. and +2 C.T., and some times with just HSC pass teachers. The policy needs a review favouring appointment of teachers at least with trained graduate qualification. Minimum teaching aptitude must be ensured before they are licensed and inducted into the profession of teaching.

Continued education of teachers and staff development programmes are much below satisfaction. Very few teachers are observed to upgrade and enhance their educational status during service periods. As such teachers become outdated and irrelevant both in respect of subject matter knowledge and pedagogical skills. In the recent past staff development programmes under the joint sponsorship of the Central and the State Government aimed at addressing the said issues. Teacher Orientation through INSET, SOPT, training courses by ELTI, BSE(O) orientation programmes were much beneficial to the teachers and pupils as well. However, a systematic policy of staff development, operational strategy, monitoring and feedback mechanism is needed.

Appointment of contractual teachers raises issues of teachers' professional commitment and work devotion. Last but not the least, appointment of additional teachers on health education, Art Education can not be undermined as these are the most neglected areas of curriculum.

5) *Curriculum Transactional Processes*

The K.B.K. schools limit their curriculum transaction just to syllabus completion, mostly focusing the cognitive growth of the pupils. A balanced and integrated development of the affective and the psychomotor domain of student personality is yet to be duly attended. Schools do not have a well formulated distinct curriculum as needed for the balanced growth of the KBK pupils. School specific concrete curriculum would be the stepping stone for quality education in this region.

Teachers largely use the conventional pedagogy. Action

research by the teachers is a rare event. Only a few teachers are engaged in innovations, curricular and pedagogical adaptation.

In respect of text book transaction it is desired that the issues/problems as emergent in the contemporary life practices of people be deliberated upon through class room instructions. However the teachers fail to give cultural, environmental and value orientations to textual studies. The National expectations as enshrined in the National Curriculum framework for school education 2001 and 2005 are less achieved especially in areas of ICT integration, use of TLM, Life skill development, adoption of continuous comprehensive evaluation and subject related process skills. Teaching and learning processes are mostly content oriented and H.S.C. examination driven. Practices of peer sharing of the professional issues through regular meets, workshops and conferences are less frequently observed. Occasional Headmasters' Conferences are of course convened. Individual attention, Diagnosis of learner backwardness, remediation, enrichment programmes are practiced in a very limited way.

6) Assessment of Pupils' Learning

Pupil evaluation activities mostly aim at measuring memory based content knowledge. Pupils Socio-personal qualities (Non-scholastic aspects in various school subjects) are rarely assessed. Evaluation approaches are mostly summative through the practice of school Annual/promotion examination. A systematic programme of formative evaluation, comprehensive records as feedback and monitoring is not inbuilt into the school programmes. Accepting subject based achievement evaluation, diagnostic evaluation and pupil aptitude exploration and other capabilities are not in common practice in these regions. Evaluation of answer scripts in public exams. Especially at H.S.C. level has remained as an area of public resentment. Transparency and accountability in pupil evaluation is still a continued challenge for all.

7) Monitoring, Supervision and System Feedback

It is painful truth to learn about the ineffectiveness of monitoring, supervision and feedback system. The administrative authorities being overburden with routine jobs get less time for academic supervision, guidance and onsite participation and monitoring. Inspectorates of Education do not have full-fledged units of research and feedback unit and also allied enabling infrastructures. Bodies of subject specific supervisors and counsellors be raised at the Inspectorate level for efficient and effective academic monitoring and co-ordination mechanism among the B.S.E.(O), Directorate of Teacher Education, the Inspectorates will be instrumental to ensure quality education in the K.B.K. region.

B) Quality Indicators in the System's Environment

1) Public & Stake Holders Participation in Education

Public and Stake holders participation in Secondary education in K.B.K. region is least achieved. The school managing committees of Govt. schools, Aided and Recognized schools in most cases don't function or can not deliver the goods as intended. Although decentralized management is emphasized at the policy level through VEC, PTA, this remains mostly in ideas. Teachers find it very difficult to gain public co-operation for resource mobilization and management. Politically motivated and divided community are reported to make the intended results least achieved. School-community confrontations reports are not rate. Local NGO, community bodies and the P.R. institutions are yet to have sustained interest and participation in Secondary stage education of the region. For this the long standing issues of first generation learners, special issues of K.B.K. girls have not been successfully addressed. The teacher organizations although are active, yet to be oriented for more constructive roles. The local industries & NGOs need to be mobilized for greater role in rendering/extending quality infrastructure and services in the K.B.K. region.

2) Institutional Interface & Collboration in Secondary Education

Institutions and organizations related to Secondary Education say, the schools, Secondary teacher Education Institutions, the administrative units (Inspectorates), the Boards of public examination, Directorate of Teacher Education, Alternative Education systems and the Welfare Departments are to be knitted under distinctive policy directives. K.B.K. Education has not been viewed as collaborative and joint efforts of the various stake holders. Funding agencies sponsoring developmental works in K.B.K. region have not been linked with Secondary Education. Linking of Secondary level vocational education, work experience programmes, and Art Education with the community based organizations farms and industries has not been capitalizing, thus, Secondary Education in this belt is going on as an isolated enterprise.

3) Pupil Productivity and Public Motivation in Secondary Education

In respect of the syllabus based learning as assessed at the H.S.C. Examination the K.B.K. students fall behind the non-KBK students as well as the average state position. (Vide Annexure No. 6 for details). Further, large majority of K.B.K. children especially the native residents completing the Secondary Education can not acquire core life skills, higher order cognitive capabilities and intended Socio-personal qualities as compared to their counterparts from other social strata and the coastal belts. In respect of the productive skills and economic efficiencies of the girls and the tribal students the position is quite frustrating. Limited benefits of work, employment, apathy towards manual labour causes low motivation for public education among the K.B.K. inhabitants. The "NIL result" schools and consistently low performing schools add to the awful scene of Secondary Education in this belt. The Secondary Education offered at present is perceived as irrelevant for contemporary life – need – demands by the common public masses especially the tribals.

Conclusion

Secondary Education in the KBK region need to be viewed from a developmental perspective. Secondary Education has been receiving inadequate attention and emphasis as compared to the other dimensions of life in the area. A deeper analysis would reveal the isolated and dis-coordinated efforts launched to promote Secondary Education in tribal dominated region of the state. It is realized with distinctive policy, directives and strategy can address the secondary education issues in this region; mainstream the larger native population and bring forth a sustainable development of the region.

NOTE: - The trends in various aspects of Secondary Education as discussed in this paper are based on factual data and field observations.

ANNEXURE – 1

Habitatons Unsurved With Secondary Schools in K.B.K. and Non-K.B.K. Region of Orissa

Name of the District	*Total No. of G.Ps.*	*No. of G.P. having no High School*	*% of High School less G.P.*
Kalahandi	271	78	28.78
Nuapada	109	23	21.00
Bolangir	285	52	18.24
Subarnapur	96	10	10.41
Koraput	226	120	53.09
Nabarangpur	169	79	46.74
Malkangiri	108	57	52.77
Rayagada	171	99	57.89
Total	2100	518	24.66

ANNEXURE - 2

Information on Different Category of High Schools in the Following K.B.K. Districts

Sl. No.	*Category of Schools*	*Koraput Dist.*	*Nabarangpur Dist.*	*Malkangiri Dist.*	*Rayagada Dist.*	*Bolangir Dist.*	*Subarnapur Dist.*
01.	Govt.(Old)	45	15	13	19	18	04
02.	Govt. (New)	09	12	04	16	96	43
03.	Non-Govt. Aided.	09	06	02	04	29	07
04.	40% Block Grant.	06	10	07	05	39	25
05.	Recognised	16	31	16	15	69	18
06.	Govt. SSD	12	15	11	02	06	01

ANNEXURE - 3: Enrolment Position of Different High Schools of K.B.K. Districts for Last 3 Years. (Only Class-IX & X)

Year	Name of Dist.	All Community (SC, ST, others)			S.C.			S.T.		
		Boys	Girls	Total	Boys	Girls	Total	Boys	Girls	Total
2003-04	Koraput	6148	3735	9883	1314	785	2099	1243	381	1624
	Nabarangpur	4884	2709	7593	1396	795	2191	1554	569	2123
	Malkangiri	2372	1330	3702	955	561	1516	682	215	897
	Rayagada	4099	2487	6586	845	435	1280	828	336	1164
	Nuapada	6165	3617	9982	1070	605	1675	1124	664	1788
	Kalahandi	15764	9322	25086	2750	1436	4186	3268	2195	5563
	Bolangir	28917	19283	48200	5877	3844	9721	4943	2483	7426
	Subarnapur	10664	8443	19107	2366	1743	4109	845	597	1442
2004-05	Koraput	5968	3952	9920	1185	653	1838	1390	487	1877
	Nabarangpur	4859	2835	7694	1351	944	2295	1552	562	2114
	Malkangiri	2555	1400	3955	1126	662	1788	679	189	868
	Rayagada	4172	4420	8592	853	448	1301	838	344	1182
	Nuapada	7048	4308	11356	1283	730	2013	1364	696	2060
	Kalahandi	16846	10221	27067	3098	1353	4451	3009	1465	4474
	Bolangir	30789	21813	52602	5929	4175	10104	5170	2903	8073
	Subarnapur	10808	9125	19933	2604	2034	4638	855	668	1523
2005-06	Koraput	6216	3853	10069	1247	712	1959	1526	571	2097
	Nabarangpur	5277	3251	8528	1577	1065	2632	1737	796	2533
	Malkangiri	2636	1411	4047	1102	644	1746	810	279	1089
	Rayagada	4587	2854	7441	1000	496	1496	1334	447	1781
	Nuapada	7076	4332	11408	1287	738	2025	1267	695	2062
	Kalahandi	16687	10284	26971	3067	1340	4407	3002	1451	4453
	Bolangir	31148	23201	54349	5850	4395	10245	5405	3229	8634
	Subarnapur	10868	9650	20518	2521	2106	4627	839	667	1506

07. Other High Schools	07	04	—	01	06	—
08. English Medium Schools	10	—	01	07	06	—
Total	114	93	54	69	279	98

ANNEXURE - 4

Comparative Statement Showing H.S.C. Result for Last 3 Years in Respect of Some Residential High Schools and Non-Residential High Schools of K.B.K. District

Residential High Schools				*Non-Residential High Schools*			
Name of the School	*% of result for 2003*	*% of result for 2004*	*% of result for 2005*	*Name of the School*	*% of result for 2003*	*% of result for 2004*	*% of result for 2005*
Govt. SSD H/S, Haradaput.	27.27	33.33	75.00	Govt. H/S., Patraput.	20.00	27.27	17.64
Govt. SSD H/S, Bamuniput.	93.75	58.33	71.42	Govt. H/S., Ekamba.	08.00	25.00	33.33
Govt. SSD H/S, Gupteswar.	10.00	52.94	64.28	Govt. H/S., Bramhanguda.	09.09	07.14	62.50
Govt. SSD H/S, Girla.	42.85	50.00	41.66	Govt. H/S., Dolopur.	25.00	08.33	13.33
Govt.SSD H/S, S.B. Nuagam.	44.44	25.00	18.51	Govt. H/S., Kumuli.	45.45	48.57	72.72
Govt.SSD H/S, Digapur.	25.00	11.11	16.66	Govt. H/S., Dhamanahandi.	11.36	29.16	21.73
Govt.SSD H/S, Lima.	75.00	69.23	76.47	Govt. H/S., Nandahandi.	19.23	13.33	14.28
Govt.SSD H/S, Gumuda.	20.00	42.85	35.71	Govt. H/S., Tentulikhunti.	12.96	38.59	22.38
Govt.SSD H/S, Badamasigam.	66.66	30.76	50.00	Govt. H/S., Jamuronda.	11.76	05.88	40.00

Govt.SSD H/S, Dongriguda.	16.66	25.00	40.00	Govt. H/S., Kundei.	06.25	Nil	12.50
Govt.SSD H/S, Dabugam.	77.77	40.00	63.63	Govt. H/S., MPV-21.	18.18	20.00	30.76
Govt.SSD H/S, Patraput.	11.11	17.85	37.50	Govt. H/S., Podia	07.14	05.00	10.00
Govt.SSD H/S, Badaambada.	70.00	16.66	46.66	Govt.(New) H/S.,Digisalapa.	23.80	26.66	33.33
Govt.SSD H/S, Kodinga.	96.96	25.71	34.14	Govt.(New) H/S., Anchalgumma.	29.41	25.00	39.13
Govt.SSD H/S, Manigam.	11.11	25.00	30.76	Govt.(New) H/S., Kukudabai.	20.00	Nil	22.22
Govt.SSD H/S, Bhamini.	61.53	65.00	73.33	Govt.(New) H/S., Tumborlla.	Nil	21.05	Nil
Govt.SSD H/S, Badabharandi.	58.82	45.00	87.50	Govt.(New) H/S., Serpalli.	16.66	16.66	23.07
Govt.SSD H/S, Belgam	56.00	70.00	80.95	Govt.(New) H/S., Anlapadar	26.92	22.72	17.64
Govt.SSD H/S, Dhodipani.	45.00	28.00	26.92	JELC H/S., Kotpad.	12.05	25.00	34.61
Govt.SSD H/S, Raighar.	67.56	64.00	57.14	M.J. H/S., Modeigam.	22.22	03.44	28.57
Govt.SSD H/S, Kali aguda.	42.85	80.00	100.00	G. H/S., Amalabhata.	03.33	23.33	04.76
Govt.SSD H/S, Mahupadar.	66.66	85.71	90.00	Chandili H/S, Chandili.	08.00	07.69	33.33
Govt.SSD H/S, Govindpalli.	58.82	46.42	75.00	S.K. H/S., Batasana.	Nil	Nil	14.28
Govt.SSD H/S, Satiguda.	85.71	80.00	88.88	Porli H/S., Parli	08.00	06.25	28.57
Govt.(New) SASN, Kundra.	82.14	70.37	80.95	Mahadev H/S., Bikrampur	47.61	16.66	44.44

S.L.N. H/S., Dhodra.	37.50	56.00	72.41	Kodobhatta H/S.,Kodobhatta.	26.53	15.00	26.66
Govt.(New) H/S., Chandahandi.	68.18	52.94	70.27	S.M.Baji H/S., Bijapur.	16.66	25.00	Nil
Lachanaguda H/S., Lachanaguda.	76.92	70.96	82.14	Paten H/S., Patakhalia	Nil	20.00	05.88
Ananta Bidyapitha, Dangarpaunsi.	48.00	48.00	59.25	S.L.N. H/S., Udayapur.	12.85	28.57	22.22

ANNEXURE - 5

Abstracts of Vacancy Position of Teachers of K.B.K. Districts as on 01-05-2006

Sl. No.	*Name of the Dist.*	*H.M OES-II SES*	*H.M. Sr,*	*TGT Arts*	*TGT PCM*	*TGT CBZ*	*LSES Trs.*	*Classical Tr.*	*Hindi Tr.*	*PET*
01.	Koraput	02	03	67	19	26	18	16	04	08
02.	Nabarangpur	01	02	33	11	04	11	05	—	06
03.	Malkangiri	—	02	29	04	04	04	02	—	03
04.	Rayagada	01	02	41	20	10	21	07	03	—
05.	Bolangir	02	03	82	35	36	21	26	16	11
06.	Subarnapur	02	10	25	14	09	04	08	03	02

ANNEXURE - 6

Comparative Statement of Result of H.S.C. Examination for the Last 5 Years Among K.B.K., Non-K.B.K Districts and State

Year	*Dist./State*	*Students appeared*	*No. of result published*	*No. of students passed*	*% of Pass*
2001	K.B.K.	29406	29210	8926	30.05
	Non-K.B.K.	234211	231732	91231	39.36
	State	263617	260942	100157	38.38

2002	K.B.K.	28641	28484	9363	32.87
	Non-K.B.K.	218162	216658	91165	42.07
	State	246803	245142	100528	41.01
2003	K.B.K.	29399	29267	11846	40.47
	Non-K.B.K.	211996	210293	107937	51.32
	State	241395	239560	119783	50.00
2004	K.B.K.	32062	31921	14804	46.37
	Non-K.B.K.	233021	231776	123738	53.38
	State	265083	263697	138542	52.54
2005	K.B.K.	35247	34987	17843	50.99
	Non-K.B.K.	248403	247037	139123	56.31
	State	283650	282024	156966	55.66

REFERENCES

1. Report of the committee on India Vision – 2020, Planning Commission, Govt. of India, New Delhi – December, 2002.
2. Vision 2020, "On agenda for School & Mass Education" the report of Task force, Deptt. Of School & Mass Education, Govt. of Orissa, 2003.
3. National curriculum framework for school education, 2000, NCERT, New Delhi.
4. National curriculum frame work for school education, 2005, NCERT, New Delhi.

12

EDUCATIONAL DEVELOPMENT OF SCs AND STs AND TAMIL NADU GOVERNMENT BUDGET: A CRITIQUE

DEBAJANI DHAL

1. Introduction

India with a population of 989 million is the world's second most populous country. Of that number, the Scheduled Castes (SCs) and Scheduled Tribes (STs) in the country today are more than 200 million[1]. According to the 1991 census, the country's population was enumerated to be 846 million, of which S.Cs constituted 16% of total population, which is 138 million, and S.Ts accounted for another 8 percent or 68 million[2]. In Tamil Nadu, SCs and STs are named as Dalits and Tribals respectively. The SCs and STs together account for about one fifth of Tamil Nadu population, the former constituting 19 % and latter 1.03%[3].

Historically, Dalits and Tribals have been among the most subordinated and poorest people in Tamil Nadu who have been structurally subjected to various kinds of social, economic and educational deprivation. It is also a fact even after 56 years of independence and with the completion of 'Nine Five Year Plans', efforts to ameliorate the conditions of Dalits and Tribals have not been successful. The efforts of the state and the expenditure incurred on the programmes and policies for the uplift of them have not produced results and therefore, there has not been any marked improvement in the socio-economic conditions of the Dalits and Tribals[4]. The plight of the Dalits can be inferred from the prevalent poverty, illiteracy and a high percentage of school drop outs among them. The socio-economic and cultural inertia and lack of what Pierre Bourdieu calls 'Culture Capital' are internal reasons for the arrested development of the Dalits and Tribals in Indian society. As regards Tamil Nadu, Dalits and Tribals are far away from the general sections of the society[5]. The welfare of marginalized population groups has always featured prominently in India's plans and policies. Such welfare, it has been recognized, needs to be with respect to programmes, as mentioned elsewhere, that are geared for developing human resources. The policy makers realize that real development cannot take roots if it bypasses SCs/STs, who represents the very kernel around which social change must take shape[6].

Various schemes have been developed under various plans and programmes. There is a Special Component Plan for dalits, initiated during the 6th Five Year Plan, which is a revolutionary concept in the sphere of social development of SCs. Similarly, Tribal Sub-Plan was also developed for the upliftment of STs in India. It envisages a radical redefinition of planning and budgeting for dalits and tribals with their economic empowerment as a concrete goal. Like other states in India, in Tamil Nadu too hundreds of schemes and plans are announced every year for the social development of SCs/STs. In the state budgets of every year, lakhs and crores of rupees are set apart for these schemes. However, the awareness of SCs and STs about these schemes and plans is basic to achieving development in each sphere. Without the fullest cooperation and participation by the people, any good scheme of the government is not sustainable. Yet over the last 50 years, improvement in the socio-economic status of the majority of SCs and STs in Tamil Nadu has only been tardy. There have been, in recent years, increasing number of struggles by SCs/STs demanding their due share in the resources of Tamil Nadu. The basic problem with budgeting for SC/ST is not merely the amounts allocated, but the very approach to SC/ST welfare. Successive governments have always highlighted their 'achievements' in the field of SC/ST welfare, often, the criterion is simply an increase in the amount spent for the welfare of SCs and STs. Educating them still remains very crucial.

2. Objective of the Paper

The present paper aims to understand: *(a)* Educational status of SCs and STs in Tamil Nadu, especially the literacy rate among SC and ST boys and girls. *(b)* To understand the various programmes which have been implemented for SCs and STs, such as Special Component Plan (SCP) for SCs and Tribal Sub Plan (TSP) for STs. *(c)* To highlight the Tamil Nadu Government Budget provision on educational development for SCs and STs. *(d)* To understand the gap between plan allocation and budget allocation for SCs and STs, and their due rights in the share of budget provision.

3. Data and Methodology

The present study is based on secondary data collected from government sources. The required information was collected from the various issues of annual reports of Tamil Nadu government. Documentary sources of information, published and unpublished documents including Census reports, reports of governmental agencies and public and private reports have been used.

4. Literature Review

A number of writers have dealt with the subject of SCs and S.Ts as outcastes, untouchables, tribals and harijans. The Researcher confines itself to a brief insight into the literature on educational status of SCs and STs, plans and programmes and policies for the educational development of SCs and STs.

4.1. Education

Goyal, B.R., (1981) has conducted a Study on Harijans with respect to their education. He has taken due account of both stimulants and impediments in the way of education of Harijans, while, cataloging government, efforts in educating Harijans and improving their lives[7]. Das (1985) analyzed the expansion of education among STs and opening of various types of schools, including technical and vocational, award of scholarships and stipends, provision of hostel facilities, boarding grants, mid day meals, uniforms and other assistance to the students at various levels. He concluded that the more affluent sections of the community utilizing and stocking up more and more benefits of the welfare programmes and the poorer sections are left behind. He suggested that in order to stop this and to reduce the gap, it was necessary to fashion future welfare programmes in an integrated way so that, poorer sections would get a sound economic footing[8].

4.2 Welfare Programme

Jhunjhunwala (2001) in his article describes the real causes behind the Indian social order. He argues that 'for the betterment of the dalits two things need to be done, first is to rely upon the law to undo equality, secondly, is to create morality in the society and encourage the rich and powerful to use their wealth for common good. He concludes by saying Dalit welfare has lost its importance due to 'superior morality' held by the dominant castes in society[9]. Pundir (1987) observes in a village in Western U.P, that education is the major factor in the mobilization of the SCs. The state policy in the past two decades has contributed to the educational development of SCs. He concludes that such educational policies of the government can enhance the status of the SCs in the society[10]

4.3 Budget Allocation

Mistry, M.D., in his report Budget Analysis at State and Local levels, points out the government priority for the weaker sections. He has been one of the pioneers in the application of budget analysis for advocating the rights of the tribal and other marginalized sections in Gujarat. In his presentation, Mr. Mistry highlights the effectiveness of Budget analysis as a tool for detecting irregularities in government spending. He also focuses on the monitoring of funds allocated by the State budget for different sectors, schemes or programmes. In his view, Budget analysis is a potential tool in the hands of the voluntary organizations to promote greater state accountability and responsiveness to the needs of the poor. He concludes that Budget analysis is an effective tool for detecting irregularities in government spending[11].

4.4 Special Component Plan and Tribal Sub Plan

Ahmed (2004) in his book 'Five Decades of Planning and Tribal Development' has mentioned the development of Tribal Sub Plan Strategy in Five Year Plans. He opines that, Five Year Plan periods, cannot be fully appreciated if the special situation in tribal areas is not fully discussed. Five Year Plans were launched with special priority for S.Ts and weaker sections of the society. The TSP strategy in the Fifth Five Year plan gave a fillip to the outlay and expenditure on S.Ts in the planning process. He concludes that Tribal Sub Plan has been a failure over time[12]. Alexander, Varghese V., (1983) in 'Tribals and Sub-plans' has mentioned that tribals constitute the vulnerable sections of society. They are being exploited over a long period of time. The age old exploitation and the repression of the tribals have cut them from the mainstream of socio-educational development of the country as a whole[13].

Gandhi (2004) has given a clear picture of Special Component Plan and also talks of allocation of money for S.Cs. In his view, the SCP is an instrument for S.Cs, whereby money allotted for them is not to be given as a residual exercise. Government usually allocated money for the S.Cs from what was left after money was allocated to the departments that government thought to be crucial. Therefore SCP is meant to take away this kind of discretion from the government or planning bodies[14]. Venkatesan (2004) opines, the SCP and its schemes by itself are very good and that it is meant for the Scheduled Castes and not for others. He has also cited the impact of various schemes on the SCs population. He says that any scheme may be good but the key for its success is beneficiary identification. Wrong identification can lead to scheme failure. He states that due to certain reasons the deserving people do not get the benefits of the scheme. He concludes that there should be better evaluation of various schemes undertaken by the government. It should reach the people who are in need[15].

The above review captures some major studies on the education of SCs and STs, backwardness, and plans and programmes for SCs and STs.

5. Data Analysis and Data Interpretation

The importance of human resource development, especially its educational component, has been recognized as vital both in the developed and developing nations because human resource contributes to economic growth like any other factors of production. Education of the downtrodden sections of society especially SCs and STs occupies top priority in society[16]. As regards Tamil Nadu, the positions of SCs and STs are still deplorable, to say the least. They are at the lower layers of society; they are not even aware of the constitutional provisions. They are deprived of getting their share in educational development, especially human resource development.

5.1. Education in Tamil Nadu

Tamil Nadu is an educationally better placed state with general literacy rate of 62.66% compared to the national average of 52.21%. It ranks third among the major states with regard to general literacy and female literacy rate. The 1991 Census shows that literacy rate of Tamil Nadu is higher than other states yet, in absolute terms, the number of illiterates in Tamil Nadu has increased from 238 lakhs in 1951 to 253 lakhs in 1991. The growth of literacy has been very uneven over the decades in the state. And the vast variations of literacy rates across different sections of Tamil society make one to sit up and make notice. Even if the state of Tamil Nadu is having higher literacy rate than other states, the literacy rate among SCs and STs are lower than the general sections of society[17].

5.2. Dalits and Education in Tamil Nadu

Right to education for dalits has been denied historically. This is so not only in Tamil Nadu but also in other states of India. Though, Tamil Nadu has a higher educational rank, within Tamil Nadu there is a large gap between Dalits and general sections of society[18].

Census of India, 1991, shows that, there are 29 districts in Tamil Nadu. Regionally, male literacy among SCs is higher in Chennai at 76.20% and the lowest in the Erode district (39.92%). Female literacy among SCs is similarly high in

Chennai at 58.48%, and the lowest level is seen in Erode at 22.28%. The overall literacy rate of S.Cs is less than that of the general population in all the districts. In the case of S.Ts, literacy rate for male and female is highest in Chennai (73.65% and 52.37%) and is lowest in the district of Sivagangai (5.28%) in the case of males and district of Tiruvannamalai (11.26%) in the case of females[19].

5.3. *School Drop Outs*

Tamil Nadu has been recognized for having achieved near total enrolment of children of school going age. Tamil Nadu has been hailed as holding the second rank in the whole country, in terms of enrolment at primary level. 'In recent times, the percentage of children enrolled is near complete. The percentage of enrolment of girls and boys in standard 1 is 94.43% and 98.50% respectively. It is gratifying to note that the trend continues to progress towards near full enrolment of children.' (Tamil Nadu: 2001) The issue of children dropping out of school at various levels has been given serious consideration. The drops out rates are more among SCs and STs boys and girls than the general sections of society. In spite of the declining trend, drop out rates among both SCs and STs are much higher than those of Non-SC/ ST students.

5.4. *Adivasis/ Tribals and Education in Tamil Nadu*

"There are 36 Tribes and their population as per 1991 census is 5.74 lakhs, representing 1.03% of the Tamil Nadu population" (Tamil Nadu: 1997-2002). The plight of STs is more tragic than that of SCs. There is a wide gap between standards of social development between tribals and Non-tribals sections of the Tamil Nadu population. Educational status of S.Ts in Tamil Nadu is worse than other states of the country. Hardly any education takes place in the tribal schools run by the government for the simple reason that no teacher comes to the school[20].

5.5. *Educational Incentives Provided by the Government of Tamil Nadu*

It was only after the independence that greater thrust had

been made towards the educational development of SCs/STs. It was realized that the reservation of seats and posts is not only solution for their age old apathy towards education but prevention of continuing atrocities against SCs and STs is a major requirement for the development of education among SCs and STs in society. In the year, 1948-49, the Govt. of Tamil Nadu introduced the scholarship scheme. More incentives such as free education, free textbooks, uniforms, scholarships, reserved seats, hostel facilities were provided for SCs and STs.

During the First Five Year Plan, importance was given to the expansion of facilities and provision of schools and teachers in the remote areas. Thereafter, in the Fourth Five Year Plan, the scheme of economic incentives was started. In the Fifth Five Year Plan, the major thrust was to offer equality of opportunities as part of overall plan of ensuring social justice and improving the quality of education imparted. Emphasis was also laid on the need for orientation of the curriculum to meet the special needs of children of SCs and STs. A landmark in the Sixth Plan was the inclusion of education of SCs and STs as one of the major programmes under the overall programmes for the development of SCs and STs in Tamil Nadu. The Seventh Plan envisaged restructuring of the educational programmes so that curricula was rid of any gender bias. Similarly, the 8th Plan had also led to a few more development programmes for SCs and STs. The 9th Plan stressed the upliftment of the backward and marginalized sections of the society. (Tamil Nadu: 2003)

Both the State and Central Government are running different welfare activities to spread educational progress among the minority sections of population, especially the SCs and STs. Various schemes and programmes were developed by Tamil Nadu government to provide better education.

5.6 Special Component Plan and Education of SCs/Dalits in Tamil Nadu

Tamil Nadu government has been implementing SCP, TSP from the 1980s. Thousands of crores of rupees have been spent in the name of SC/ST welfare every year. Though various programmes have been implemented, the benefits had hardly reached the people for whom they were intended. Therefore, there is no significant change in the lives of the majority of SCs in Tamil Nadu. Therefore, SCP was introduced as an effort to radically rework the whole strategy of SCs welfare and their empowerment. The Government of India introduced the plan during 6th Five Year Plan and the plan was made obligatory for all the State Governments and departments as well as Central Government Ministries[21].

In Tamil Nadu, SCP strategy has been implemented since 1980-81 with the following objectives: To assist SCs families to cross above the poverty line and to provide basic amenities and facilities in their habitations. With a view to achieve these objectives, the resources of more than 20 departments are pooled and schemes are implemented by fixing targets for each scheme. The schemes, which are implemented by these departments, include educational advancement and socio economic development of SCs[22].

5.7 Tribal Sub Plan and Education of STs/ Adivasis in Tamil Nadu TSP

Like SCP for Schedule Caste, TSP was developed as a major source to develop the educational background of STs in Tamil Nadu. The TSP strategy was continued during the sixth plan period with greater emphasis on specific objectives, namely: Development of human resources and up gradation of education, Elimination of exploitation of tribals in the field of education, Development of adequate infrastructure. A few programmes have been introduced under TSP for enhancing the position of tribals in Tamil Nadu. Tribal residential schools were built for the development of S.Ts. However, even after 20 years of TSP strategy in Tamil Nadu, many policy analysts argue that no perceptible improvement has been noticed in the tribal areas and in the living standards of tribals[23].

5.8 Tamil Nadu Government Budget at Glance

The annual budget (i.e. the 'Annual Financial Statement') of a government is a major instrument, by which government balances its intention with available resources. The budget is an important pointer to the government's priorities, performances, decisions and intentions. The budget is also an articulation of the existing power relations in society. It has an impact on the weaker sections of society, especially SCs and STs[24].

5.9 Dalits (SCs) and Budget Dynamics

Budgeting for Dalits is a major issue. The problem with budgeting for Dalits is not merely the amounts allocated, but the very approach to Dalit welfare. The tragic situation of Dalits in the state needs special attention. A cursory look at successive budgets of the Schedule Castes sector in the Centre as well as in the constituent States of the country reveals that 'change' is an arena, planners and programme executives still fear to tread upon. They feel safe wearing the mantle of a status-quoist. They excel in 'exercising extreme caution before putting one step forward. 'Change' is the only turn of leaf that SCs has been aspiring for centuries together.

In their strategic planning, it is anathema to provide scope for SCs to frog-leap others and frog-leaping SCs, in the opinion of planners and bureaucrats, will lead to chaotic social upheavals. None of these budgets did consciously provide for integration of SCs in the mainstream. On the contrary, the modus operandi of programmes has been strengthening SCs isolation and sustaining their segregation[25]. Successive governments have always highlighted their 'achievements' in the field of S.Cs and S.Ts Welfare. Often the criterion is simply an increase in the amount spent for the welfare of Dalits. After traversing a long path of more than four decades of development, it would be worthwhile to mention the level of development of S.Cs and S.Ts so far[26].

5.10 Budget Provision on Education for Welfare of SCs and STs

As education being the most effective instrument for socio-economic empowerment, high priority continues to be accorded to improve the educational status of SCs and STs in Tamil Nadu. Tamil Nadu government implemented various plans, programmes and schemes that included the needs and interests of SCs/STs. Both Central and State governments have a role in the implementation of various schemes for the welfare of SCs and STs education. Budget allocation manifests the government's real commitment to the well being of the people, especially the weaker sections of the society such as SCs and STs.

Statistics are presented below to show how the allocation for SCs and STs welfare has come down during the Ninth Five Year Plan. Several questions have answers: Is the amount allocated, even if it is increasing, just and adequate, given the genuine rights of Dalits and Tribals in Tamil Nadu? Where does all the money allocated go? Is it due to the lack of awareness among people, or gap between SCs/STs and general sections of society or lesser priorities of the government for SCs and STs? The following pages will be providing in detail in reality, how much Tamil Nadu government allocated for the educational development of SCs and STs during the period 1997-2002.

Various state schemes developed for the education of SCs, especially educational development during pre-school or high school. Tamil Nadu government has also provided laboratory equipment to Adi-dravida children. On the basis of merit of students, government has also given grant to SCs/STs students including higher secondary students. Buildings were also constructed for the boys and girls hostel. Educational concession is also given to the students studying in schools. For the literacy of SC girls studying 3-5 and 6th standard, special incentive scheme has also been implemented. Scholarships and stipends were also given to SC boys and girls under SCP.

Government has also upgraded the Adi-dravidar welfare middle school into high schools. Government has also given programme for the opening of single teacher Adi-dravidar welfare elementary schools under SCP. Scout and scout uniforms have also been provided to the scout and scout master. Free bicycles have been given to all girls belonging to SCs/STs studying in 11th and 12th in the government aided Higher Secondary schools. Typing centre has also been set up for SCs/STs students under SCP. The programme also takes care of the additional cost of food charges in hostels.

Textbooks are also supplied to the education of the SCs. As per Plan-Budget link during Ninth Five Year Plan starting from 1997-2002, various programmes have been formulated for the education of SCs. Among several programmes, only those dealing with primary and secondary school education are considered for the following analysis.

The programmes like coaching of SCs/STs students studying in colleges under SCP is not considered here, as it is post-school scheme. Similarly, loans to SCs/STs for pursuing professional and post graduate courses, loans to SC converts to Christianity for courses of professional courses, as it deals with professional courses have also been excluded. Many other schemes have also been excluded because they are concerned with post- secondary or on the job training/ education. During 1997-98, 16.87 crores rupees were allocated for the welfare of S.Cs Education. In 1998-99, 24.94 crores rupees were allocated for education. During 1999-2000, 21.23 crores rupees were allocated for the welfare of the S.Cs education. In 2000-2001, 17.46 crores rupees were allocated for the welfare of S.Cs education and during 2001-2002, 20.81 crores rupees were allocated for the welfare of SCs education.

5.11 Budget Allocation for STs Education under Various Heads

Various programmes are being implemented for the welfare of S.Ts Education. These programmes include building schools, residential schools, and houses for teachers, uniforms for scouts and scout masters, girl's hostel including their maintenance and upkeep, adhoc merit grant for students in higher secondary schools. Other programme relating to post-secondary education and training have not been considered for this presentation. During 1997-98, 71.64 lakhs money were allocated and in 1998-99, 76.57 lakhs rupees were allocated. During 1999-2000, 1.18 crores have been allocated. During 2000-2001, 96.1 lakhs was allocated for the STs education and in 2001-2002, 1.65 crores were allocated for the welfare of STs education. It can be said that there is some increasing trend in amount allocated during five years.

5.12. *Various Plans and Programmes under Special Component Plan (SCP) for Education of SCs*

Under Special Component Plans, various schemes and programmes have been formulated for the upliftment of S.Cs in Tamil Nadu, such as, scholarships and stipends were given for the welfare of S.Cs education under SCP. School education, upgrading of Adi-Dravidar middle school into higher schools, hostel facilities, excursion to school pupils have also been provided by the Tamil Nadu Government. The allocation under SCP by the Tamil Nadu Government was 9.2 crores in 1997-98 and slipped to 5.55 crores in 1998-99. However, in 1999-2000, the allocation became lower at 3.82 crores and went up to 6.26 crores in 2000-01. In the last year of the Plan period, the amount stayed at 6.94 crores.

5.13. *Budget Allocations under Tribal Sub Plan for Primary and Secondary School Education, 1997-2002*

Unlike SCP, Tribal Sub Plan (TSP) was formulated for the welfare of S.Ts. The programmes covered opening and maintenance of residential schools, pre-schools and construction of school buildings. The amount varied from 1.53 crores in the first year of the Plan to 11.71 lakhs at the last year of the Plan period.

5.14 *Sub Total of All the Allocations During 9th Five Year*

The total amount allocated for the welfare of S.Cs, S.Ts, SCP, TSP during 9th Five Year Plan can be seen from Table 1. It shows, during 1997-98, the amount of rupees 28.15 crores money was allocated for the education both SCs and STs, where as in 1998-99, it was Rs. 31.66 crores. During 1999-2000, 26.16 crores were allocated. In 2000-01, the amount was 24.81 crores. In 2001-02, the amount was 29.41 crores. The annual allocation during the five years has remained same through the Plan period.

Table 1. Total Allocation of Resources for the Welfare of SCs and STs Education During 9th Five Year Plan

(In Lakhs)

Departments	*1997-98*	*1998-99*	*1999-00*	*2000-01*	*2001-02*
Welfare of SCs Education	16,87.83	24,94.99	21,23.14	17,46.37	20,81.89
Welfare of STs Education	71.64	76.57	1,18.85	96.01	1,65.92
Special Component Plan	9,02.76	5,55.42	3,82.31	6,27.64	6,94.07
Tribal Area Sub Plan	1,53.42	39.60	-8.27	11.71	Nil
Sub Total	28,15.65	31,66.58	26,16.03	24,81.73	29,41.88

Source: Tamil Nadu Government, Department of Finance, and Annual plan, Plan-Budget Link: Supplementary to the Detailed Budget, Chennai: 1999-2004.

5.15 Financial Rights of Dalits and Tribal in Tamil Nadu

A careful look at the respective allocations in the Tamil Nadu state budget (During 1997-02) reveals, how inadequate the allocations for Dalits and Tribal welfare, vis-à-vis their legitimate dues. As per 1991 census, SCs constitutes 19.18% of the total Tamil Nadu population and S.Ts constitutes 1.03% of the total population. As a whole, the overall percentage of SCs and S.Ts is 20.21%. As per rule, 20% amount should be given to the both SCs and STs. In all the heads under which allocation is made during the 9th Plan, at least 20% should be given for welfare of SCs and STs under each head. This is according to the SCP and TSP schemes.

5.16 Tamil Nadu Government Budget—A Critical Look

Tamil Nadu government always shows its priorities towards SCs and STs in government records and reports. Tamil Nadu government always has a perception that 70% is being spent for the welfare of education of SCs and STs. But, the amount spent is not producing the desired results. The reason for a state of affairs can be seen from the careful review of Table 2.

Table 2. Overall Pictures of the Tamil Nadu Government's Priorities for the Welfare of S.Cs and S.Ts. on Educational Point of View

Year	*Total Amount Realised (In Lakhs)*	*Amount For S.Cs And S.Ts Due (20% Of Total Amount) (In Lakhs)*	*Amount Released Actually For S.Cs and S.Cs In Real (In Lakhs)*	*Amount Denied (In Lakhs)*	*Denied Amount In Percentage*
1997-98	14609.34	2921.868	2815.65	106.218	3.63%
1998-99	18400.34	3680.068	3166.58	513.488	13.95%
1999-00	19129.78	3825.956	2616.03	1209.926	31.62%
2000-01	17501.27	3500.254	2481.73	1018.524	29.09%
2001-02	17647.92	3529.584	2941.88	587.704	.16.65%

Source: Tamil Nadu Government, Department of Finance, and Annual plan, Plan-Budget Link: Supplementary to the Detailed Budget, Chennai: 1999-2004.

The table 2 shows that how SCs and STs are deprived of their assured development shares in the budget allocations. As per Plan Allocation (General Education) Tamil Nadu, an amount of Rs.146.9 crores was allocated during 1997-98, where as in 1998-99, Rs.184 crores money were allocated as a whole for general education. During 1999-2000, Rs. 191.29 crores was allocated. In 2000-01, 175.1 crores rupees have been allocated as a whole. During 2001-02, the amount of Rs. 176.47 crores was allocated for the total population of the Tamil Nadu state. The actual allocation for SCs and STs is presented in the column 4 of Table 2. The shortfall in allocation is given in column 5 and the shortfall as percentage of the due share is given in column 6. The shortfall varied from an insignificant 3.6% in the first year of the Plan period increased to around 30 percent in the last but one year of the Plan period and decreased to 16 percentages in the last year of the plan period.

Amount that should accrue to the SCs and STs according to SCP/TSP is indicated in the column 3 of Table 2. The figures have been arrived at by taking 20 percent of the total allocation for the each year. It is to be reminded that S.Cs and STs constitute 20 percent of the total population. From the above-mentioned data, it becomes clear that SCs and STs are denied of their due share promised in SCP and TSP in Tamil Nadu. Such denial of their due share may result in slower pace of development for the S.Cs and S.Ts and therefore SCs and STs are not able to catch up with the rest of the population. This probably explains the difference in school drop out rates of SCs and STs and those for rest of the population[27].

6. Conclusion

The SCs (dalits) and STs (Adivasis), which are part of Tamil Nadu population, constitute 20 percentages. Dalits and Tribals are the poorest sections of society. They still live in abject poverty, misery and human deprivation as marginalized sections. Education of SCs and STs is not only necessary for a single state or but also for all the states. Human resource development is a major instrument for the empowerment of the weaker sections of society. Drop out rates are also higher among SC/ST boys and girls than general population of the state. It seems to imply that government has only a low priority for the educational development of SCs and STs, even if Tamil Nadu government always claims that it ranks very high in literacy level among the States of India.

SCs and STs are receiving various types of protective treatment for the past three decades to enable them to attain parity with the advanced sections. Like other states in India, Tamil Nadu too has various schemes for their upliftment. Tamil Nadu government has adopted two mechanisms viz., Special Component Plan (SCP) for SCs and Tribal Sub Plan (TSP) for STs. SCP is designed to channelise the flow of benefits and outlays from the general sectors in the plan of the States and Central ministries for the development of SCs. TSP is used as a strategy for tribal development in states. The major objective was to address the issue of backwardness in tribal areas and tribal population.

The annual state budget gives an indication of Government's priorities, performances, decisions and intentions and it can also be considered as an articulation of the existing power relations in society. It has also an impact upon the weaker sections of society, especially the SCs and

STs. Budget allocations for them can change in long run their status in the state. Tamil Nadu government has provided various provisions for the educational development of SCs and STs. Various schemes and programmes have been implemented over the years. The forgoing analysis of the budget allocation and expenditure shows that there is an overall gap between plan allocation and what rightfully should have been allocated to them. Lack of interest and government will are a major hurdle in educating them. It also does not benefit the SCs and STs due to non-availability of timely financial support such as free ships, scholarships and fellowships, due to inadequate and untimely disbursements.

From the above said analysis, it becomes clear that SCs and S.Ts are denied of getting their due share promised in SCP and TSP in Tamil Nadu. Such denial of their due share in budget allocation may result in slower pace of development for the SCs and STs and therefore they will not be able to catch up with the rest of the population in Tamil Nadu in the near future. Therefore, it is likely the exiting differentials in educational attainment between SCs and STs and the rest of the population will continue for some more time.

REFERENCES

1. SSS Social Study Circle di (ESTD) - Dalit India, A Comprehensive Outline for the Development of SCs and STs, 1982, www.dalitindia.com.
2. The Growth and Development of SC and ST Population in Gujarat and Future Prospects, www.iussp.org/2001/brazil
3. Radhakrishnan, P. 'Sensitising Officials II', *The Hindu*, 4 Dec. 2001.
4. Kumar, Vivek. 'Alternative Economic Survey 2002-2003: Liberalisation Sans Social Justice', in *Dalits*, Ed. Alternative Survey Group, Rainbow Publishers.
5. *Ibid.*, p. 154.
6. India—A Welfare State, Policies and Programmes for Women Welfare and Advancement, www.hcidhka.org.
7. Goyal, B.R., *Educating Harijans*. Haryana: The Academic Press, 1981.
8. Das, A.K., "Educational and Economic Achievement and Trend Thereof among the ST of West Bengal", in *Tribal Transformation*

in India, Ed. Buddhadeb Chaudhuri, New Delhi: Inter India Publications, 1985.

9. Jhunjhunwala, Bharat. "Dalit Welfare: Moral Duty of the Rich and Powerful", *The Statesman*, 30 June, 2001, p. 6.
10. Pundir, Naresh Singh, "Social Mobility among Chamars in a North Indian Village", M.Phil. dissertation, Meerut University, Meerut, 1987.
11. Mistry, M.D., "Budget Analysis at State and Local Levels", *Budget Analysis and Policy Advocacy in India*, Ed. Abha Shankar & Mark Robinson, Courtesy of The Times of India, the Ford Foundation.
12. Shakeel, Ahmed, M., *Five Decades of Planning and Tribal Development*, New Delhi: Gyan Publishing Development House, 2004.
13. Alexander, Varghese V. 'Tribals and Sub Plans'. Seminar, 1983: Feb, P. 33.
14. Abraham, Princy M., "A Descriptive Study of the Special Component Plan with References to Animal Husbandry Ship Scheme", M.A. dissertation, Stella Maris College, Chennai, (2004): pp. 77-86.
15. *Ibid.*, pp. 87-91.
16. Kaushik, Vijay, & Bela Rani Sharma, *Encyclopedia of Human Rights and Women's Development*, Vol. 2, New Delhi: Sarup and Sons, 1998, pp. 74-75.
17. Tamil Nadu. Tamil Nadu people's Forum for Social Development. Tamil Nadu Social Development Report 2000. Chennai: Social Watch, 2000; pp. 41-42.
18. Ibid., p. 116.
19. Tamil Nadu. Department of Economics and Statistics. Statistical Hand Book of Tamil Nadu 2003. Chennai: State of Tamil Nadu, 2003, p. 443.
20. Tamil Nadu. Tamil Nadu people's Forum for Social Development. Tamil Nadu Social Development Report 2000. Chennai: Social Watch, 2000; pp. 117-120.
21. India, Govt. of, Report of the Steering Committee on empowerment of the S.Cs and other backward classes and minorities, Tenth Five Year Plan (2002-2007)
22. Tamil Nadu People's Forum for Social Development: S.C.P, Dalit Hopes Betrayed? Social Watch Tamil Nadu, March 2003.
23. Tribal Sub Plan,www.tripurainfo.com/opinion/exp-op2./nagaraju.html
24. Tamil Nadu People's Forum for Social Development: Social Development of Dalits and the Tamil Nadu Government

budget—A Critique. Chennai: Tamil Nadu people's Forum for Social Development, 1999.

25. *Ibid.*
26. Basic Profile to SC/ST welfare, http://www.upportal.com/
27. Tamil Nadu Government, Department Of finance. Annual Plan. Plan-Budget Link: Supplementary to the Detailed Budget. Chennai: 1999-2004.

13

SELF-GOVERNANCE AND NATURAL RESOURCE MANAGEMENT DURING REFORMS PERIOD: EVIDENCE FROM THE SCHEDULE AREAS OF ORISSA

NIHAR RANJAN MISHRA

Sustainable development poses a great challenge for the developing countries like India with their increasing pace of industrialization, urbanization and income growth that put tremendous pressure on natural resources for products and services, on one hand, and, shrinking common property resources base, rapid increasing human and livestock population, poverty, on the other, are responsible for the tremendous pressure of degradation on the existing resources. No doubt, this problem of resource degradation is a challenge before any disadvantage community in India, but in tribal areas, it has assumed alarming protections because the traditional means of obtaining livelihoods are being increasingly threatened. Traditionally, tribal families earned their livelihoods from surrounding natural resources by using different means and methods. However, in last fifty years, access to and control over the natural resources has undergone radical changes. On the other hand, the state sponsored and private sector national and multinational companies have steadfastly corded the land, water and forest rights of local communities (Gadgil and Guha, 1992). Because of the current onslaught of globalisation, the power of money and market has begun to distort democracy and natural resources are being exploited o meet the ever increasing requirements and aspirations of the affluent groups. Alongside, the process of ecological degradation has continued unabated. The present paradigm of development, emphasizing urbanization, and industrialization has not only accentuated this process but has also caused displacement of tribal populations from their habitats (Bokil, 2002). As a result, local communities have virtually been transformed from a relatively independent, self-reliant and self-determining entity to one dependent on the vagaries of money market, labour contractors and government agents (Fernandes, 1992).

However, realising the situation, for last three decades many scholars like Hardin (1968), Olson (1965), Ostrom (1990), Wade (1988), Vandana Siva (1991) and others have studied various aspects of Common Property Resources in different parts of the world and have prescribed various solutions for the management of this resources. Realising the local self-government as strong grass root level democratic institutions, most of he scholars have given emphasis on self-governance and people's participation (Rasmussen and Dick, 1995). There is a general consensus that successful development outcomes depend, in part on beneficiary involvement in programme and planning and execution. In light of this decentralized governance has been conceived as an institutional arrangement for involving people and, there by, for achieving better implementation of development programmes at the grass root level. As part of achieving this goal, Panchayat Raj pattern of local self-government has been enforced in the country by granting constitutional recognition of these rural local self-governing institutions under the 73rd constitutional Amendment Act, 1992. However, in the beginning at was not introduced in the tribal areas. With certain modifications Panchayat Extension to Scheduled Areas (PESA) Act, 1996 was introduced in the scheduled areas of India.

Taking certain studies from secondary sources, the personal experiences and literatures into account the present paper makes an attempt to understand the real picture of self-governance during the reform periods in the schedule areas of Orissa. It also tries to critically compare the State Conformity Act with Central PESA Act, 1996.

Approaches and Constitutional Provisions for Scheduled Tribes

The social and economic conditions of the people belonging to the scheduled tribes have been the concern of Indian political and social movements before Independence. Indeed to Gandhiji, the father of the Nation, freedom was not a mere political objective but raising the mass of people from poverty and degradation. The mainstream political and social movements, which were profoundly influenced by Gandhian approach emphasised the imperative need to transfer the scheduled tribes. The Cripps Mission of 1942 and he Cabinet Mission of 1946 had enormous influence in the formulation of special policies for the tribal people.

Soon after Independence, the basic principles for the development of the scheduled tribes were clearly set out by Pundit Jawaharlal Nehru, the first Prime Minister of free India, in the form of five principles known as 'Tribal Panchasheel', which was later endorsed by the Renuka Roy team (1959), Dhebar Commission (1961), and Shilu Ao committee (1969). Starting from the Special Multipurpose Tribal Blocks of 1956, the measures taken for development of scheduled tribes are multifarious. Tribal Development Blocks, Large-scale Multipurpose Cooperative Societies (LAMPS), Tribal Development Agencies, Integrated Tribal development Area Projects (ITDA), Modified Area Development Approach (MADA), Tribal Sub-plan Strategy (TSP), 1974-75, Micro Projects for Primitive tribal Groups reflected the course of tribal development administration in the country (Rao, P.V., 2001). A Variety of approaches and strategies like top-down approach, regional planning, target group approaches, integrated development, participatory development, Joint Forest Management, watershed Management, poverty alleviation programmes have formed as part of the development approach.

The Constitution of India enshrines a number of important provisions for the safeguard as well as promotion of the interests of the scheduled tribes. Broadly speaking, it envisages a tripod schemata comprising: *a)* policy goals and objectives in the shape of Directive Principles in the Article 46; *b)* the legislative and physical infrastructure in the fifth and sixth schedule; and *c)* financial support in Article 275 for funding schemes of tribal development and welfare (Mohanty, P.K., 2000:538). The main provisions relating to schedule tribes are contained in the Articles 15(4), 16 (4), 19 (4), 19 (5), 23,29, 46, 164, 275 (1), 330, 332, 334, 335, 338, 342, Fifth and Sixth schedule of the constitutions. In order to assist the tribal in enjoying their existing rights without any hindrance by others through summary process and to protect and promote the interests of the schedule tribes, the President of India has issued two orders I, e., the Schedule Areas (part A States) order, 1950 and the Schedule Areas (part B States) order 1950 (as amended).These two orders of scheduled areas which are included in the fifth schedule of the Indian constitution (Article- 244) declares certain tribal areas as schedule areas in the respective states of Andhra Pradesh, Orissa, Madhya Pradesh, Bihar, Himachal Pradesh, Maharashtra, Gujrat and Rajsthan .Similarly Article 244(2) provides various provisions under sixth schedule for the administration and control of schedule tribes in North-Eastern sates.

History of Self-Governance in India

It is widely recognised that self governing village communities characterised by agrarian economics had existed in India form the earliest times. Not only are they mentioned in the Rig Veda, which dates from approximately 1200 B.C., there is also definite evidence available of the existence of village "Sabhas" (Council or Assemblies) and "gramins" (senior persons of the village) until about 600 B.C. In course of time, during pre-colonial period these village bodies took the form of Panchayat (an assembly of five members) which looked after the affairs of village. They had both policy and judicial powers. Besides these village Panchayats, there were also caste Panchayats to ensure that persons belonging to a particular caste adhered to its code of social conduct and ethics. Although under the Mughals their judicial powers curtailed, local affairs remained unregulated from above village offices and servants were answerable primarily to the Panchayats.

With the advent of the British, the self-contained village communities and their Panchayats ceased to get sustenance. In course of time, formally constituted institutions of village administration replaced them. It is a historical fact that local self-government in India, in the sense of an accountable representative institution, was the creation of the British. In 1870 the Viceroy, Lord Mayo, got a resolution passed by his council for decentralization of power to bring about administrative efficiency in meeting the demands of the people and to add to the finance of the "existing imperial resources which will not suffice for the growing wants of the country" (Venkatarangaiya, M. *et al*, 1969:97). The government resolution of 18 May 1882 during the Viceroyalty of Lord Ripon, providing for local boards consisting of large majority of elected non-official members and presided over by a non-official chairperson, is considered to be the *magna carta* of local democracy in India.

In 1906, the Congress, under the presidency of Dadabhai Naoroji, accepted self-government as the political goal for the country. Recognising the importance of self-governance in Indian context, Royal Commission on Decentralization in 1907, recommended that "it is most desirable, alike in the interest of decentralization and in order to associate the people with the local tasks of administration, that an attempt should be made to constitute and develop village affairs" (Malavia, H.D., 1956). But, like the Ripon resolution, the recommendations made by Royal Commission on Decentralization also remained largely on paper. Montague-Chelmsford reforms of 1919, proposed a scheme in bringing the local self-government under the domain of Indian ministers in the provinces. The Government of India Act, 1935 and the inauguration of provincial autonomy under it marked another important stage in the evolution of Panchayat in the country. With popularly elected governments in the provinces, almost all-provincial administration felt duty bound to enact legislations for further democratization of local self-government institutions.

In the post independence period, the government of India has brought about certain constitutional provisions to strengthen local self-governments. Article 40 of the constitution reads "the state should take the steps to organize village Panchayats and endow them with such power and authority as may be necessary to enable them to function as units of self government. Emphasising the role of local-governance, the Balvantray Mehta committee in 1957 recommended that in order to get real progress in rural development the public participation in community works should be organized through statutory representative bodies (Balavantray, M., 1957:23). In 1978, Asoka Mehta Committee gave emphasis on block level organization said that Panchayat Samiti at block should be formulated for all round development (Mehta, A., 1978:4). Unlike many other states of India, Orissa has also passed the Gram Panchayat Act of 1948 to form local authorities like District Boards or Joint Committee. Similarly, the Zila Parishad and Panchayat Samiti Act of 1959 have led to the formation of the Orissa Panchayat Samiti at block level and Zila Parishad at district level. Village level democracy became a real prospect for India in 1992 with the 73rd amendment to the constitution, which mandated that resources, responsibility and decision making be devolved from central government to the lowest unit of the governance, the Gram Sabha or the village assembly. A three-tier structure of local self-government was envisaged under this amendment.

Panchayat Extension to Scheduled Areas (PESA)

The constitution (73rd) Amendment Act, 1992, in corporating many path-breaking provisions for effective local self government practices, was not automatically made applicable to the scheduled areas (Article 243M) because of their unique characteristics and special needs as also recognizing the special features of the tribal people. Subsequently, on the basis of expert advise as contained in the Bhuria Committee Report, 1995, an Amendment Act was enacted in December 1996 enabling extension of the 73rd Amendment Act, 1992, in a modified form to the schedule areas. The Act extends Panchayats to the scheduled areas of eight sates namely, Orissa, Andhra Pradesh, Madhya Pradesh, Himachal Pradesh, Gujrat, Bihar, Maharashtra, and Rajasthan, which intends to empower the Gram Sabha and Gram Panchayats in tribal society to preserve and conserve their traditional right over natural resources.

The Provisions of the Panchayats
(Extension to the Scheduled Areas) Act, 1996

(*An Act to provide for the extension of the provisions of Part IX of the Constitution relating to the Panchayats to the Scheduled Areas*.)

1. This Act may be called the Provisions of the Panchayats (Extension to the Scheduled Areas) Act, 1996.

2. In this Act, unless the contest otherwise required," Scheduled Areas" means the Scheduled Areas as referred to in clause (1) of Article 244 of the Constitution.

3. The provisions Part IX of the Constitution relating to Panchayats are hereby extended to the Scheduled Areas subject to such exceptions and modifications as are provide in section.

4. Notwithstanding anything contained under Part IX of the Constitution, the Legislature of a State shall not make any law under that Part, which is inconsistent with any of the following features, namely:-

(a) A State legislation on the Panchayats that may be made shall be in consonance with the customary law, social and religious practices and traditional management practices of community resources;

(b) A village shall ordinarily consist of a habitation or a group of habitations or a hamlet or a group of hamlets comprising a community and managing its affairs in accordance with traditions and customs:

(c) every village shall have a Gram Sabha consisting of persons whose names are included in the electoral rolls for the Panchayat at the village level;

(d) every Gram Sabha shall be competent to safeguard and preserve the traditions and customs of the people, their cultural identity, community resources and the customary mode of dispute resolution;

(e) Every Gram Sabhas shall :

(i) approve the plans, programmes and projects for social and economic development before such plans. Programmes and projects are taken up for implementation by the Panchayat at the village level;

(ii) Be responsible for the identification or selection of persons as beneficiaries under the poverty alleviation and other programmes;

(f) every Panchayat at the village level shall be required to obtain from the Gram Sabha a certification of utilization of funds by that Panchayat for the plans, programmes and projects referred to in the clause.

(g) the reservation of seats in the Scheduled Areas at every Panchayat shall be in proportion to the population of the communities in that Panchayat for whom reservation is sought to be given under Part IX of the Constitution;

Provided that the reservation for the Scheduled Tribes shall not be less than one-half of the total number of seats;

Provided further that all seats of Chair-persons of Panchayats at all levels shall be reserved for the Scheduled Tribe;

(h) the State Government may nominate persons belonging to such Scheduled Tribes as have no representation in the Panchayat at the intermediate level or the Panchayat at the intermediate level or the Panchayat at the district level: Provided that such nomination shall not exceed one-tenth of the total members be elected in that Panchayat;

(i) the Gram Sabha or the Panchayats at the appropriate level shall be consulted before making the acquisition of land in the Scheduled Areas for development projects and before re-setting or rehabilitating persons affected by such projects in the Scheduled Areas; the actual planning and implementation of the projects in the Scheduled Areas shall be coordinated at the State level;

(j) planning & management of minor water bodies in

the Scheduled Areas shall be entrusted to Panchayats at the appropriate level;

(k) the recommendations of the Gram Sabha or the Panchayats at the appropriate level shall be made mandatory prior to grant of prospecting license or mining lease for minor minerals in the Scheduled Areas;

(l) the prior recommendations of the Gram Sabha or the Panchayats at the appropriate level shall be made mandatory for grant of concession for the exploitation of minor minerals by auction;

(m) while endowing Panchayats in the Scheduled Areas with such powers and authority as may be necessary to enable them to function as institutions of self-government, a State Legislature shall ensure that the Panchayats at the appropriate level and the Gram Sabha are endowed specifically with-

(i) the power to enforce prohibition or to regulate or restrict the sale and consumption of any intoxicant;

(ii) the ownership of minor forest produce;

(iii) the power to prevent alienation of land in the Scheduled areas and to take appropriate action to restore any unlawfully alienated land of a. Scheduled Tribe;

(iv) the power to manage village markets by whatever name called;

(v) the power to exercise control over money lending to the Scheduled Tribes;

(vi) the power to exercise control over institutions and functionaries in all social sectors;

(vii) the power to control over local plans and resources for such plans including tribal sub-plans;

(n) the State legislations that may endow Panchayats with powers and authority as may be necessary to enable them to function as institutions of self-government shall contain safeguards to ensure that Panchayats at the higher level do not assume the powers and authority of any Panchayat at the lower level or of the Gram Sabha;

(o) the State Legislature shall endeavor to follow the pattern of the Sixth Schedule to the Constitution while designing the administrative arrangements in the Panchayats at district levels in the Scheduled Areas.

5. Notwithstanding any-thing in Part IX of the Constitution with exceptions and modifications made by this Act, any provision of any law relating to Panchayats in force in the Scheduled Areas immediately before the date on which this Act receives the assent of the President which is inconsistent with the provisions of Part IX with such exceptions and modifications shall continue to be in force until amended or repealed by a competent Legislature or other competent authority or until the expiration of one year from the date on which this Act receives the assent of the President; (II) Provided that all the Panchayats existing immediately before such date shall continue till the expiration of their duration unless sooner dissolved by a resolution passed to that effect by the Legislative Assembly of that State or, in the case of a State having Legislative council, by each House of the Legislature of that State.

Before examining the real picture of self governance in natural resource management in the scheduled areas of Orissa, let us have a look at the tribal profile and scheduled areas of Orissa.

Tribes of Orissa

Orissa, which is said to be the land of multi ethnic groups, is famous for tribals. There are 62 scheduled tribal communities in Orissa having 81,45,081 (males 40,66+females 40,78,298) persons i.e. 22.13 percent of the total population of the state with a sex ratio of 1003 females per 1000 males (2001, Census of India). About 10.38% of India's scheduled tribe population is in Orissa, the third in terms of tribal concentration, only next to Madhya Pradesh, Maharashtra. About 98.86 %of the tribal population lives in rural areas. The percentage of the tribal population to the total population is highest in Malkangiri (58.54) and lowest in Puri (0.27 %) (1991, Census). The districts dominated by tribal populations are Malkangiri (58.54%), Mayurbhanja (57.87%), Nawarangapur (55.26%), Rayagada

(54.99%), Sundaragarha (56.74%), Koraput (50.67%), Phulabani (50.13%), whereas, the district which covers a sizeable tribal populations are Keonjhar (44.62%), Gajapati (47.88%), Nuapada (35.95%), Jharsuguda (33.88%), Deogarh (33.31%) (1991, Census). About 22.21 % among the tribal of the state are reported to be literate (2001, Census). These tribal communities belong to Austro-Asiatic, Dravidian, and Indo-Aryan language families. Though most of the tribal communities of the state have their own dialect, some of them speak Oriya. The patrilinial decent system, and patriarchal system of authority is still predominated among them. They believe in animism, animatisms, nature-worship, and ancestor worship.

Out of these 62 tribal communities, 13 communities such are Bonda, Chukia, Bhunja, Didayi, Dongiria Kandha, Hill Kharia, Juang, Kuia Kandha, Lanjia Saora, Lodha, Mankiridia, Paudi Bhuiyan, Saora and Birhor considered as Primitive Tribal Groups (PTGs). These PTGs are living in 20 parts of blocks of 12 districts and for their economic development,17 micro projects were set up at different period of time. Out of 17 micro projects in Orissa, 13 are established within the Tribal Sub Plan (TSP) areas and rest 4 are established outside the TSP areas. For the total tribal population in the state 21 Integrated Tribal Development Agencies (ITDA) are in operation covering 118 blocks. The tribal economy of Orissa is basically considered as subsistence economy. Around 75% of them are staying bellow poverty line (2001 Census). The habitat is largely forest clad. Though the tribal of Orissa are engaged in different activities, the land and forest, particularly the Minor Forest Produces (MFPs) have been playing as a major source of their livelihood (Malik *et al*, 1996).

Most of the tribal population in Orissa is confined to scheduled areas of the state. The scheduled areas cover 69,613.80 sq. k.m. which is about 44.70 per cent of the total area of the state. Its total population is 88, 71,071 out of which the population of scheduled tribe is 47, 62,207 constituting 53.68%, as per 1991 census. The tribal population of he scheduled areas is 67.72 % of the total tribal population of the state as per the 1991 census. Consequent to the creation of 17 new districts, the scheduled areas now cover 7 districts fully and 6 districts in part, out of 30 districts in the state.

The details of the scheduled areas of the state are given in table-1.

Table 1. Distribution of Scheduled Areas in Orissa

Sl. No.	District	Details of the declared scheduled areas	Areas of the tract under scheduled areas (sq.km.)	Total population of the tract covered under scheduled areas	Population of ST in the tract covered under scheduled areas	Population of SC in the tract covered under scheduled areas
1.	Mayur-bhanj	Whole district	10,416.60	18,45,580	10,90,626	1,31,765
2.	Balasore	Nilagiri block	223.60	106468	53,080	10,780
		Nilgiri sub-division				
3.	Keonjhar	1-Tahasils of Keonjhar sub-division namely:				
		(I) Keonjhor Tahasil	5,350.20	6,46,857	3,54,605	52,498
		(II) Telkoi Tahasil	1585.40	3,28,437	1,52,986	32,487
		2-Tahsils of champua subdivisions namely:				
		I.Champua Tashil				
		II. Barbil Tahasil				
4.	Sambal-apur	Kuchinda Tahasil of Kuchinda Sub-divisions	2,367.30	2,25,086	1,25,741	27,263
5.	Sundar-garh	Whole district	9,921.40	15,73,617	7,98,481	1,38,157
6.	Gajapati	I-R. Udaya-giri Tahasil of Parlakhe-				

		mundi sub-division				
		II-Guma Block of Khemundi Tahasil of Paralakhe-mundi sub-division	2,498.80	2,87,799	1,95,497	12,525
		III-Rayagada Block of Parala-khemundi sub-division				
7.	Ganjam	Suruda Tahasil excluding Gazaibadi and Ghoshha Gram Pancha-yata in Ghum-sur sub-division of Bhanjanagar	912.00	1,42,649	12,852	29,076
8.	Kalahandi	2 Blocks namely:				
		(i) Th. Rampur of Bhawanipa-tana sub-division	323.80	55,777	31,042	14,170
		(ii)Lanjigarh of Bhawanipa-tana sub-division	999.70	60,974	29,832	14,189
9.	Koraput	Whole district	8534.00	10,29,986	5,21,849	1,38,169
10.	Rayagada	Whole district	7584.70	7,13,984	4,00,097	1,01,956
11.	Nawaran-gapur	Whole district	5135.30	8,46,659	4,67,919	1,27,800
12.	Malakan-giri	Whole district	6115.30	4,21,917	2,46,214	84,208
13.	Phulbani	2 Tahasils namely:				
		i-Khandamal Tahasil of Kandhamal sub-division	2017.60	1,60,205	76,587	36,180
		ii-Balliguda Tahasil &				

iii-G-Udayagiri Tahasil of Balliguda sub-division	5628.10	3,86,076	2,04,799	63,319
Total Scheduled Areas	69,613.80	88,71,071	47,62,207	10,14,542
State Total	1,55,707.00	3,16,59,736	70,32,214	51,29,314
Percentage of Scheduled Areas to that of the State	44.70 %	28.20 %	67.72 %	19.78 %

Source: ST and SC Development Department, Government of Orissa.

If we look into the traditional management system in the scheduled areas of Orissa, it is found out that the tribal communities are traditionally well-versed in the regulation, control and conduct of their domestic, religious, socio-economic, political and judicial affairs through the combined wisdom of their leaders and village councils. They have their own system of governance, law and justice system. They have a system of democracy through which they address to their various problems, be they intra-tribal, inter-tribal or between the tribal and non-tribal. They usually have the council of elders of lineages, clans or tribal groups at a higher level. The traditional tribal political organizations designated differently in different tribal communities perform their role as regard to village administration, maintaining socio-cultural harmony, imposing punishment on the social deviants and in redressing the grievances.

Orissa Conformity Act

Pursuant to the Panchayat (Extension to Scheduled Areas) Act (1996), the state government of Orissa amended its earlier legislations as: *i)* Orissa Gram Panchayat Amendment Act (1997) (Act 15 of 1997), *ii)* Orissa Panchayat Samiti Amendment Act (1997) (Act 16 of 1997), and, *iii)* Orissa Zila Parisad Amendment Act (1997) (Act 17 of 1997), and this was notified in the Orissa gazette dated 22nd December 1997.

A comparative analysis of state acts and central act in their extension to scheduled areas makes it clear that while incorporating some of the provisions of the central act, the government of Orissa has in many ways, deprived the tribals of their community control over local natural resources and hence diluted the very essence of the central PESA Act 1996.

Table 2

Panchayat (Extension to the Scheduled Areas) Act, 1996- Functional Devolution on Panchayats

Sl	*Components*	*Mandatory Provision*	*Status*
1	Definition of Village	A village consists of a habitation or a group of habitations or a hamlet or a group of hamlets comprising a community and managing its affairs in accordance with traditions and customs	A village consists of a habitation or a group of habitations or a hamlet or a group of hamlets comprising a community or different communities having distinct socio-cultural practices and managing its affairs in accordance with traditions and customs.
2	Status and Functions of Gram Sabha	Every village will have a Gram Sabha which will be competent to safeguard and preserve the traditions and customs of the People, their cultural identity.	Along with central Act the Orissa Act adds that it should be consistent with the relevant laws in force and in harmony with the tenets of the Constitution and Human Rights.
3	Constitution of Panchayat	Panchayat will be constituted at village level with reservations for Scheduled Tribes in the manner prescribed in Part IX of the Constitution.	Orissa adopted the same provision.
4	Acquisition of land for development projects and resettlement of displaced persons	Prior consultation with Gram Sabha or Panchayat at the appropriate level shall be made mandatory.	Orissa assigned the power to Zilla Panchayat with no role for the Gram Sabha/ Gram Panchayat
5	Planning and Management of Minor Water Bodies	Entrusted to Panchayat at the appropriate level	Orissa assigned power to Zilla Parishad instead of Gram Sabha/Gram Panchayat
6	Grant of Prospecting license or mining lease	Prior recommendations of Gram Sabha or the Panchayats at the appropriate level shall be made mandatory	Orissa gives powers to Zilla Parishad.

	for minor minerals		
7	Grant of concession for exploitation of minor minerals by auction.	Prior recommendation of Gram Sabha or Panchayats at appropriate level shall be made mandatory.	Orissa assigned the power to Zilla Parishad.
8	Enforce prohibition/ regulate or restrict sale & consumption of any intoxicant	Panchayats at the appropriate level and the Gram Sabha to be endowed with the powers	Gram Sabha (to control & supervise Gram Panchayat to execute).
9	Legislation	State legislation shall make necessary provision to enable them function as institutions of self-government and shall caution safeguards to ensure that Panchayats at the higher level do not assume the power and authority of any Panchayats at the lower level of the Gram Sabha.	No safeguards are provided in the Act
10	Administration	The State legislation shall endeavor to follow the pattern of sixth schedule of the constitution while designing the administrative arrangements in the Panchayats at district level in Scheduled Areas.	No safeguards are provided.

Critical Analysis of State Conformity Act

If we unfold he history of self governance in India, it could be seen that the experiment in decentralized governance in India, which aims at empowering the people for effective participation in local governance, has hardly given the tribals any power to have control over these resources. Despite the constitutional provision of special powers vested with the governors wherein they can exclude any act of parliament or of the state legislature to the 'schedule areas' by notification, or extend them with such exceptions and modifications, which they think necessary for peace and good governance, none of the governor of states having scheduled areas have applied their discretion in enforcing such provisions. On the contrary, all the acts and enactments passed by parliament as well as state legislatures have been extended to the scheduled areas without making suitable modifications to suit he socio-cultural and politic-economic ethos of the tribals. Even the Panchayat Raj Acts for decentralized governance in various states, in the past, were extended to the scheduled areas without taking into consideration the customs and traditions, and their system of governance.

However, the latest Panchayat Extension to Scheduled Areas (PESA) Act, 1996 which was aimed to empower the Gram Sabha and Gram Panchayat to take control of their destinies and ensure grass root participatory democracy in scheduled areas of India is also not able to bring the desired result in a tribal dominated state like Orissa. A cursory reading of the central PESA Act shows that empowerment of the Gram Sabha is the core principle of PESA and this sanction of Gram Sabha stands on entirely different footing from empowerment of Gram Panchayat, though the two terms "Gram Sabha" and "Gram Panchayat" are being used interchangeably. Most of the state legislations including Orissa, reading the two terms as synonymous, have empowered the Panchayat, which for all practical purposes, actually disempowers the Gram Sabha. Hence, any adoption of the PESA by states must be aware of this ambiguity and discern the two institutions in the right sense.

While giving a comparative analysis of both state act and central act, which have been extended to the scheduled areas, attempts have made to highlight the major distinctions therein. Section 4(b) of this Act defines that a village shall consist of one or more habitations or hamlets comprising a community and managing its affairs in accordance with its traditions and customs. Since a community in tribal areas is to take into consideration a functioning collectivity and face-to-face habitational relationship. Under the New Scheduled Area Act, the formal recognition of the community and the assembly of its members as 'Gram Sabha' is the most significant achievement in the history of democratic institutions build so far. Further, the significance of command over community natural resources as recognised by the act is not in isolation or a mere economic issue, but in relation to the cultural identity of the people. Since the 'community' in the form of 'Gram Sabha' enjoys the constitutional recognition, its authority cannot be questions any more. Under the Extended Panchayat Act in Scheduled Areas, whereas, according to section 4(iii) in the context of the state of Orissa, Gram Sabha has been conferred with this power to plan and approve the programmes in various matters of socio-economic development. Moreover, by defining the Gram Sabha as a community or communities consisting of a large number of people with different cultures and customs, the state has also not bothered to safeguard and preserve the traditions and customs of people, their cultural identity, community resources and the customary mode of dispute resolution.

Regarding he traditional rights and customs of tribal people, their cultural identity and community control over resources etc., as mentioned under section 4 (d) of the central Act, Orissa provides rights to 'Gram Sabha' making it competent to safeguard and preserve the traditions and customs of people, their cultural identity, community resources and the customary mode of dispute resolution consistent with the relevant laws in force and in harmony with the basic tenets of the Constitution and human rights (originally not provided under the central PESA Act, 1996).This in fact implies that in case of any disputes, the hold of Criminal Procurer Code, Indian Penal Code, Orissa Forest Act etc. would prevail over the customary laws of these communities. By this, the state practically does not give any right to tribal people to safeguard, exercise and preserve their traditional rights and control over resources.

The primary resources other than agriculture in the traditional economy are: forests, pastures, waste land and water on which the tribal people depend for their living. The wrong entitlements over resources of all descriptions started getting established during the British period. It was in that period the intimate relationship between the resources and the local community, which was like that between the mother and the child, was ended and the state acquired monopoly rights their own. The colonial process of centralization has unfortunately got further reinforced under the tutelage of new paradigm of development, which has been adopted in our country after independence. The Forest Act (1927) did not recognize the symbiotic relationship between forest and forest dwellers and the forest became the property of the state. It is clear that the right to life at the individual level and the human right of maintaining the identity at the community level in the case of tribal people have been ignored in the Indian Forest Act. The interventions of new economic reforms in the form of globalization, liberalization, and privatization have brought about enormous effect on tribal economy. These have forced fundamental changes in policies across all natural resources. The biggest irony of this change was that the forest dweller, which has a life-long relationship with the forests, which are their very homes, their religion, their culture, and their everything, was conspicuous by its absence in the policies. In this formal structure, which recognizes only administrative and market relations, an all out effort has been made to see that these life-long mother-child relationships are transformed into market relationships. The establishment of industrial and mining complexes in the name of development, construction of highways, heavy influx of outsiders, supply of forest produces for meeting new demands, proved to be a big burden on the forests. Consequently, there was ruthless destruction of the forest. The worst effect of this mindless destruction has been on the life of tribal people. Thus, backward communities, and more particularly people in tribal regions have been most affected in this process of development since they live in resource rich regions. Tribal areas produce most of the country's coal, mica, bauxite and other minerals. Due to rapid industrialization in tribal areas, most of the tribals have been displaced from their ancestral lands. In addition to direct displacement, mining activity also affects the livelihoods of thousands more as water table gets disrupted, an excessive burden is dumped on fertile agricultural land and forest are cut (Mohapatra, 1991).Not only are communities deprived from their vital subsistence resources, their long term sustainability is also jeopardized. The very basis of their life is getting destroyed. But, unfortunately, no attention has been paid to save these tribals from these disasters. Though the introduction of PESA Act (1996) brought certain hope for them, it was not able to bring about desired results due to certain factors, which we have discussed here.

In the context of natural resources, Central PESA Act specifically grounds the Gram Sabha control over prospecting of mines minerals, planning and management of water bodies, management of minor forest produces, leasing mines and alienation of land (including the power to restore land any alienated land of a scheduled tribe). These appear to be substantial rights at least on paper. In practice, however, the benefits of PESA have not materialized at al. In a detailed analysis of the operationalization of PESA in 4 states, Upadhyay (2004) shows how the intent of PESA has been stymied by the states through exploitation of loopholes, omissions, reinterpretations, temporizing and ambiguity in the rules or orders that they have passed in response to PESA.

In the case of land acquisition, PESA mandates that the Gram Sabha or the Panchayat at the appropriate level, needs to be consulted before acquiring lands for development projects and before resettling or rehabilitating persons affected by such projects in the scheduled areas. The requirement of this law would be completed with if either the Gram Sabha or the Panchayat at the appropriate level is consulted. Orissa Government Amendment Act of 1997 impinges this right of Gram Sabha by exclusively giving power to Zila Parishad, which provides enough scope for manipulation at the state level. The use of the word 'consultation' under PESA instead of 'consent' significantly waters down the power vested with the Panchayat. The critical examination of the operationalization of this act in this context shows that though the government has given power to the Zila Parishad, the real power lies in the hand of government. There is no prior consultation with Gram Sabha and also with Zilla Parishad. The evidences from southern Orissa show that the government, which formulated the act itself, is violating the acts giving different justifications in the name of development. For instance, the sterlite project in Kalahandi district which falls in a 5th scheduled area, runs counter to the spirit of the Supreme Court judgment in Samatha versus state of Andhra Pradesh, which not only prohibits sale of land, government or private, in 5th scheduled areas to non-tribals but also bars mining leases or prospecting licenses to mining companies. However, the Orissa government performed illegal sleight of hand by deciding not to emulate the Andhra example, as it argued; the existing laws in the state are adequate to protect the rights and the interests of the tribals. It backed up its decision with the thesis that "transfer of land for development activities, establishment of industries and operation of mining leases etc. in scheduled areas should bring about encouraging socio-economic development of the tribal population" (Padel and Das, 2004; Samal A: 9). Secondly, the law does not permit the state to acquire any scheduled land without the prior informed consent of the Gram Sabha. This too has been thrown to the winds with sheer arrogance (source: PESA- a reality check by Vidhya Das). Recently, some news in the national newspaper 'The Hindu' shows that there are lots of manipulations in the consent of Gram Sabha in the scheduled areas of southern Orissa, where the mining projects of Utkal Alumina, Aditya Alumina and Vedanta Alumina are going on (Das, 2004). However, some internet sources (info@agragamee.org) show that the approval of mining projects by Gram Sabha meeting of Lanjigada and Batelima village of Kashipur block, called by collector on June 28th 2002 is baseless. The Gram Sabhas manufactured by hiring people in truck loads from nearby townships and keeping the actual Gram Sabha members out with the help of an ever loyal police force.

The opening remark in the draft National Policy for Rehabilitation by the government of India that "with the advent of new economic policy, it is expected that there will be large scale investment, both on account of internal generations of capital and increased inflow of foreign investments, thereby creating an enhanced demand for land to be provided within a shorter time span in an increasingly competitive market ruled economic structure" (GOI, 1994) shows that government is more concerned about globalization rather than the struggle of the displaced person. Due to the displaced induced development policy of the government, natural resources and livelihood of tribals are in great danger. People depend upon the land, forest and other natural resources for their livelihoods have been dispossessed of their subsistence through land acquisition and displacement. Evidence shows that displacement from the large scale projects has virtually pushed the tribals to the object of poverty and hunger. As a result, the tribals and people in the scheduled areas are forced to migrate. There are numbers of examples on migration coming from tribal dominated districts. The report published in a local daily "The Sambad" dated 28th July 2003 on situation of Kalahandi by district officials bears testimony to this fact. There are 48 thousand people in state of hunger and unemployed youths are forced to migrate to the neighbouring states Andhra Pradesh and Chattisgarh for jobs and livelihoods. The state, instead of safeguarding the rights of the tribals, has been acting as an alley, protector or promoter of the private companies. This has been demonstrated in Kasipur block of Rayagada district and Lanjigarch of Kalahandi district. Profit making companies are provided with the entire ready-made infrastructure, government security, the administrative assistance, while the voice of the affected people is suppressed even by restoring to repression and brutal police action. The case of Maikanch (Kasipur block), which held on 26th December 2002 where police brutally gunned down three unarmed tribal people and injured many more is nothing more but state's repression on the tribal movement by defying all democratic norms. And this is only for the benefit of two corporate houses (Hindalco of India and Alcan of Canada) involved in Bauxite mining and processing (Sarangi, D. *et al*, 2005).

In the case of land alienation, which is considered to be of enormous significance in the case of tribals, the state has again made the procedures subservient to the powers already conformed by other legislations to various authorities such as the collectors and other existing laws. Though the state has given power to Gram Sabha for recommendation through Panchayat to prevent alienation of land in scheduled areas and to take appropriate action to restore any unlawfully alienated land of scheduled tribe. In real life, Gram Panchayat is taking decisions with higher authorities. No consultation with Gram Sabha is seen.

While as per the central PESA act, the power to plan and manage 'minor water bodies' exclusively vested with the Panchayat at appropriate level, the Orissa state Conformity Act has given this right to Zila Parishad. However, the first obstacle in this management is on the definition itself. No legal definition of minor water bodies exists in the statute books. And the state has left the matters undefined as well. The provision of national water policy and state water policies are at variance with PESA when it comes to the management of CPRs, particularly to the minor water bodies. The PESA is focused with regard to community's traditional and customary rights over CPRs and seeks empowerment of Gram Sabha to manage these, leaving water policies to the Panchayats. To this extent, the National Water Policies also entrust Panchayat with planning and management of minor water bodies. Since the term 'minor water bodies' remains vaguely undefined in the large body of laws governing water and water bodies, it created a scope for confusion at local level. The Pani Panchayat and Watershed Management Act enacted in the state where water users' associations and watershed committees have been formulated has no linkage with the local self-government units and more so in the scheduled areas.

PESA recognizes the forest and forest produces are critical components of livelihoods, and it makes radical provisions of grating ownership of minor forest produces (MFP) to the Gram Sabha in the scheduled areas. But again, the provision has been rendered ineffective by the state governments either by living ambiguity about which forest rights are to be exercised in or making the provision subservient to the JFM rules or other MFP rules and legislations, or completely ignoring the provision (as in the case of Madhya Pradesh). The analysis of state act in the context of MFP shows that, while devolving the power of MFP to Gram Sabha to Panchayat to different level, the government itself stands in a contradictory place. While has given the power of control and supervision in the hands of Gram Sabha, the executive that is the ownership right in the hand of Gram Panchayat

[Orissa Gram Panchayat (minor forest produce administration) Rules 2002]. This rule has also given right to Panchayat Samiti for fixation of price of MFP. Though the Gram Panchayat has ownership rights and the Gram Sabha has supervision right of MFP, none of them belong to the price fixing committee at Panchayat Samiti level. Whereas the representative of District Forest Officers (DFOs), Tribal Development Cooperation Committee (TDCC), Orissa Forest Development Committee (OFDC) and Tribal Cooperative Marketing Development are part of this committee. It shows that thought the law has given emphasis on self-governance, the bureaucratic dominance is still continuing. Just like the central PESA act, the Orissa act does not give a legal definition of MFP. In Orissa, *Kendu* leaves, *Sal* seeds, bamboo, have been nationalized. These are not included under MFP. These are being produced and managed by state. This is contrary to the common sense definition of MFP "which is that part of a tree that can be sustainable harvested without damage to the survival of the tree." More significantly, it denies access of bamboo to poor tribal artisans on which their livelihoods more critically depend. On the other hand, the state policies have subsidized bamboo for private industry. As some of the MFP in Orissa is managed by private traders, the tribals are getting very low compensations for their produces. The revised JFM guidelines do not even mention PESA indicating the low importance given to its provisions and their potential bearing on the JFM framework in 5th scheduled areas. PESA coexists with totally contrary legislations such as the land acquisition, wildlife protection, forest conservation and the Indian Forest (1927) Acts with no clarity about which is to prevail over others (Sarin *et al*, 2003). However, the conferral of the right of ownership of MFP on the community is significant. When the fruit belongs to a person, can some one else have are absolute right over the tree which produce that fruit? The answer is clear no. Thus, the absolute authority of the state on the forest area and the tree, which produces the so called minor items, is automatically circumscribed.

In Orissa, after giving the responsibility to Gram Sabha and Gram Panchayat, no efforts have been taken to educate the people to own, control and manage MFP. The real sprit of PESA has not been properly understood and internalized by the Gram Sabha. Even the government officials are not aware of PESA (Behura and Panigrahi, 2004). Matters concerning ownership and use of minor forest produces and preventing land alienation and restoring alienated land of a scheduled tribe, which has been entrusted to the Gram Panchayat, can be implemented until and unless the existing regulations like Orissa Forest Act (1972), Orissa Land Reform Act (1960) and Regulation 2 of 1956 regarding the transfer of immovable properties in scheduled areas are amended according to the new state acts.

In the context of role of Gram Sabha in resource management in Orissa, some of the studies have highlighted certain factors for which the Gram Sabha is not functioning as it would be. While Behura and Panigrahi's study in Kalahandi, Malkangiri and Kandhamal districts shows that lack of awareness, educational backwardness are the main causes of lack of participation (2004). Though the same kind of statement was also raised in the studies of Menon and Sinha (2003) in Keonjhar district, they emphasized on certain other factors. They said that, the long distances on foot to attend meeting due to lack of transport facilities, no prior information by the Sarpanch and Panchayat secretaries regarding the date of meeting and lack of knowledge regarding the role of Gram Sabha are the major factors in unsuccessful functions of Gram Sabha. However, a different kind of reason was shown in the studies of Vidhya Das (2004) in southern Orissa. He said that the manipulation of Gram Sabha's decision by higher authorities is the main cause of absence of members in the Gram Sabha meetings.

Conclusion

It is clear from the above analysis that the Gram Sabhas, which are the functional decision making units in the Central PESA Act (1996), have received a small space of deciding the various welfare schemes in the state of Orissa. Self-governance and consequently a vibrant people's democracy has become a dream for the tribals in the state. Most, if not all, development decisions for tribals are top-down, including the land to be given to the companies, leasing mines, managing water bodies etc. In most of the cases, the major portion of development resources are controlled by the Zila Parisad, and the Zila Parisad is controlled by the local MLAs and MPs, which means that the party in power controls the districts and blocks. Even, while in some cases the government has gone for giving wide ranging power to the people, they have not provided an enabling environment by changing the world archaic laws or the bureaucratic mindset and attitude that come in conflict with the new sets of laws under the PESA Act in the state. The enforcement of the general laws in the tribal areas has virtually eclipsed their rights on natural resources. While the Panchayat acts for the scheduled areas acknowledged the competence of tribal communities to manage the resources, the application of laws such as Land Acquisition Act, Forest Act, Land Reform Acts, etc. have been applied indiscriminately against the interest of tribals. This has made it difficult for Gram Sabhas or Panchayats to operate in an independent and autonomous manner creating conflicting situations in many cases.

Further, the introduction of New Economic Policy in the form of globalization, privatization and liberalization has made the situation more complex, which brought a lot of disasters in the natural resources in the tribal areas of Orissa by violating all the PESA and environmental acts.

However, it is too late for the state like Orissa to understand the significance of communities living close to natural resources upon which they depend. It is only a matter of time when the nation-state would come about in their approach to realize that for any effective governance and developmental activities including managing out natural resources, and establishment of industries, they have to integrate communities closest to natural resources by a total paradigm shift in their approach.

Suggestions

1. PESA should be implemented in true sprit.
2. Gram Sabha and Gram Panchayat should be endowed with powers for implementation of development and

socio-economic activities.

3. To mobilize tribal people and create awareness among them about their rights, duties and responsibilities, sensitization campaigning and regular training programmes are registered and in this context local NGOs should be involved by giving some financial assistance from the government.
4. The rights on land, forest, and water should be given to the tribal people so that they may administer these resources judicially through Gram Sabha.
5. In accordance with the State Conformity Act (1997) in the scheduled areas, it is necessary that all regulations, acts and laws operating in scheduled areas such as land alienations, joint forest management, watershed management and forest acts, etc. be suitably amended within stipulated time.
6. The MFP should be defined properly.
7. The Kendu leaves and bamboo should be included under MFP.
8. The minor water body should be defined properly.
9. It has to be clear as to when the Gram Panchayat needs to consult Gram Sabha.
10. Gram Sabha should be given power to prevent land alienation and restoring the alienated lands. For this, suitable provision should be made in PESA act.
11. There should be a federal law system and not a centralized law because each tribal community has distinct tradition and culture. Acts should be properly amended to safeguard their customs and traditions.
12. In order to save the poor tribals from the clutch of globalization, the government should change its attitude. It should be more tribal friendly rather than friendly to the multi-national companies.

REFERENCES

Behura, N.K. and N. Panigrahi, 2004, Status of Panchayat Raj Institutions in the Scheduled Areas of Orissa:An Empirical Study, *Man in India*,Vol. 84(3&4), pp. 179-96.

Bordi and M.S. Bolkil, 2002, Tribal communities and sustainable Livelihoods: Lessons from Tamil Nadu, *Journal of Rural Development*, Vol. 21 (2), pp. 163-86.

Das, V., PESA-A Reality check, *http://www.agragamee.org/newinitiatives_pesa.htm*

Das, P., 25.04.2005, Call for Review of Alumina Projects in Orissa, *The Hindu*.

Fernandes, W., 1992, *National Development and Tribal Deprivation*, New Delhi: Indian Social Institute.

Gadgil, M. and R. Guha, 1992, *The Fissured Land*, New Delhi: Oxford University Press.

Menon, P.S.K. AND B.D. Sinha, 2003, *Panchayat Raj in Scheduled Areas: A Critical Study*, Concept Publishing Company, New Delhi.

Menon, M., 20.04.2005, The Battle for Bauxite in Orissa, *The Hindu*.

Mohanty, B, 2005, Displacement and Rehabilitation of Tribals, *Economic and Political Weekly*, Vol.XL, No. 13, pp. 1318-1320.

Mohanty, P.K., 2000, Development of Scheduled Castes and Scheduled Tribes in Independent India: Leads and Lags, *Journal of Rural Development*, Vol. 19 (4), pp. 535-572.

Ostrom, E. (1990), *Governing the Commons*, Cambridge University Press, Cambridge, New York.

Rasmussen, L.N. and R.M. Dick, 1995, Local Organizations for Natural Resource Management: Lessons from Theoretical AND Empirical literature, *EPTD Discussion Paper No. 11*, International Food Policy Research Institute, Wasinton, U.S.A.

Rao, P.V., 2001, Reflections on Tribal Development, *Journal of Rural Development*, and Vol. 20 (1), pp. 87-97.

Samal, A., Institutional Reforms for Decentralized Governance and the Politics of Control and Management of Local Natural Resources: A Study in the Scheduled Areas of India. *http://dlc.dlib.indiana.edu/archive/00001084/00/Avinish_Samal.pdf*.

Sharma, B.D., 1999, *A Letter to the President*, Sahyog Pustak Kuteer, New Delhi.

Sharma, B.D., 1997, *Tide Turned*, Sahyog Pustak Kuteer, New Delhi.

Sarin, M., N.M. Singh, N. Sundar and R.K. Bhogal, 2003, *Devolution as threat to democratic decision-making in forestry ?Findings from three states in India*, ODI Working paper no. 197, Overseas Development Instutute, London.

Sarangi *et al*, 2005, State Repression in Kashipur, *Economic and Political Weekly*, Vol. XL, No. 13, pp. 1312-1314.

Upadhyay, S., 2004, *Tribal Self-rule Law and Common Resources in Scheduled Areas of India: A new paradigm shift or another ineffective sop*, Paper presented at "The Commons in an Age of Global Transition: Challenges, Risks and Opportunities; 10th Biennial Conference of IASCP", Organised by Association for the Study of Common Property at Oaxacs, Mexico, during August 9-13.

Verma, R.C., 1995, *Indian Tribes through the Ages*, Ministry of Information and Broadcasting, New Delhi.

Wade, Robert *et al* (1988), "The Management of Irrigation System: How to Evoke Trust and Avoid Prisoner's Dilemma", *World Development*, Vol. 16 (4), pp. 489-500.

An Apple to Civil Society, *http://www.agragamee.org/newinitiatives_pesa.htm*

14

DEMOCRATIZATION WITH INCLUSION: REPRESENTATION AND EMPOWERMENT OF SCHEDULED TRIBES THROUGH PANCHAYATS

SATYAPRIYA ROUT & PRATYUSNA PATNAIK

I

Democracy, Decentralisation and Inclusion

In recent years, many states in the developing world have reconsidered their projects of democratic governance, and have brought up political reforms, favouring increased inclusion, participation, and empowerment. Democratic decentralisation, therefore, has emerged as the process of reforming the existing democratic governance systems, which promises devolution of power to the people and a more accountable form of government. This ongoing process of political reform has made it clear that democracy, by itself, does not automatically benefit the poor, the under-privileged, the disadvantaged and weaker sections of society—and/or the group/s, which have long faced social, economic and political exclusion.

Such realisation about failure of democracy, partial or otherwise, is related to the recognition that poverty and powerlessness are same sides of the coin, and poverty is not just an economic phenomenon implying low income and scarcity of material assets. The non-economic manifestations of poverty have increasingly become public with current emphasis on socio-political aspects of development, including educational attainment, health status, living patterns, capacity to raise voice and representational status of under-developed groups. It has now been acknowledged that economic conditions intrinsic to poverty has also a social face in terms of low education and healthcare, as well as a political face manifesting lack of voice, power and representation. Poor people along with suffering from problems like illiteracy, malnutrition and disease, also face many other socio-political disadvantages that impede their ability to share in the benefits of democratisation (Manor, 2004). People with less income also tend to be less organised, less capable of articulating their interest and gain benefits from political and policy process, and less powerful to influence public policies that affect their lives.

The inability of the poor, underprivileged, backward and weaker sections of society to involve themselves with the democratic political and policy processes, and gain benefits that democracy provides often originates because of the very nature of democracy that is in practice in most countries of the world, i.e. the liberal representative model of democracy. The modern meaning of the term democracy tends to emphasise its procedural aspect like periodic elections to choose representatives to take decisions on behalf of the common citizens. A historical trajectory of the term, however, may suggest otherwise. As a form of government, democracy has had a different and more challenging meaning than it has lately acquired. Until the nineteenth century, by democracy what was understood is what we now tendentiously call direct or popular democracy, as was in vogue in ancient Athens in Greece (Arblaster, 1999).

In contrast to the Athenian model of direct or popular democracy, which emphasised on the direct and active participation of all citizens, and on their political equality, the liberal representative model emphasised political contestation, and rational decisions through democratically chosen institutions of periodic elections. Parallel to the distinction between popular or participatory democracy and liberal representative democracy, Luckham *et al.* (2000) make a distinction, between democratic politics and democratic institutions. While notions like popular participation, equality and emancipation are part of the realm of 'democratic politics', 'democratic institutions' encompass methods and procedures of legitimating rules and assuring political contestations through free and fair elections. Democratic politics, based upon a culture of participation, are therefore, broader than the methods and procedures of political contestations, which form the crux of liberal representative democracy.

The modern liberal representative model of democracy tends to lay greater emphasis upon the procedural aspect of democracy rather than the substantive aspect. It also tends to concentrate more on the consolidation of democratic institutions, than on the spread of democratic politics. Such procedural democracy in the broader framework of liberal representative model, most frequently, has ignored the political struggles of marginalised groups, including poor, women, and other excluded categories, to gain a voice in the matters of decision making. The neglect of democratic politics by liberal representative democracy, therefore, has paved the way for further democratic reforms or 'democratisation of democracy' (see, Castaneda, 1994). In the absence of these reforms to incorporate democratic politics into the mainstream liberal political institutions, representative democracy becomes redundant, with little scope for disadvantaged and excluded categories of society to gain any benefit out of it.

A growing understanding of these problems calls for immediate action to address them in a right way. Policy makers, academicians, researchers and development practitioners alike have realised that poor and other excluded sections of society like Scheduled Castes, Scheduled Tribes and women have great developmental needs, but their needs by itself do not imply the awareness and the ability to take collective action in an increasingly democratised system (see Coelho *et al* 2002). Democratisation with progressive inclusion of the hitherto excluded sections of society through decentralisation reforms, therefore, has emerged as a new governance paradigm to address the drawbacks of liberal representative democracy, and the persisting problems of exclusion, poverty and powerlessness. Just as the earlier discussions on development recognised the need for growth with redistribution, the current problems and priorities come to see the need for democratisation with inclusion (Manor, 2004).

Recognising the need for greater democratisation and progressive inclusion, many governments carried out political reforms ensuring decentralisation to promote empowerment and inclusion. In its attempts for democratisation, the Indian state enacted the 73rd Constitutional Amendment Act in 1993, making provisions for devolution of power to the local levels, and gave a constitutional status to the panchayats. The new decentralisation efforts were coupled with inclusive policies of reservation of seats for weaker sections such as Scheduled Castes, Scheduled Tribes and women. This opened a new chapter in the history of democratic decentralisation in India, which gave an opportunity to the hitherto excluded categories to raise their voice, and in turn, include themselves in making of decisions that affect their lives.

In the backdrop of above discussion, the present paper focuses on the issues of inclusion and empowerment of Scheduled Tribes in the democratic local governments or Gram Panchayats. It perceives inclusion as a process and tries to explore the potentials of the decentralisation policies for such inclusion. The objective of the paper is to examine the process of inclusion and empowerment of Scheduled Tribes through decentralised governance. The empirical work for the paper has been carried out in *Saptasajya* gram panchayat of Dhenkanal district in Orissa. The panchayat was chosen for detailed analysis with the criterion that the post of president of the panchayat should be reserved for Scheduled Tribe. Case study method followed by group discussions and personal interview with key informants were adopted to elicit relevant data for the purpose of research. Including the president and vice-president, Saptasajya gram panchayat comprised 14 elected representatives, out of which 7 members belonged to Scheduled Tribes.

The paper is divided into four sections. Following this introduction, which posed the background for the paper and discussed the objectives and methodology of research, the second section engages itself with a conceptual discussion of exclusion, inclusion and empowerment. The third section explains the case study and analyses representation, participation and empowerment of scheduled tribes in the chosen panchayat. The fourth section highlights the pitfalls of the decentralised governance in ensuring inclusion and empowerment, and puts forth some of the suggestive measures for transforming symbolic inclusion to meaningful representation. The paper concludes by way of emphasising the potentials of decentralised system for inclusion and empowerment.

II

Conceptualising Inclusion and Empowerment

Possibilities of achieving social justice and social cohesion in a world subject to chronic and apparently irresistible forces of inequality and exploitation are central to the contemporary social and political agenda of inclusion. Any discussions for conceptualising 'inclusion' should, therefore, throw some light on the contexts, process and practices that generate conditions of exclusion. It is, thus, appropriate to begin with a brief analysis of the concept of 'social exclusion' as it appears in social science literature.

Social exclusion is one of the relatively recent concepts used in social science literature, which was first used in France and then moved to other parts of Europe. René Lenoir (1974), who looked after the social affairs of the French Government, is given the credit for authoring the term (see Sen, 2000). Use of the term became popular in Europe in the wake of prolonged and large scale employment difficulties, which gave rise to criticism of the welfare systems for failing to prevent poverty, and for hindering economic development (Loury, 1999). Scholars using the concept of social exclusion intend towards dissolution of social cohesion, denial of equal rights and protections to all sections of population, and link the idea of exclusion with conventional ideas of inequality, deprivation, etc. Poverty and unemployment, and the other forms of inequality and deprivation that accrue from these two fundamental problems have been the major concern of social exclusion scholars (see e.g. Bhalla and Lapeyre, 1997;

De Hann, 1998; Sen, 1997; Silver, 1994). Although the theory and concept originated in developed countries, increasing attention has been paid to the possible relevance of the concept of social exclusion to social policy analysis in developing countries (see IILS, 1997 and IDS, 1998).

Analyzing the concept of social exclusion in the context of low and middle income countries, the recent IILS (1997) work referred to: *a)* problematic groups, including beggars, rural landless, asset-poor, unemployed, retrenched women workers, and ethnic minorities; *b)* problematic conditions, such as poverty, unemployment, ghettoisation, family breakdown and isolation; and *c)* problematic social, economic and political processes. Such an analysis of social exclusion captures important dimensions of experiences of certain groups, who are in the process set apart or excluded from participation in social life of a country.

In many occasions, social exclusion is a product of institutional failure. Kabeer (2000) mentions that disadvantages result in social exclusion when various institutional mechanisms through which resources are allotted and value assigned operate in such a way as to systematically deny particular groups the resources and recognitions that would allow them to participate fully in social life. Different institutional mechanisms of society, including the political institution of state, often generate, perpetuate and reproduce different sources of inequality, which generate various forms of exclusion in society. Institutions, which guide human behaviour and assigns rules of membership and access, produce exclusion, at the first instance, by designating some as non-members, to whom access to resources and recognition are denied.

The central issue, to the analysis of causes, characteristics and possible remedies for social exclusion, pertains to the context within which exclusion is generated. Kabeer (2000) attempts a systematic review of some of the relevant literature pertaining to the concept, and distinguishes three categories of practices that generate patterns of inclusion and exclusion in society. The first one is termed as 'mobilisation of institutional bias', which refers to 'a predominant set of values, beliefs and institutional procedures that operate systematically and consistently to the benefit of certain persons and groups at the expense of others' (see, Lukes, 1974). Many of our social institutions and normative practices function in such a way that it favours certain sections of society, and in turn, excluding the rest. Marginalized groups such as women and *dalits* are in most occasions subject to exclusion because of institutional bias. The second category of practices which functions as exclusionary mechanism is that of 'social closure', through which 'social collectivities seek to maximize rewards by restricting access to resources and opportunities to a limited circle of eligibles' (see also, Parkin, 1979). Social closure is a deliberate strategy of exclusion, where resources and opportunities—mainly economic—are monopolised by privileged sections of society, and denied to the underprivileged. The third category of practices, Kabeer mentions, that generate exclusion is that of 'unruly practices', which refer to 'the gap between rules and their implementation occurring in practice in most institutional domains' (see also, Fraser, 1989; Gore, 1993). The public provisioning of services are mostly subject to this unruly practices, and thus, the poor and marginalized sections of society remain far away from accruing the benefits which are even meant for them.

The project of inclusion—a possible remedy for exclusionary practices—should be based upon a through understanding of the context of exclusion, and thus, different inclusionary projects may be formulated depending upon the context of exclusion. In this regard, Fraser's (1997) analysis of various forms of injustice offers a useful framework to understand the concept of social exclusion, and the responses that they offer for the project of inclusion. Fraser's framework provides a conceptual spectrum stretching from primarily economic forms of injustice at one end to primarily cultural forms of injustice at the other. Explaining Fraser's analysis of ranges of injustice, Kabeer (2000) adds that, primarily economic forms of injustice deal with exploitation, marginalization and deprivation, where exploitation is originated from appropriation of the fruits of one's labour, marginalization from exclusion from the means of livelihood or confinement to poorly-paid, undesirable forms of work; and deprivation from being denied an adequate standard of living. Similarly, at the cultural end of the spectrum are forms of injustice stemming from social patterns of representation, interpretation and communication. These forms of injustice are manifested in the ways in which the dominant groups impose dominant values and ideologies, systematically devalue and disparage certain categories of people, and routinely reduce the chance of these categories to participate in public space.

Notwithstanding the positioning of the primarily economic forms and primarily cultural forms as two poles of injustice, the distinctions made between them depict just an analytical construct, rather than being real. Not only these two forms tend to be inter-related and sometimes inseparable, at occasions one generates the other, or, in turn, is generated by the other. Acknowledging this, Fraser (1997) adds that somewhere between primarily economic and primarily cultural forms of injustice, lie certain hybrid forms of injustice, which he terms as 'bivalent collectivities'. These include groups for whom economic injustice is combined with cultural injustice. Gender, ethnicity, race, caste are forms of inequality, which may be included in the bivalent collectivities, where economic injustice encompass to elements of injustice, that stem from the dominant values and ideologies of a society.

These different forms of injustice generating exclusion in society, as mentioned by Fraser, have their own strategic responses for the project of inclusion. Where exclusion occurs due to primarily economic forms of injustice, the project of inclusion should be based upon mobilisation of interests of the disadvantaged groups, and should formulate them in terms of 'redistribution'. Similarly, where exclusion generates due to primarily cultural forms of injustice, policies of inclusion should revolve around question of 'identity', and should formulate the demands of excluded in terms of 'recognition'. However, where exclusion is hybrid, attempts towards inclusion should encompass material interests and questions of identity, and inclusionary policies, therefore, should include politics of redistribution as well as recognition (Kabeer, 2000).

Arguing in a similar tone, for having a deeper understanding of the contexts of exclusion before designing inclusionary policies, Ruth Levitas (1998) mentions that fundamentally different inclusionary projects are embedded in different discourses of exclusion. Levitas (1998) further identifies three different approaches to inclusion, which are related to three distinctive discourses of exclusion. The first one is that of 'Redistributionist Approach', which revolves around practices of exclusion originating out of poverty and other socially generated inequalities of access to power and resources. The second approach to inclusion-exclusion is a 'Moral Underclass Discourse', which identifies the causes of exclusion with the moral and cultural characteristics of those who are excluded—the so-called global underclass. The moral underclass discourse of Levitas is quite similar to Fraser (1997) category of exclusion, which originates out of primarily cultural forms of injustice. This approach demands inclusionary policies valorizing paid work (as opposed to unpaid/underpaid labour) and welfare benefits for the excluded. The third approach that Levitas (1998) identifies is that of 'Social Integrationist Discourse', which prioritises economic efficiency and social cohesion, and tries to link both.

Having discussed the various approaches to the project of inclusion—the apparent possible remedy for the problem of exclusion—we may now proceed further to emphasise upon the political context of the project of inclusion. Stewart (2000) identifies two issues as centrally important in considering the political context of inclusion: the question of state power and the question of difference. The inclusionary projects, which continue to see general socio-economic inequality as of central relevance to build upon any inclusionary possibilities and thus, argue for 'redistributionist strategies' require an organised state power for implementation of such strategies. Further, those demanding welfare benefits for the excluded also share similar requirement of an organised state power. Therefore, equal citizenship rights, in the form of equal rights to vote and associate with the state, are often regarded as central inclusionary practices followed by a progressive state.

However, there are several limitations to sole emphasis on organized state power and redistributionist approaches for addressing the problems posed by social exclusion. The equal citizenship rights, in many occasions, remain far from being realized owing to the gross inequality and difference that groups within a democracy share among themselves. Equal voting and representation rights to groups which are well organized and empowered mean quite different from assigning the same rights to marginalized and disempowered groups. Owing to their differential historical experiences, these two groups may derive different benefits even from the same rights offered by state. We, therefore, should insist that inclusion is not necessarily a matter of an adequate and equal share in resources, but fundamentally of equality of participation in the determination of both individual and collective life chances (Stewart, 2000). The limitations of organized state power and redistributionist approach, thus, point out to the second political context of project of inclusion, i.e. 'the politics of difference'.

Perhaps the most visible proposals for democratic inclusion indicate towards the politics of difference as the context for the project of inclusion. Where as the politics of redistribution expresses a universalism of structural inequalities, politics of difference highlight that 'people are different from one another in fundamental ways, and to treat them as similar—i.e. by granting them all the same political rights and access to politics—effectively extinguishes any political manifestation of difference (see Young, 1989, 1990). These groups of scholars—or 'difference democrats' as they are called by John Dryzek (1996)—who emphasise the politics of difference, believe that 'universality erases everything that is particular, different and valuable in the experience and identity of the oppressed' (Dryzek, 1996: 476). Difference democrats, therefore, often suggest measures for setting aside quotas of seats in parliaments for particular category of groups in their proposal of inclusion.

Including people in the realm of government has been integral to democracy since long, and has been much emphasised by American pluralists like David Truman (1951) and Robert Dahl (1956). However, there exists a clear distinction between these plural democrats and those of difference democrats in their approach towards inclusion within the framework of a democratic state. Dryzek rightly points out that '...where as US pluralism is passively inclusive in its pattern of representation in that it is prepared to accept whatever constellation of groups emerge from society to enter into politics, difference democrats are more attuned to the need for actively inclusive representation, in which efforts are made to promote the ability of the groups to recognize an interest and pursue it in politics' (1996: 477).

Difference democrats, therefore, point out the main challenge before the project of inclusion, i.e. recognizing an interest and pursuing it through a political manner. In most occasions, the marginalized and excluded sections of society, due to their historical experience of exploitation and submissiveness, lack the awareness and ability to recognize what really constitute their interests. Such inability and lack of awareness often replicates exclusion in an otherwise inclusive state, which provides equal rights, both of voting and representation, to all the citizens.

Difference democrats believe that desirable patterns of interest organisation and representation, amongst the excluded groups, do not arise automatically; and therefore, urge that 'the state should play an active role in sponsoring and certifying groups, removing obstacles to their exercising political influence, and creating channels for that influence to be felt in government' (Cohen and Rogers, 1992: 426). Arguing in a similar manner, Young (1992) demands the state to 'promote self-organisation of members of oppressed groups where such organisation is week, or to provide greater resources to existing associations representing oppressed or disadvantaged groups, and to create compensatory political forms to ensure that such groups have an equal voice in agenda setting and policy formation' (Young, 1992: 532).

We may now summarise that the project of (political) inclusion is perceived as a befitting response to the problems of poverty, powerlessness and oppression, which are usually by-products of social and political exclusion. In a context, where inclusion is in the top of political agenda in most of developing nations, democratization through the politics of decentralisation promises progressive recognition and inclusion of different groups in the state. Such inclusion, however, do not limits itself to the state politics, rather, they exhibit in a more prominent and visible manner in the political life of society. Because in many occasions pressure and demands for democratization and inclusion has originated from outside the framework of state – i.e. in civil society (see, Dryzek, 1996). Therefore, civil society, in any form, has a significant role to play in the whole process of inclusion. Inclusion, thus, doesn't only entail a notion of association with the dominant imperatives of state politics; it also portrays the notions of empowerment, self-realisation, expressing voice, representation, etc.

III

Inclusion, Representation and Participation in the Panchayat: *Unfolding the Case Study*

Democracy, as mentioned in the previous section, has always been a project of inclusion, albeit its limited scope for such a process. However, the recent reforms introducing decentralisation has enlarged the scope of democracy to emerge as a real inclusive form of governance. Despite several attempts for decentralisation since independence in our country, the project of inclusion has not been in the state agenda before the 73rd Amendment to the Constitution in 1993. The 73rd Amendment is crucial from the perspective of inclusion on two counts: first, it devolved power to the people at the grassroots and institutionalized the local governance system; and second, it ensured inclusion of hitherto excluded sections of society by creating provisions for reservation of seats for SCs, STs and women in local bodies, i.e. panchayats. In accordance with the provision of the amendment, while Article 243G of the Constitution empowered the State Legislatures to endow the panchayats with such powers and authority as may be necessary to enable them to function as institutions of self-government; Article 243D made provisions for reservation for Scheduled Castes, Scheduled Tribes and women, and gave an opportunity to the hitherto neglected sections of society to raise their voice and, in turn, be a part of the decision making process.

It is worth mentioning here that the reforms amending the constitution, attempted to fulfil the limitations of democracy, by way of devolving power and resources to the local level, and creating an institutionalised structure for practising inclusion. Attempts for inclusion will have limited success, as it has been the case within the framework of democracy, without devolving sufficient power and resources to the people or the social categories, which the state intends to include. The following paragraphs in this section explore the possibilities of inclusion of Scheduled Tribes, by way of analysing a case of representation and participation of Scheduled Tribes in one Gram Panchayat (*Saptasajya Gram Panchayat*) in Dhenkanal District of Orissa.

Saptasajya Gram Panchayat: Location and Structure

Saptasajya Gram Panchayat is situated towards the south-west of Dhenkanal town at a distance of nearly 30 kilometers. A narrow *pakka* road links Saptasajya village with the Dhenkanal town. Known for its scenic beauty, Saptasajya finds a place in the tourist map of Orissa. Saptasajya—the bed (valley) of seven mountains —is home to a beautiful waterfall, which attracts several tourists to the locality.

Saptasajya panchayat consists of six villages, out of which one is uninhabited. Politically as well as demographically, Patrabhaga, Saptasajya and Padmalavpur are the three important villages of the panchayat. Saptasajya has comparatively a higher concentration of Scheduled Tribes, who constitute nearly 37 per cent of the total population of the village (see Table 1). Scheduled Castes constitute only 8 per cent of the total population of Saptasajya panchayat. The concentration of Scheduled Tribe was the highest in Kamining village, which accounted for nearly 53 per cent of the total population of the village. All the villages are multi caste villages with the inclusion of Scheduled Tribes. The villages in this panchayat, except Saptasajya, are not well connected to the main road. There are a few petite grocery shops and tea shops on the main road that connected to these villages of the panchayat.

Table 1. Population Division of Saptasajya Panchayat

Name of the Villages	*Scheduled Caste*	*Scheduled Tribe*	*General*	*Total*
Patrabhaga	209	763	1045	2017
Padmalavpur	43	279	455	777
Saptasajya	2	237	387	626
Kamining	13	185	153	351
Baradapali	55	25	102	182
Jorabati	-	-	-	-
Total	322	1489	2142	3953

Source: (Census of India, 1991), District Panchayat Office, Dhenkanal.

The president's post of the Saptasajya Gram Panchayat was reserved for the Scheduled Tribe category. The Panchayat president (*sarpanch*) was a retired school teacher from Saptasajya village, and was not active in politics. When the seat was reserved for ST, he was requested by his fellow community members and local elites from the panchayat to contest the election. Local elites had a profound influence on the working of this Panchayat. The Naib-Sarpanch was from Patrabhaga village, whose husband was a party worker of the Biju Janata Dal (BJD). Both Patrabhaga and Padmalavpur had influential persons, controlling the functioning of the Saptasajya panchayat. In Padmalavpur, we observed, several members of the traditional elites, who possessed substantial land, and had a greater say in matters concerning panchayat.

The Saptasajya panchayat consisted of 14 elected representatives including the president and the vice president (Naib-sarpanch), out of which 11 seats were reserved for various marginalised categories. One of the major reasons for selecting this panchayat was that out of the 14 seats, six (43 %) were reserved for Scheduled Tribe communities. The following table depicts the reservation pattern of the Saptasajya panchayat.

Table 2. Reservation Pattern of Saptasajya Panchayat

Constituency	*Saptasajya*
Unreserved	3
Res (Women)	-

Res (Scheduled Castes)	
Res (Scheduled Tribes)	4
Res (Scheduled Caste Women)	1
Res (Backward Class Citizens)	2
Res (Scheduled Tribe Women)	2
Res (Backward Class Citizen Women)	2
Total	14

Saptasajya panchayat consisted of a large number (50 %) of Scheduled Tribes and Scheduled Castes representatives: thanks to the reservation policy of 73rd Amendment to the Indian Constitution, which ensured their representation in local bodies. The 3 unreserved constituencies in Saptasajya panchayat were occupied by representatives belonging to the upper castes of society. Thus, it was only due to the affirmative action policy, that inclusion of Scheduled Tribes was made possible in local governance and decision-making. The landholding pattern of the panchayat representatives was perfect reflection of their social status. Majority of the representatives, being from ST and SC categories, were either landless, or had minimal acres of land. All the Scheduled Tribe representatives, except one were landless. The president of the panchayat was the only landed ST representative, who possessed less than 2.5 acres of land.

Participation and Representation in Saptasajya Panchayat

The affirmative action policies of the 73rd Amendment to the Indian Constitution has enabled the Scheduled Tribes to ensure their inclusion in rural political institutions, who otherwise are excluded from the rural public sphere including political. However, inclusion in the rural political institutions and increased presence in terms of number do not automatically guarantee empowerment of these communities. Whether this political inclusion has been resulted in successful representation—through participation of elected members in the functioning of the panchayat—forms the point of departure for the present piece of research.

The participation of the representatives, more particularly those belonging to Scheduled Tribes, in the Saptasajya panchayat was assessed by examining the way in which they acted in regular panchayat activities. The participation in panchayat activities was gauged by looking into factors such as attendance in regular gram panchayat meetings; participation in setting the agenda, which involved identifying issues and problems of the constituencies, raising them in panchayat meetings and participating in the discussions; and finally their involvement in the decision making process, such as taking decisions in planning, budgeting, location of developmental projects, and selection of beneficiaries in the panchayat.

Attendance in Gram Panchayat Meetings

Attendance of elected representatives in regular gram panchayat meetings was found to be very low in the Saptasajya panchayat. Almost all the Scheduled Tribe representatives, except the panchayat president, did not attend the meetings regularly. Panchayat meetings were reduced to informal gatherings of the president, one or two representatives belonging to the upper castes and the locally influential persons, who were observed to play an active and decisive role in panchayat related matters. Even though the representatives stated that they were irregular in attending panchayat meetings, the panchayat records, however, showed regular attendance of elected representatives. On further enquiry, it was found that participation in the panchayats has been minimised to signing the registers, which was done at home, when the registers were carried to the houses of representatives to collect their signatures, or otherwise the representatives were asked to come to the president's residence to sign the register. Such an observation from the present study is corroborated with similar findings from Northern India by Lieten (1996), who confirms from his study in Western Uttar Pradesh that the *pradhan* usually sends the documents for signature or thumb impression to the elected members' houses, who apparently never physically attend the meetings.

Along with Scheduled Tribes, the women representatives also opined that they remained irregular in attending Gram Panchayat meetings, making the panchayat meetings an overwhelmingly male-dominated event, albeit policies targeting towards empowering women by giving them one-third representation. The limited attendance of elected representatives was found to be associated with the ambiguous nature of the meetings themselves. In most occasions panchayat meetings were formalities to be completed, and marked only in records without their actual occurrences. Such an observation can be substantiated by the fact that the meetings were most often called without prior and adequate notice. Often, proxy meetings were held and the proceedings were recorded even without the knowledge of those who apparently attended them. However, these proceedings were endorsed by all the members with their signature, including those who were absent from the meetings.

Participation in Setting the Agenda

Identifying issues of the locality, raising specific problems in the meetings and discussing them are some of the important activities in the functioning of the panchayats. Social divisions in terms of caste, category and gender decisively influenced representatives' performance in these activities. The Scheduled Tribe representatives of Saptasajya Gram Panchayat occasionally raised the problems of their localities. Only the panchayat president was observed to be comparatively vocal from among the ST representatives.

In order to gauge the capacity of the representatives in raising issues, the respondents were asked about the manner in which they raised issues in the panchayat meetings. The capacity to raise issues in the panchayat meetings was low among those belonging to marginalised groups, such as Scheduled Tribes, women, and Scheduled Castes. These members, in a majority of the cases, did not raise any question of their locality themselves; instead they sought the help of other members to do so. Some of these members preferred to discuss their constituencies' problems with the president and/or other politically influential persons of the panchayat after the meetings, and outside the panchayat office. The representatives belonging to disadvantaged groups could not discuss issues of their constituency in the panchayat meetings. Rather, the discussions during the meetings were observed to be communication between president, husband of the vice-president and other politically influential persons of the panchayat, without active involvement of representatives.

Low attendance in panchayat meetings and limited capacity to raise issues often came in the way of discussing the problems of the panchayat, and in turn, in the process of decision making. Simply sitting and listening to the proceedings of the meetings and nodding their heads have been the form of participation for most Scheduled Tribe representatives. Active participation, which means initiating and being involved in the discussions in the meetings was found to be very rare in Saptasajya Gram Panchayat.

Participation in Decision Making

We identified several areas of participation in panchayat decision-making activities, and the respondents were asked to indicate how they participated in those identified areas. The participation of ST representatives was found to be very low in important decision making activities like 'where should a developmental project be located', 'whom to give benefits from a developmental programme' and 'whom to give contracts'. Only a few influential panchayat members took active role in making important decisions in the panchayats. Others were just asked to put their signatures once the decisions were taken. It was observed that Scheduled Tribe representatives knew some of the key terms like 'planning', 'budgeting', 'developmental work', etc. without knowing anything else, or the importance of these activities in the functioning of the Panchayats.

The influence of local elites and other political leaders from outside the institutional structure of panchayat was observed to be very much explicit in Saptasajya Gram Panchayat. Being a member of tribal groups, the sarpanch could not exert much influence in panchayat matters. It was observed that the local elites were taking decisions on behalf of the sarpanch, reducing his position to just a rubber stamp.

Factors Contributing to the Limited Participation in Panchayat

Several factors contributed towards low attendance of Scheduled Tribe members in panchayats meetings as well as low participation in the panchayat decision making process. Among other factors, economic compulsions, socio-historical experience of oppression and powerlessness, social disabilities and household work were found to be major reasons for irregular attendance and limited participation in panchayat meetings.

Economic compulsion was reported as one of the major cause of low participation in panchayat activities. Much of the Scheduled Tribe representatives were landless, and the main source of income for them was manual or daily labour. Attendance in gram panchayat meetings, in such a situation, often came in the way of their livelihood. Respondents were very straightforward in this regard and stated that they cannot afford to miss a day's income, and hence regular attendance becomes difficult if not impossible.

The historical experiences of powerlessness and social closure were more than enough to be overcome so easily through a mere visibility in panchayat by dint of reservation policy. The Scheduled Tribes, and more so the women representatives of these communities, who had been excluded from village public sphere in most part, found it difficult to exert their position as representatives. Their political identity as representatives of the panchayat was in many occasions not compatible with their social and economic identity as members of marginalised, facing several social disabilities. The political identity as panchayat members, which was based on the principles of egalitarianism and equality, was in direct conflict with their social identity, which has its origin in social inequality and a hierarchical social order.

The women representatives belonging to the Scheduled Tribe community were twice marginalised, in the sense that they had to face the limitations of being Scheduled Tribes as well as being women. Household work and distance of the Gram Panchayat office were found to be the other reasons for the low participation of these representatives. In all the cases, women representatives in general, hardly got any time for panchayat activities after fulfilling their household responsibilities of cooking and child rearing. This made it difficult to attend panchayat meetings, which could take several hours, especially if they were taking place in another village. It is a well known fact that women have to shoulder greater responsibilities than men in bringing up children and looking after household work. Therefore, active participation by women in panchayat matters meant that a perfect balance has to be maintained between the dual roles of women, i.e. their private roles as housewife and the public roles as panchayat members. Women representatives belonging to all castes stated that negligence in fulfilling their private role as housewives may have adverse consequences in family ties.

Besides these specific factors, several common factors like illiteracy, lack of awareness, having less interest in panchayat related matters and village politics, also acted as bottle-necks to effective participation of Scheduled Tribe elected representatives in panchayat related matters.

IV

Beyond Symbolic Representation: ...*Making Inclusion Work*

The above analysis of participation of elected representatives in one of the gram panchayats of Orissa – described in somewhat unenthusiastic manner – reveals that ensured inclusion and visibility in rural political institutions through policies of affirmative action could not help the Scheduled Tribe representatives to perform as better representatives of their constituencies. Representation and participation are closely linked concepts in panchayats, where once elected as representatives, the members are expected participate in the functioning of the panchayats, and in turn, assert their position in the panchayats. Participation of elected representatives in panchayats can, therefore, be stated as a manifestation of representation, which gives them scope to make their position as representatives explicit and obvious (see also, Inbanathan, 2001). However, our observation from the case study of one panchayats in Orissa point towards the fact that limited participation in panchayats related activities impeded the process of representation of Scheduled Tribe representatives.

Such an observation raises a question as to why inclusion through state intervention failed to work in the context of rural political institutions. Before attempting to answer such a question, it is apt to highlight the contexts and processes which propagated exclusion of these categories. The exclusion of Scheduled Tribes from mainstream of rural political arena can be analysed adhering to Kabeer's (2000) framework of 'institutional failure'. The functioning of the state and the development practices followed by the state since independence has operated systematically and consistently to the benefit of certain section of society at the expenses of Scheduled Tribes. The exclusion of Scheduled Tribes as a result of 'institutional bias' has always juxtaposed with 'social closure', which restricts the access of these communities to that of the rural public sphere. What could have been more to depict social closure of these communities, than what we observed from our case, in terms of specific seating arrangements of members in gram panchayat meetings and other social gatherings. During the course of inquiry, we observed that seating patterns in panchayat meetings and/ or any other social gatherings are determined by social divisions in terms of caste, category or gender. The Scheduled Tribe representatives were seen to cling to each other, and the other higher caste members visibly maintained a distance—a distance which was both spatial as well as social. Finally, exclusion of Scheduled Tribes in rural political institutions in particular and rural society in general could be analysed in terms of 'unruly practices', where exclusion has been perpetuated and accelerated because of wide gap between rules of the state and their implementation by agencies of state in various institutional domains. Despite policies for tribal development and empowerment since independence, these sections of society, to a larger extent, have remained far away from accruing the benefits meant for them, a fact which points towards failure of implementation mechanisms and agencies of state. Owing to all these, exclusion for Scheduled Tribes has ranged from economic forms of injustice on one side to cultural forms on the other, and involving other forms like social, political, etc. in between.

Assured representation through state policy of affirmative action may have served to address the issue of cultural exclusion by means of providing visibility, recognition and identifying identity of tribal communities in rural political institution of panchayat in particular and/or rural public sphere in general, however, its potentials for addressing exclusion which arises out of economic forms of injustice has always remained limited. In the absence of appropriate attempts to pursue redistributionist inclusionary projects, politics of recognition in terms of increased visibility in panchayats was proved to be a failure in tackling *hybrid* forms of exclusion, which most tribal communities face.

Active vs. Passive Inclusion

Having discussed the contexts of exclusion and the political measures to address them, we may now turn towards our original question as to why inclusionary policies failed to work towards empowering these communities. We may here adhere to Dryzek's (1996) framework of active and passive inclusion for analytical purposes. The political project of inclusion that the state followed through decentralisation measures attempted to re-organise state power through inclusion of Scheduled Tribes within its framework, which provided them with additional resources to function as representatives. The state even recognised the 'politics of difference' and provided the excluded communities with added privileges of assured share of resources of the state to make inclusion possible. However, these inclusionary policies, which we may term as 'passive', could not automatically generate norms of participation among excluded communities, which seems to be more important than provision of additional resources.

The minimal participation of Scheduled Tribe representatives as members of panchayat, as we observed from our case study, was the sole bottleneck towards making inclusion work in panchayats of Orissa. What was missing from the whole project of inclusion was an 'active' attempt to promote the interests of these excluded communities and to sensitise them to pursue those interests through politics and structures of decentralisation. The Scheduled Tribe communities owing to their historical experience of submissiveness, powerlessness, and backwardness in terms of education, information, awareness, etc. failed to identify their interest, despite having structural arrangements to pursue those interests. Lack of capacity of these members to organise their interest and participate in an effective manner, which could have been addressed through an active inclusionary policies, were observed to be important factors, for which inclusion could not turned out to be empowerment for these categories.

Having identified the fact that lack of capacity on the part of Scheduled Tribe representatives and absence of measures to promote active inclusionary policies by state as crucial factors for failure of inclusion in decentralised governance in Orissa, we may now highlight some of the suggestive measures for a successful and active inclusionary policy.

Promoting Active Inclusion

i) Positive attitude and genuine attempt

Promoting active inclusion first and foremost requires a positive attitude, and a genuine attempt towards the whole process of decentralisation by the state. In many occasions, the state devolved power and responsibilities to lower tier of government without devolving sufficient financial resources. Quite often the representatives in our case study opined that panchayat did not have sufficient financial resources to carry out the developmental works of their constituencies, which the constituents demanded to the representatives, and also which they themselves sincerely desired to do. Therefore, the state should endow the panchayats with more financial resources and sufficient autonomy to decide over those resources at their level. Besides these, an active inclusion for Scheduled Tribes in the context of decentralisation, would also mean constructive policies, which will work to counter the powerlessness of these communities. Policies giving additional and sufficient focus for their education, health, and environment would work in creating self-respect among them and, in turn, sensitising them about their rights. One of the major reasons for minimal participation of tribal members in the panchayat was that they were less assertive about their positions as well as their rights. Such an additional attention towards their education, health and environment through adequate policy measures and investments would definitely generate assertiveness among these communities.

ii) Capacity building measures

Second, any attempt towards promotion of an active inclusionary project should begin with building and enhancing capacities and capabilities of the hitherto excluded groups. We must highlight that capacity building is not a one-time affair; rather it is a process, which should be given constant efforts both by the state and other civil society organisations. As we pointed out in the previous section, added investment and attention for their education, health and environment would be the first step to prepare them as active citizens. Besides, there should be awareness building campaigns about the structure, functioning, duties, and responsibilities of the gram panchayats as the third tier of decentralised governance. Similarly, the Scheduled Tribe representatives should be sensitised about their rights and responsibilities as members of the panchayat. Capacity building measures for Scheduled Tribe representatives should also include sufficient training of these representatives, which will not only help in making them aware about the activities of decentralised governance system, but will also build confidence and self-respect among them to be assertive citizens, who can stand for her/his rights. Gender sensitisation is another activity, which should be given top priority in capacity building measures. The representatives at the panchayat level in general and those belonging to disadvantaged categories in particular should be sensitised about gender equality, and the capability of women representatives. And the women representatives, more so to speak of, should be trained to realise their potential as representatives.

iii) Civil society intervention

The third suggestive measure that we offer to promote an active inclusionary project in panchayat is to ensure greater civil society intervention in the whole process of governance. Presence of an active and vibrant civil society would make lot of differences in making inclusion possible and work in the context of decentralisation. The capacity building measures that we identified in the previous section requires working in close proximity with local communities and tribal representatives, which the civil society can perform more efficiently than any other agency including state. From an historical perspective too, civil society has been more inclusive in its structure and functioning than that of state. Lack of awareness and limited participation in panchayat related activities were observed to be important hurdles on the way of increased and active inclusion of Scheduled Tribe representatives in our case study. We must understand that participation is a process, which requires certain egalitarian ethics and past experience, that most of these representatives lack. The socio-historical experience of inequality, submissiveness and exploitation couldn't prepare these members to participate in equal terms with other members of panchayat. Further, the past developmental experience since independence, where these communities have always remained at the receiving end of government programmes, has made them 'takers' of benefits offered by state, where as the current decentralised paradigm expects them to behave as 'makers' and 'choosers' of their own development. In such a context, civil society has a great scope to manoeuvre, and help in making inclusion work in panchayats. Civil society can play an active role in building capacity among these representatives, by way of training, creating awareness, sensitising about gender equality, teaching norms of participation, etc. An active collaboration between state and civil society would definitely make a difference in decentralised governance, and would work towards making inclusion possible in rural political institutions.

Conclusion

In this paper, we tried to explore the process of inclusion and empowerment of Scheduled Tribe in decentralised governance structure. Our case study in one of the tribal headed gram panchayats in the state of Orissa revealed that numerical visibility and assured inclusion through policies of affirmative action did not automatically resulted in empowerment of these members in rural political institutions. Lack of awareness, capacity and capability, coupled with limited participation created sufficient hurdles on the way of effective inclusion and empowerment of these representatives. We identified that the attempts by the state to promote inclusion has largely remained passive in nature. There has not been enough attempts to mobilise the interests of the Scheduled Tribes, who themselves lack such ability to mobilise their own interest. The exclusionary project of decentralisation may have been successful in providing recognition of interests of tribals, but such acknowledged interest has to be mobilised and attempts should be made to pursue it through frameworks of decentralised governance. Further, recognition of interest and identity and provision of visibility in rural political sphere in no way address the question of economic inequality, which produce sufficient exclusion in rural communities.

To conclude, we may say that the political reform of decentralisation possesses enlarged potential and scope for effective and active inclusion. However, such potential has to be realised and worked out to transform symbolic representation to meaningful inclusion, with promotion of an active exclusionary politics by the state, and increased intervention of civil society in the whole process.

REFERENCES

Arblaster, A. (1999): 'Democratic Society and its Enemies', *Democratisation,* Vol. 6 (1), 33–49.

Baviskar, A. (1995): *In the Belly of the River: Tribal Conflicts Over Development in the Narmada Valley,* Delhi: Oxford University Press.

Bhalla, A. and F. Lapeyre (1997): 'Social Exclusion: Towards an Analytical and Operational Framework', *Development-and-Change;* 28(3): 413-33.

Castaneda, J. G. (1994): *Utopia Unarmed: The Latin American Left after the Cold War,* Vintage Books, New York.

Coelho, V.S.P.; I.A.L. De Andrade and McMontoya (2002): 'Deliberative Fora and the Democratisation of Social Policies in Brazil', *IDS Bulletin,* 33 (1).

Cohen, J. and J. Rogers (1992): 'Secondary Associations and Democratic Governance', *Politics and Society,* 20 (4): 393-472.

Dahl, R.A. (1956): *A Preface to Democratic Theory,* Chicago: University of Chicago Press.

De-Haan, A. (1998): 'Social Exclusion: An Alternative Concept for the Study of Deprivation?' *IDS-Bulletin,* 29 (1): 10-19.

Dryzek, J.S. (1996): 'Political Inclusion and Dynamics of Democratisation', *American Political Science Review,* 90 (1): 475 – 87.

Fraser, N. (1989): *Unruly Practices: Power, Discourse and Gender in Contemporary Social Theory,* Cambridge: Polity Press.

Fraser, N. (1997): *Justice Interruptus: Critical Reflections on the 'Post-socialist' Condition,* London and New York: Routledge.

Gore, C. (1993): 'Entitlement Relations and 'Unruly' Social Practices: A Comment on the Work of Amartya Sen', *Journal of Development Studies,* 29 (3): 429–60.

Ghatak, M. and M. Ghatak (2002): 'Recent Reforms in the Panchayat System in West Bengal: Toward Greater Participatory Governance?', *Economic and Political Weekly,* Vol. 37 (1), 45–58.

Ghosh, B.N. (2000): 'Women Leadership in Gram Panchayat: Prospects and Constraints', *Journal of Indian Anthropological Society,* Vol. 35, 47–52.

IDS (1998): 'Poverty and Social Exclusion in North and South', *IDS Bulletin,* 29 (1).

IILS (1997): 'Social Exclusion and Anti-poverty Policy: A Debate', *Research Series No 10.* Geneva: International Institute for Labour Studies.

Inamdar, N.R. (1991): 'Panchayati Raj Leadership: Emerging Dimensions', *Journal of Rural Development,* Vol. 10 (5), 561–73.

Inbanathan, A. (2001): 'Representation and Accountability in Local Government: The Panchayats of Karnataka', *Working Paper No. 96,* Institute for Social and Economic Change, Bangalore.

Kabeer, N. (2000): 'Social Exclusion, Poverty and Discrimination: Towards an Analytical Framework', *IDS Bulletin,* 31 (4).

Lenoir, R. (1974): *Les Exclus: Un Francais Sur Dix,* Paris: Editions du Seuil.

Levitas, R. (1998): *The Inclusive Society? Social Exclusion and New Labour,* London: Macmillan.

Lieten, G.K. (1996): 'Panchayats in Western Uttar Pradesh: 'Namesake' Members', *Economic and Political Weekly*, vol. 31 (39), 2700–5.

Lipset, S.M. (1960): *Political Man*, Heinemann, London.

Loury, G.C. (1999): 'Social Exclusion and the Ethnic Groups: Challenges to Economics'. Paper presented at the *Annual World Bank Conference on Development Economics*, Washington, D.C., April 28-30, 1999.

Luckham, R., A.M. Goetz and M. Kaldor (2000): 'Democratic Institutions and Politics in the Context of Inequality, Poverty and Conflict', *IDS Working Paper No. 104*, Institute for Development Studies, Sussex.

Lukes, S. (1974): *Power: A Radical View*. London: Macmillan.

Mander, H. (1999): 'Towards Direct Democracy: The Legal Empowerment of Gram Sabha', *Kurukshetra*, Vol. 48 (1).

Manor, J. (1999): *The Political Economy of Democratic Decentralisation*, World Bank, Washington D.C.

Manor, J. (2004): 'Democratisation with Inclusion: Political Reforms and People's Empowerment at the Grassroots', *Journal of Human Development*, 5 (1): 5–29.

Pal, M. (2004): 'Haryana: Caste and Patriarchy in Panchayats', *Economic and Political Weekly*, August 7.

Parkin, F. (1979): *Marxism and Class Theory: A Bourgeois Critique*. London: Tavistock.

Saward, M. (1992): *Co-optive Politics and State Legitimacy*, Aldershot: Dartmouth.

Schumpeter, J. (1943): *Capitalism, Socialism and Democracy*, Allen & Unwin, London.

Selznick, Philip. [1949] (1966): *TVA and the Grass Roots: A Study in the Sociology of Formal Organization*, New York: Harper and Row.

Sen, A. (1997): 'Inequality, Unemployment and Contemporary Europe', *International Labour Review*, 136 (2): 155-172.

Sen, A. (2000): 'Social Exclusion: Concept, Application and Scrutiny', *Social Development Paper No. 1*, Manila: Asian Development Bank.

Silver, H. (1994): 'Social Exclusion and Social Solidarity: Three Paradigms'. *International-Labour-Review*, 133(5-6): 531-78.

Singh, Y. (2002): 'Decentralised Governance in Madhya Pradesh: Experiences of the Gram Sabha in Scheduled Areas', *Economic and Political Weekly*, Vol. 37 (40), 4100–4.

Stewart, A. (2000): 'Social Inclusion: An Introduction', in P. Askonas and A. Stewart (ed.) *Social Inclusion: Possibilities and Tensions,* New York: Palgrave.

Truman, D.B. (1951): *The Governmental Process: Political Interests and Public Opinion,* New York: Knopf.

Walzer, M. (1991): 'Constitutional Rights and the Shape of Civil Society', In Robert E. Calvert (ed.) *The Constitution of the People: Reflections on Citizens and Civil Society,* Lawrence: University Press of Kansas.

Walzer, M. (1994): 'Multiculturalism and Individualism', *Dissent* 41 (2):185-91.

Young, I.M. (1989): 'Polity and Group Difference: A Critique of the Ideal of Universal Citizenship', *Ethics,* 99 (2): 250–74.

Young, I.M. (1990): *Justice and the Politics of Difference,* Princeton: Princeton University Press.

Young, I.M. (1992): 'Social Groups in Associative Democracy', *Politics and Society,* 20 (4): 529-34.

15

SUSTAINABLE LIVELIHOOD OF TRIBALS: ISSUES AND CONCERNS

DR. J.K. MOHANTY

Tribal Development has been one of the priority areas of the government ever since independence. The focus has been on bringing overall development in tribal areas by creating different livelihood avenues for these weakest communities. However, reality shows that many of the development programmes failed due to lack of proper implementation and coordination among various government and non-government departments. An attempt has been made to analyze the emerging issues and prospect of tribal development through various livelihood programmes in Koraput district of Orissa.

Koraput is one of the tribal dominated areas of KBK districts (Undivided Kalahandi—Bolangir--Koraput) of Orissa, burdened with persistent poverty, malnutrition, high infant and maternal mortality. As per the Scheduled Area Order 1977, Orissa is one of the scheduled areas. The order again specifies that Koraput district is one of the major scheduled areas of the state. Koraput was the largest district of Orissa till 1992 (undivided districts of Koraput), and was divided into four districts—Koraput, Nabarangpur, Rayagada and Malkangiri on 2nd October, 1992. According to the 2001 census, the total population of Koraput district is 11, 77,954. The district ranks 15th among the districts in Orissa in terms of population and contains in it 3.21% of the total population of the state. According to 2001 census, 83.18% of the total population of Koraput district lives in rural areas.

The tribal communities live throughout the length and breadth of the district. 62 types of tribal communities inhabit the Koraput district. The major types of the primitive tribes are Paraja, Kondha, Soura, Gadaba, Halva, Bhumia, Koya, Kotia, Pentia, Santala and Bhatada. According to 2001 census the total tribal population of the district is 5, 85,830 which constitute almost 50% of the total population of the district.

Poverty—an enigma illustrates that mankind has been willing to give tribal everything but a healthy and qualitative life. Tribal constitute almost half of the district's population, which has been deprived of self-respect and living in miserable conditions. The persistent poverty and lack of livelihood facilities undermine the socio-economic and health conditions of tribal people. Most of the tribals are classified either as marginal workers or non-workers. A majority of the population i.e. 87 percent lives below poverty line (the Statistical Handbook, 1993) and 50% of the total BPL families are tribal. They neither have productive assets nor do they have any meaningful productive activity. They are mostly manual labourers, work in unorganized sector and have no purchasing power.

Causes of Poverty and Lack of Livelihood

1. *Imbalanced Regional Development*

Development in present scenario means improving the standard of living of people. Raising socio-economic condition, education and health are all significant components of development. Certainly, economic growth is an essential means of enabling development. But the development in Orissa is highly coastal centric. Even after fifty-nine years of independence the most of the areas of western and southern Orissa are highly undeveloped. The KBK area in general and Koraput district in particular has been one of the most backward areas of India. Development should be an overall development. It should not be development of one region at the cost of another.

2. *Lack of Sustainable Development*

The sustainable development as defined by the World

Commission on Environment and Development, is "meeting the needs of present generation without compromising the needs of future generations". In brief, sustainable development means the development that lasts. But the present scenario shows that a vast deforestation is taking place in Koraput, which has jeopardized the life of tribal people. Tribals mostly depend on forest and it provides safety net to these forest dwellers. There is a firm symbiotic relationship exists between tribal and forest. In the face of inflation, reduced wages in real terms, unemployment, sickness, and reduced productivity from land etc. forest acts as a safety net to these people. It plays a vital role in protecting these communities against food shortage, livelihood insecurity, illness, pollution, high prices etc. But the rapid deforestation in tribal areas has raised a big question about the sustainability of tribals of Koraput district. This issue is very serious because the future generation of tribes would not only inherit just the pollution but also the depleted natural resources and physical capital. The impact of this on tribes is also reflected in loss of habitat, exploitation, expropriation and threats from outside agencies for their socio-economic life. Much has been talked about tribal development, but development is meaningless if it is not sustainable. The quest of development adversely affected the indigenous people causing deprivation, displacement and devastation, and drastically altered the relationship of tribes with their natural environment and its resources, which invariably led to the pauperization of tribes.

3. *Heavy dependence on Primary Sector*

Before going to discuss the nature of livelihood pattern of a particular area, it is essential to discuss the occupational pattern of its main workers. It serves as an economic indicator to measure both the level of development and extent of backwardness. It also shows the prospect of development for an area in the coming years. Occupational pattern of main workers in Koraput district is given below in Table 3.1.

Table 3.1: Occupational Pattern of Main Workers in Koraput District (Figures in lakh)

Types of occupation	*Rural*	*Urban*	*Total*
a) Cultivators	6.02(55)	0.10(10)	6.12(51)
b) Agricultural laborer/Allied activities	3.93(36)	0.17(17)	4.10(34)
Total Agricultural	9.95(90)	0.27(26)	10.22(85)
c) Non-Farm sector (ISB and tertiary)	1.07(10)	0.75(74)	1.82(15)
Total main workers	11.02(100)	1.02(100)	12.04(100)

(Figures shown in brackets indicate percentages to total main workers)

Source: District Statistical hand book, Koraput, Rayagada, Malkangiri and Nowrangpur, 1993.

The above table reveal that 51% of main workers in the district are cultivators, 34% are agricultural labourers and workers in allied activities to agriculture like animal husbandry, pisciculture etc. Thus in agriculture there is 85% of main working force. This indicates that in Koraput district the livelihoods pattern is heavily dependent on primary sector. Only 15% of main workers in the district depend on Non-farming activities. Unavailability of livelihood in other sectors viz. secondary and tertiary sector has forced the tribals to live in stark poverty and misery.

4. Inadequate Farm Practices

Farm sector has occupied a prominent place in the development of tribal economy. It is a well-known fact that most of the tribals depend directly or indirectly on agriculture for their livelihood. But the district has an *Unsatisfactory Land-Resource.* The presence of hills, undulating terrains and Forests in large part does not offer an environment for better farming practices. Only 16% of net area sown in the district during Khariff season has got irrigation potential. The tribal areas are mostly deprived of irrigation because of hilly tracts and mountains. Most of the land in tribal areas is favorable for one crop during monsoon.

The tribal agriculture in general suffers from *primitive and under-developed techniques of cultivation.* Tribal farmers are familiar with traditional equipment of cultivation as these are simple in make, easy to operate and cheap to purchase. They don't follow crop rotation in hill slopes and un-irrigated lands. Traditional shifting cultivation is widely practiced among them. Thus the backward nature and minimal level of farming have made the tribal farmer's economy largely insufficient to support their livelihood. As there is no surplus farm produce they are unable to save anything for development. This has played havoc in their economic life.

Since agriculture is the major source of livelihood of the tribal, it is essential to study the size of operational holding in the district. Operational holding is classified as: Marginal (0.5 to 1 hectares), Small (1 to 2 hectares), Semi medium (2 to 4 hectares), Medium(4 to 10 hectares) and Large (More than 10 hectares).

Size of operational holdings of the total social group and that of tribal group in the district is given below in table 4.1

Table 4.1: Size of Operational Holding

Size	*Total Social Group*	*Tribal Group*
Marginal	63730 (46%)	37855 (44%)
Small	40795 (29%)	26860 (31%)
Semi Medium	24725 (18%)	15985 (19%)
Medium	7905 (6%)	4780 (5%)
Large	1160 (1%)	735 (1%)

Source: District Statistical handbook, Koraput, 2001.

The above table reveals that the size of operational holding of the tribal group is very less as compared to that of the total social group. Among the tribals, 44% are marginal farmers and 31% are small farmers. Thus 75% of the tribals are small and marginal farmers having land of less than 2 hectares. Small size holding does not provide proper scope for scientific cultivation. Farmers with small operational holding cannot engage themselves in farm activities throughout the year and thus it has not contributed much to improve their financial conditions.

Farm Support System viz. the scope of irrigation, better seeds, fertilizer, use of scientific tools and methods of cultivation etc. is also limited. Even though for some areas there is abundant scope to yield 2 to 3 crops during an agricultural year, the poor economic condition of farmers do not allow them to do so. Lack of financial support to irrigate the land has forced them to harvest a single crop during monsoon and the crop produced from such small holding is not sufficient for a family even for one year.

The above facts reveal that the nature of agricultural land as well as the size of operational holdings has not been able to support adequately the livelihood of tribals in this district.

5. Shifting Cultivation

Shifting cultivation occupies a distinct place in the tribal economy of Koraput district. It is extensively practiced by most of the tribes at a primitive level of operation under certain ecological constraints. It is done by cutting trees on hill tops and slopes by burning the fallen trees and bushes and dibbling or broadcasting the seeds in the ash covered soil. The rest is left to nature's care. Crops are harvested for the first two or three years at a diminishing rate and then the land is left until it regains its fertility. This process continues until the fertility of the land is completely exhausted due to soil erosion. The land is then finally abandoned leaving only bald hills devoid of any economic or environmental importance. Tribals then go for a new clearing of hill slope for fresh cultivation. This kind of cultivation is thus shifted from one patch of hilly land to another ultimately abandoning one hill after another bringing large scale deforestation and massive degradation of topsoil, which severely affect the ecological balance of the region. It is a wasteful, ruinous practice, destroys valuable forests, deprives the people of availing the benefits of forest and forest produce, affect rainfall and threatens the future livelihood avenues by making the land completely barren and unusable for further agriculture.

6. Problem in Financing

It is another hurdle for the growth of livelihood pattern of tribal in the district. Poor farmers usually depend on outside financial agencies for their requirement. In Koraput finance is made mainly by Regional Rural Banks, Commercial Banks and Co-operative Banks. But the number of these financial institutions is not sufficient and they are unable to provide adequate financial support to these tribal farmers.

Suggestion

Prosperity and development of our rural and tribal areas, where millions of people live in extreme penury, can be accomplished only through development of livelihood programmes.

1. Agricultural research and education, is one of the principal engines of our economic strength. The diminishing land resources, increasing biotic stress, threat to bio-diversity, shrinking natural resource base etc. are some of difficulties now we are going to face in agricultural sector. These difficulties should be handled scientifically to increase agricultural production and sustainable use of our scarce land resource.
2. Farm resources in the district, though favorable to some extent, are neither proficiently used for farm development nor for and livelihood. Farmers don't follow crop management and they lack agro-modernizations. Timely farm support is very much essential to increase the production of crops at any area. Agro support system is weak in the district. By providing various farm support systems like irrigation, high yielding variety of seeds, fertilizers, pesticides etc., agricultural production can be increased in this region.
3. Due to scarcity of lands, lack of financial support to purchase developed agricultural implements, absence of alternative means of gainful livelihood in the region, religious belief and tradition etc. most of the tribals are forced to depend on shifting cultivation in this region. Introduction of viable alternative source of livelihood deserve more attention in the scheme of tribal development to reduce the heavy dependence on shifting cultivation.

4. The state has been emphasizing to promote farm sector so that farm produce can increase and will benefit the rural tribals. Nationalization of commercial banks for social control, intensification of co-operatives, lead bank scheme, formation of Regional Rural Banks, District Credit Plan, agricultural subsidy, promotion of self help groups and many other concepts have come to the picture when one thinks over rural development and tribal development. In Koraput district 83% of the population live in rural areas and nearly 50% of it are tribals. Thus tribal development should be considered as a prerequisite for an overall economic development of the district. Agriculture has been considered as the main economic activity of tribals. So proper financing to farm sector is essential to open various livelihood opportunities for tribals.
5. Slowly and steadily education should spread among tribals. There is a need of skill and capacity building of tribals through education, organizing self-help groups, arranging economic activities, and providing agriculture extension activities. The aim should be to build tribal's capacities, give information and construct a positive perspective of society. Some amount of development has taken place during the planned era and lot more needs to carry out. It is to be considered as a joint effort of government, official, local politicians and people. A holistic approach by taking locals into confidence and with their active participation would go a long way in making this region a paradise. Various schemes like fish ponds, vegetable cultivation, ginger cultivation, tick plantation, horticulture, petty trade, should be taken up through SHGs. Financial assistance from the government is required to implement these schemes on an experimental basis. This would go a long way in improving socio-economic status of tribes in Koraput.

Conclusion

In spite of some of the development measures taken through

years after independence no substantial progress is marked in the living standard. Due to lukewarm political patronage and lack of pragmatic result oriented approach the tribals still languish in the quagmire of ignonimity. On the contrary policy decisions regarding development through industrialization have resulted in conflict and confrontation between the aboriginals and the government. It must be taken into account that any policy decision that affects the tribal population must involve the tribals. They must be allowed to save their own destiny. The concept of development must not be conceived in the matrices of our own vision but according to the needs, ideas, contentment and acceptability of the tribals.

Tribes are part of the society and their problems should be treated as that of the society. The stakeholders in this exercise viz. government, bureaucrats, local politicians, and NGOs should take up their collective responsibilities to eradicate poverty from tribal society and try to march forward on the way to a sustainable development. The concern stakeholders should give a human approach to create livelihood and eliminate the widespread poverty from tribal society. The tribal poor must be treated as a resource rather than a burden. The need of the hour is to go for a practical approach to attack poverty through promotion of tribal livelihood.

REFERENCE

Pati, R.N and Das, J. (2002): *Tribal and Indigenous People of India: Problems and Prospectus*, New Delhi: A.P.H. Publishing Corporation.

Mahapatra, Lakshman K. (1999): *Resettlement, Impoverishment and Reconstruction in India. Development for the Deprived*, Vikas Publishing House, New Delhi.

Ramaiah, P. (1981): *Tribal Economy of India*, Light and Life Publishers, New Delhi.

Ramamani, V.S. (1988): *Tribal Economy: Problems and Prospects*, Chugh Publications, Allahabad.

Sharma, B.D. (1978) *Tribal Development: The Concept and the Frame*, Prachi Prakashan, New Delhi.

16

DEVELOPMENT DRIVEN DISPLACEMENT AND IT'S IMPACT ON TRIBALS

KRISHNA CHANDRA PRADHAN & PRAKASH CHANDRA PANIGRAHY

There are some 85 million Indians who are officially classified as "Scheduled Tribes". Of these, about 16 million live in the states of North-Eastern India, and the rest live in the heart of India, in a more-or-less contiguous hill and forest belt that extends across the states of Gujarat, Rajstan, Maharastra, Madhya Pradesh, Chhatisgarh, Jharkhand, Andhra Pradesh, Orissa, Bihar and West Bengal.

The Tribes of the north-east differ from their counter parts in other parts of India in several respects. The substantial one is their exposition to modern English education as a result their literary rates, and hence their chances of being advantageously absorbed in the modern economy, are much higher than that of their counterparts elsewhere in India. Second, unlike the tribal of the mainland they have been largely exempted from the trauma caused by dispossession.

Orissa figures predominately in the list of underdeveloped states in India have been a victim of some ill thought-out development strategy. Despite being a rich state in terms of its mines and minerals and natural resources. Orissa has not made any real progress as for as the development of the state and its people are concerned. Nature has bestowed Orissa with plenty of mines and mineral resources. The state is blessed with 99 percent chromate ore, 92 percent nickel ore, 65 percent of graphite and pyrophylite, 66 percent of bauxite 31 percent of mineral sand, 32 percent of manganese, 28 percent of iron ore and 24 percent of coal resources of the country. Yet Orissa is one of the poorest states of the country. Ironically, the under developed and Tribal dominated western and southern belts of Orissa are the store house of most of mines and mineral deposits of the state. Over the years several industries, big and small, as well as several irrigation projects have come of in these areas, resulting, huge displacement and dispossession of tribals from their traditional means of life and livelihood.

Development and Displacement in Orissa

Development activities in Orissa gained momentum in the early 1950s. Officially, 81,176 families from 1,446 villages were displaced due to development projects from 1950 to 1993 that required the acquisition of 14,82,626 acres of land. The major development projects which induced large scale displacement in the state during this period were industrial projects-such as Rourkela Steel Plant (RSP), the Hindustan Aeronautics(HAL) and the National Aluminum Company (NALCO).

However 80 per cent of displacement has been for multipurpose dam projects like the Hirakud hydroelectric dam in the early 1950s which displaced 22,000 families in Orissa as well as Madhya Pradesh. When the Rengali Dam project came up in1971, the resettlement issue raised its head again; In 1973 Orissa came up with its first resettlement policy and in 1977 conceded land for land as the basis for rehabilitation. In 1989 the first mining sector policy was formulated and 1994, Orissa formulated it first comprehensive, and for its time, progressive policy for all water resources projects.

Over the last decade, both development and its accompanying displacement have accelerated. The focus has been on industrial and mining projects till now. UNDP estimates that till date, one lakh people in Orissa have been displaced since independence while 20 lakhs have been affected by development projects.

The Hirakud multipurpose river valley project on the river Mahandi in Sambalpur district was the first major project to be conceived after independence. The project started in 1948 and was completed in 1957. The main purpose of the project was to facilitate intensive cultivation, increase productivity, and ensure security against uncertainty and loss of agriculture, The reservoir resulted in the sub-mergence of 74,300 hectares of land including 23,988 hectares of forest cover and 49,888 hectares of agricultural land, The project affected 285 villages of which 249 villages were (108 fully and 141 partly affected) in Orissa and 36 villages (3 fully and 33 partly) in Madhya Pradesh. Due to displacement, the livelihood of 22,141 families consisting of 1,10,000 people was disrupted. Around 4,744 families, all belonging to the scheduled castes and scheduled tribes, were displaced forcible with the help of the police. Only 2,185 families were resettled in17 rehabilitation camps; 3,134.71 acres of private land and 221.91 acres of forest were acquired for the resettlement of displaced persons.

Impact of Globalization

Under the auspices of liberalization and globalization tribals continue to be displaced from the land they own on cultivate, as the non-tribal leadership of the state has signed a series of leases with mining companies both Indian and Foreign. As a consequence of Government policy of opening up peoples natural resources to foreign capital in the mid-1990s, and greater privatization of mining companies, there are a huge number of large Indian and foreign transnational Corporations (TNCs) trying to tap natural resources in Orissa and in the region. In the last five years, the Orissa Government has signed 43 MoUs. Requiring 1600 million tones of iron ore in the next 25 years. MNCs like BHP-Billiten, Vedanta Alumina, Rio Tinto Mining Alcon, Hindalco, Jindal, POSCO, Bhusan had queued up to exploit the states resources. The state government has already given lease to mine 1,000 million tones of bauxite ore to different companies. These are but misleading signs of development in Orissa. One can not take this massive industrialization and mining activity as the scale to judge the rise in human development indicators among the people in the remote areas of Southern and Western Orissa.

Present Scenario

Excess land acquired for projects results in larger avoidable displacements. This has been a constant feature of every project in Orissa. Excess than needed land for a commercial entity in capital investment with assured returns through it is ostensibly acquired for future expansion. The HAL was established in 1963 at Sunabeda in triabal-dominited Koraput district for manufacturing defense components. HAL acquired 9301 acres of land, displaced 468 families from 10 villages. HAL has originally acquired this huge area for the establishment of all five units of its fighter plane MIG Project. However, only one unit was established and the other four units were not shifted to this site; the extra land acquired by HAL from the villages has never been used. This extra land has been allotted to private parties instead of being returned to the displaced people. A boundary wall was then built around the entire acquired land thus cutting off the displaced people from important access routs and restricting out side access to the villagers still residing inside in their original homestead areas.

NALCO acquired a total of 10,058 acres of land of which 2427.30 acres was for bauxite mines, 2638.96 acres for construction of the township and 6992.50 acres for setting up of the alumina plant. The following is an example of the common but gross injustices that take place during implementation of otherwise fair R & R polices-NALCO in Koraput district paid compensation for land and houses to 59 displaced families in Champadar and 16 families in Koraguda village in 1982. When these two villages were finally and physically shifted to Sahid Laxman Nayak Nagar Colony, Damanjodi on December 23,2003, 42 families have swelled their numbers in the intervening 21 years , families who in enumeration paper simply did not exit. Hence they had no existence in the resettlement colony in 2003. In fact they belonged no where.

Denial of Constitutional Rights

The land resources of the scheduled tribes are being rapidly depleted by the government, which has a constitutional responsibility to protect the tribes. The displacement will mean, deprivation of the privilege and protection guaranteed to the Scheduled Tribes under the 5th schedule of the constitution with reference to Article 244 and other allied articles for constitutional governance, Legal principles of tribal self-rule envisaged under Panchayatas Extension to Schedule Areas Act, (PESA) and Tribal Protective Land Transfer Regulation.Confering special powers rights to tribal development authorities.

Exploitation, zero health care and educational facilities, malnutrition, inhuman torture, rising unemployment, inordinate delay in disposal of land cases are the cruel realities which speak to us about the development syndrome of the area.

Compensation for Displaced

Development projects for irrigation, wildlife sanctuaries and national parks invariably displaced large population while they have little or no alternate source of livelihood to offer, unlike industrial projects which have the potential to provide jobs, even if in limited numbers.

Hence this is the only category of projects where the land for land offer has been made to those evicted. Because these projects have invariably come up in tribal dominated areas, the rehabilitation offers more for the scheduled tribe category of displaced in the form of two acres of irrigated land and three acres of non irrigated land, an acre more of the latter than what general category of displaced persons get. In addition, all displaced persons (DPs) get one-tenth of an acre for homestead and Rs. 25,000 for self relocation. All DPs get in addition another 50,000 for house and cattle-shed construction. In case of unavailability of land, Rs. 30.000 and 15,000 per acre of irrigated and non-irrigated land respectively will be given. Reclamation cost of land-usually grazing land is converted for this purpose-will also be given. An allowance of Rs1,000 will be given for 12 running months for temporary shed and transportation.

Project Affected Peoples (PAPs), other than DPs, too get land for land even if they still retain their homestead. They get an equal area of irrigated land and double the area of non-irrigated agricultural land of what they lose but the limit is set at a maximum of two and four acres, respectively, no matter if they lose more than that. If land is not available, they get Rs 50,000 per acre of irrigated land and Rs. 25,000 per non-irrigated land.

Under the category of industrial and mining projects employments is the prime rehabilitation benefit to the DPs. One assured employment per family is compulsory. Current policies left out in the cold all other sons and daughters from any benefit. What's more, the entire family with an average size of six to eight members depended on that one job-holder. In many instances it has been seen that the son sets up his separate family after the father has nominated him as the beneficiary leaving the other dependants to fend for themselves.

Realities of Displacement

Poverty, rampant corruption, failed government mechanisms are the main characteristics associated with the tribal anger and up rise of Naxal in Tribal India. Government's performance on the rehabilitation front can be simply termed as disastrous. To sum up, all the so-called development projects in no way helped the majority displaced tribal. This, rather, has alienated the rural tribal people and taking advantage of this anger and frustration among tribal, and the government's insensitivity towards tribal problems, Naxal have made a meteoric growth in tribal India.

Rehabilitation of people displaced by dams like the Hirakud in Sambalpur district, built way back in 1950s, is not yet complete. Compensation amounting to Rs15,41,46,996 has not been paid for years. Finally when some people, it was a saga of gross financial irregularity as many displaced persons have complained. People still have not forgotten this humiliation and this is one prime reason for the meteoric growth of Naxal violence in different parts of Sambalpur. As per the recently published Ghadei committee report, of nine blocks of the district, three are grossly underdeveloped, three are underdeveloped and three are developing. Hirakud is the world's largest earthen dam, thus 28 percent area of the district is irrigated whereas remaining 72 percent area have seen no sign of it. Except in some areas in Rengali, Maneswar and Jujumura Block, the rest six blocks are not linked with canal system. It is a sad reality that in all the nine Blocks of Kuchinda, Jamankira, Jujumura, Naktideul, Bamra, Maneswar, Rengali, Rairakhol and Dhankauda there is an acute shortage of drinking water facility. The electricity requirement of the state is mostly catered to by the Hirakud dam, whereas most villages in the district are yet to get proper electric connection and supply. The government continues to ignore the poor, downtrodden people of the area, which was successfully exploited by the Naxals. Today, Naxals belonging to CPI (Maoist) are very much active in most areas of Sambalpur, especially in the remote villages like Jujumura, Burda, Meghapal, Chhamunda, Khalasuni, Naktideul, Rairakhol, Badarama, Mahulpali, Karadapal, Biriaam, Debikhol, Khariyakani, Debatadahar, Dingijharan, Dhinkireduma, Hikpali and Jangula. Living conditions in these villages are simply inhuman; there is no sign of credible governance in these Naxal infested areas of Sambalpur.

It is the cruel reality borne out of the ill thought-out development strategy in Orissa that in all of the resettlement operations, the majority of oustees have ended with lower incomes; less land than before, less work opportunities, inferior housing, less access to the resources of the commons such as fuel wood and fodder and worse nutrition and physical and mental health. It is estimated that around three to five million people have been displaced since 1950 in Orissa on account of various development project; of the displaced, more than 50 percent are tribal. The Tenth Five-Year plan (2002-07) makes a very special mention on different poverty alleviation schemes and programmes; how-ever their impact on rural poverty remains dubious. When it comes to implementation, the government agenda is grossly mismanaged, and it is mostly corruption-ridden, which raises serious doubts over the government's commitment for human rights and social security. This failed state of affairs so far has been successfully exploited by Naxal groups to win over the local tribals as a formidable support base. The asymmetrical development in Orissa has fostered a conflict between values of democratic governance and aspirations of the people. The Naxal movement in Orissa has so far managed to sustain because it successfully exploits the life of marginalized people in these areas. It has established a link between underdevelopment, regional imbalance, economic disparity and gun culture. But the deplorably poor condition of the people has ironically seen the use of excessive violence and counter violence in the name of upliftment of the poor.

On the other hand, while the Naxal leadership makes a strong claim for fighting for the rights of the poor, the former has so far remained apathetic in enhancing the quality of life in villages, arguing instead that all reforms have to follow from revolution. To them development is adversarial to revolutionary consciousness. In fact, Naxal groups in these areas have vehemently opposed any type of construction work, it seems that they are afraid the government will win over the poor ignorant tribals to its side once they allow the development process to start.

A study of Naxal violence in Orissa revels that today's explosive situation has been largely fostered by a continuous absence of development, But violence itself is by no means a way to attain development, rather it is an extreme form of exploitation. To evade "maldevelopment" and to replace the existing atmosphere of chaos and terror, what is required is the creation of appropriate institutions, systems and relations. The need of the hour is to free the system from exploitation and corruption which would bring down societal tension by ensuring equality of status and opportunity. To deal with the ever-increasing Naxal problem, Orissa must sufficiently increase and properly manage fund allocation in the field of healthcare, education, nutrition programmes, disease control, irrigation, rural electrification, rural roads and other basic requirements, especially in its Naxal-affected rural areas. The state must ensure that its institutions a do not breed exploitation. It must work on a formula where there is larger democratic participation in the processes of decision making and development.

REFERENCES

Guha, R.C. (2007): "Adivasis, Naxalites & Indian Democracy", *Economic & Political Weekly*, Aug. 11-17.

Pradhan, K.C. (2006): "Tribal Development and the Provision of PESA", in Tripathy, S.N. (edited volume) Rural Development for social change, Sonali Publication, New Delhi.

Mukherjee, D. (2005): It you look after Forest people you kill Naxalism , The Asian Age, 28th June.

Fernades,W. and Thukral E.G.(eds)(1989): *Development Displacement and Rehabilitation*, Indian Social Institute, New Delhi.

Mathur, H. Mohan and D. Marsden (1998): *Devel̀opment Projects and Impoverishment Risks Resetting Project-Affected People in India*, Oxford University Press, New Delhi.

Mahapatra, Lakshman K. (1999): *Resettlement, Impoverishment and Reconstruction in india. Development for the Deprived*, Vikas Publishing House, New Delhi.

Padhi, R. and N. Adve (2006): "Endemic to Development Police Killing in Kalinga Nagar", *EPW*, Jan. 21-27.

Kujur, R.K. (2006): "Underdevelopment and Naxal Movement", *EPW*, Feb. 18-24.

Jena, Manipadma (2006): "Orissa Draft Resettlement & Rehabilitation Policy, 2006", *EPW*, Feb. 4-10.

17

EMPOWERING WOMEN THROUGH COMBATING GENDER-BASED VIOLENCE AND DISCRIMINATION: NEPALESE EXPERIENCE OF USING PUBLIC INTEREST LITIGATION AS A STRATEGIC TOOL

CHAPAGAI, RAJU PRASAD

1. Introduction

Securing empowerment of women at the prevalence of gender based violence and discrimination in society is myth not a reality. It is unquestionable fact that violence and discrimination result in disempowerment. At the same time, disempowerment promotes and perpetuates violence and discrimination. Empowerment in fact is an outcome of the elimination of the discrimination and violence against women that are being promoted by patriarchal norms and values in society.

Throughout much of the history of Nepal, defective cultural beliefs allowed women only limited roles in society. Many people believed that women's natural roles were as mothers and wives. Women were considered to be better suited for childbearing and household work rather than for involvement in the public life. That type of socially constructed gender role resulted in gender imbalance of power between women and men.

Till 1990, Nepalese society formally denied women some significant rights and freedoms accorded to men. Only since the promulgation of democratic constitution in 1990, women empowerment through fighting violence and discrimination has been an important part of the women's rights movement. Subsequently, Nepal also ratified "Convention on the Elimination of all Forms of Discrimination against Women 1979" along with other important human rights instruments that have further vitalized the empowerment issues.

Though the constitution doesn't explicitly incorporate the term "women empowerment" but it provides wider scope for paving the way of empowerment. The Article 11 not only guarantees formal equality but also aims at securing substantive equality that requires state to devise various measures to promote rights of women. Directive principles provided under Article 25 and 26 further impose positive obligation upon state to give priority to women's health, education and employment. Moreover, Article 9 of the Treaty Act 1990 gives the status of domestic laws to the ratified human rights conventions; therefore, women's rights guaranteed under the conventions are also equally enforceable. Scope of remedy in the case of violation is also effectively provided especially through the Article 88 as it empowers the Supreme Court with jurisdiction for "Judicial Review" and "Public Interest Litigation".

In subsequent days, PIL has been being utilized as a strategic tool for fighting violence and discrimination against women. Some of the litigations are found resulted in empowering women especially in area of property right, employment, and marriage and family life. Mostly the paper highlights major achievements of judicial intervention in term of women empowerment through critical analysis of select Supreme Court decisions. For examples: in *Mira Dhungana V. His Majesty's Government et al* (2003) the Supreme Court labeled marital rape as heinous sexual crime and endorsed the sexual autonomy of women even within marital bond. In *Sapana Pradhan Malla for FWLD V. HMG/Nepal (2002)* the Supreme Court, recognizing the right to equal protection of law against gender-based violence and discrimination irrespective of the character of the victim, overturned the No 7 of the Chapter on Rape of Country Code 1963, that constituted very nominal punishment in the case of rape on prostitute. Responding the *Sharmila Parajuli et al for Pro Public V. HMG/Nepal (2003)* the Supreme Court issued directive order to the government for the enactment of appropriate law to protect women's right to freedom from sexual harassment at work place and the public place. Recent judicial interventions on right to passport, right to dispose property, right to enjoy parental property are counted significant in this regard.

The paper finally observes that PIL has become instrumental in eliminating discriminatory laws and gender biased customary practices responsible to perpetuate violence and discrimination against women and in holding government accountable to enact new laws and ensure faithful enforcement of legal provisions aimed to protect women's right to freedom from gender-based violence. In addition, the paper reveals the fact that the PIL has also played educative role by bringing several issues to the public debate and consultation.

2. Women Empowerment as a Matter of State's Obligation

2.1 Constitutional Imperatives

To begin with the preamble, it comprises paramount objectives of the constitution as to secure social, economic and political justice through protection of basic human rights. It is obviously impossible to secure constitutional goal without getting women empowered economically, socially and politically. Therefore, a woman empowerment is also one of the mandates enshrined under the preamble.

Most significantly, the Article 11 not only guarantees "formal equality" but also pave the way to secure "substantive equality". Constitution declares that all citizens are equally entitled to non-discrimination, equal protection and equal application of laws regardless of sex. Obviously, sex is one of the prohibitory grounds of discrimination so it cannot be used to create gender injustices. So that, there is no room for any form of discrimination and injustices against women as this article relies on 'zero-tolerance against discriminations approach'. Therefore it can be said that state is charged with the constitutional obligation to eliminate all types of negative discriminations against women that inhibit their overall empowerment. Rather, constitutional mandate for accelerating substantive equality under proviso of Article 11 requires state to devise special measures for the protection and advancement of women. Fulfillment of this positive obligation of state is mostly expected to promote gender equality taking into account the biological and culture specific context of women. In *Rina Bazaracharya Vs Cabinet Secretariat of Council of Ministers et. al* Supreme Court further clarified the intent and purpose of the special protection clause that it doesn't permit any state action or measure that results in disempowerment of women; it only permits measures that are in favor of women and result in acceleration of de facto equality.

In order to materialize goal of substantive equality as envisaged under Art 11 of the constitution also prescribe positive state obligations under chapter of *directive principles*. State is charged with the responsibility to create supportive environment for protecting life, liberty and property of the people and further enjoin the government to eliminate all types of social and economic inequalities. The constitution also directs government: to pursue a policy of making the female population participate, to a greater extent, in the task of national development by making special provisions for their education, health and employment which are in fact keys to the empowerment; to make necessary arrangements to safeguard the rights and interests of children and shall ensure that they are not exploited, and shall make gradual arrangements for free education; to pursue such policies in matters of education, health and social security of orphans, helpless women, the aged, the disabled and incapacitated persons, as well as ensure their protection and welfare. Though abovementioned directive principles are constitutionally declared unenforceable but the Supreme Court through the way of interpretation has enhanced the enforceability. The court has established the judicial precedent that 'judicial intervention can be made if Public Authorities don't comply with directive principles'; therefore, state cannot refrain from fulfilling it's obligation to promote advancement of women as directed under the directive principles.

Many others constitutionally guaranteed fundamental rights could also be invoked for holding government accountable towards removing hindrances for women empowerment. Among them right against deprivation of personal liberty guaranteed under Art. 12(1) is significant one. Supreme Court has further expanded its horizon by adopting the interpretation that right to life is inherent in constitutionally guaranteed right to personal liberty. Besides, Art 22 guarantees fundamental right to privacy it is also significant to protect women's right to bodily integrity and right to freedom from physical intrusion. In one landmark case the Supreme Court held that women's right to control over their own body is a part of fundamental right to privacy.

Based on the collective reading of the constitutional provisions relevant to women's rights require two-way state interventions with regard to women empowerment. One is to eliminate all form of gender based violence and discrimination that are causes of women's disempowerment through adopting appropriate legislative, executive or any other measures. Another way is to create enabling environment for the enjoyment of fundamental rights and freedom guaranteed under the constitution through taking special measures in favor of women.

2.2 *Treaty Obligations*

Nepal has a unique legal provision regarding the national application of international instruments. A separate Treaty Act was passed by the interim government (1990-91) to regularize ratification of, and accession to, such conventions in line with the spirit of Article 126 of the *Constitution of the Kingdom of Nepal*, 1990. Section 9 of the Treaty Act provides that any treaty once ratified, acceded to, accepted and approved by the Parliament, in which the Government is a party, shall be enforceable as a national law. Treaty Act 1992 provides that the provision under the international instrument to which Nepal is a state party, are equally applicable to prevailing Nepalese laws within the territory of Nepal. Even it has also provided that if any provision of municipal law is inconsistent with the provision of such treaty the provision of treaty will get primacy. Nepal has pioneered in ratifying human rights convention in the region. It has already become party of most of the major international human rights treaties.

Gender equality and justice is generally recognized in all international human rights instruments to which Nepal is a party. The Universal Declaration on Human Rights (UDHR) recognizes the 'equal rights of men and women'. Most significantly, Article 1 of the UDHR incorporates the principle of equality stating, 'All human beings are born free and equal in dignity and rights.' Also Article 2 goes on to stress right to equality saying, 'everyone is entitled to all the rights and freedoms set forth in the declaration, without distinction of.... sex....'. This type of the prohibition on sex-based discrimination is also incorporated in Article 2(1) and 2(2) of the ICCPR and ICESCR. Similarly, Article 3 of the both covenants impose state obligation towards gender equality in same way, 'The state parties to the present covenant undertake to ensure the equal right of men and women to enjoyment of all rights set forth in the present covenant'. A similar provision on sex-based discrimination is also contained in the Convention on Rights of the Child 1989 (CRC).

Among the ratified conventions CEDAW is most comprehensive human rights instrument aimed to promote women's rights. All the relevant rights incorporated under the previous conventions are integrated under CEDAW. It is revealed from the study of its preamble that CEDAW convention is rooted in dignity and worth of the human person and equal rights of men and women as it explicitly acknowledges that discrimination against women violets the principles of equality of rights and respect for human dignity.

Article 1 of CEDAW defines discrimination against women in very comprehensive way. As a state party, first and foremost Nepal is obliged to comply with this definition. CEDAW imposes several general and specific obligations upon state party. Talking about general obligation, Nepal as a state party is charged with the obligations to combat discrimination at the national level through adopting series of measures which are: incorporating the principle of equality of men and women in their legal system, i.e., abolishing all discriminatory laws and adopting appropriate ones prohibiting discrimination.;

establishing tribunals and other public institutions to ensure the effective protection of women against discrimination; and ensuring elimination of all acts of discrimination against women by persons, organizations or enterprises. Also states parties are allowed to adopt temporary special measures aimed at accelerating de facto equality between men and women. CEDAW also imposes the specific obligations upon state parties that are as follow:

- To guarantee to women the exercise and enjoyment of human rights and fundamental freedoms on a basis of equality with men.
- To take appropriate measures to modify the social and cultural patterns of conduct of men and women, with view to achieving the elimination of prejudices.
- To take all appropriate measures including legislation, to suppress all forms of traffic in women and exploitation or prostitution of women.
- To ensure women's equal access to and equal opportunities in, political and public life, including the right to vote and stand for elections as well as to participate in the formulation and implementation of policy.
- To take steps to eliminate discrimination against women in order to ensure equal rights with men in the fields of education, employment, health care and in other areas of economic and social life.
- To ensure the application of the provisions of the convention to women in rural areas.
- To accord to women equality with men before the law.
- To take all appropriate measures to eliminate discrimination against women in all matters relating to marriage and family relations including reproductive rights of women.

3. *Legal Impediments to Women Empowerment*

Despite the constitutional and international obligations, there are various legal impediments for achieving women empowerment in substance. Enjoyment of most of the above said rights are still dream for Nepalese women; in fact, these are only limited within the texts; very few legislative and executive efforts have been made to materialize these Rights in living reality. It is shameful to say that on the one hand, there is presence of various state protected discriminatory laws that are resulting in disempowerment of women. On the other hand, some of the positive legislations aimed to empower women are also remained either non-implemented or inefficiently implemented. In addition, several areas are still left behind from legislative enactments, which are really urgent to be covered by legislation.

It is notable here that the constitution itself recognizes gender-based discrimination in term of citizenship rights. Article 8 of the constitution deprives woman from right to transfer their citizenship to her children and husband that is unquestionably responsible to render women subordinated to men in society. On the one hand, it is big hurdle for women to enjoy freedoms and rights concerning marriage and family life, on the other hand it is playing role to keep patriarchal dominance going. As right to citizenship is considered "right to have rights" it also negatively affects the enjoyment of all other fundamental rights and freedoms. Very unfortunately, Supreme Court judgment in *Chandra Kanta Gynwali V. HMG Cabinet Secretariat et al.* along with some of the other judgments also legitimized constitutionally protected gender-based discrimination in citizenship rights.

Nepal has still failed to perform its duty to guarantee non-discrimination as provided under the Constitution and the ratified international conventions. Many legal provisions are seemed problematic in term of meaningful realization of women's rights. Under Chapter on Homicide of Country Code women are still mostly prohibited from exercising freedom of abortion. Very limited freedom of choice is provided to women as 11th amendment of Country Code allow women to abort pregnancy in the first trimester (12 weeks). Penal provisions concerning abortion are also found discriminatory. Voluntary abortion is severely punished rather than forced abortion. Recently Supreme Court asked government to avoid unjust penal provision taking into account the constitutional and treaty obligation for gender equality.

Though 11th amendment of Country Code increased the penalty in the case of child marriage, this is scanty, as child marriage is still not declared void According to law; child marriage is viodable upon the age of eighteen only if no child is born to the couple. However, statistics reveals the fact that law has become failure to combat the child marriage. Even 30 percent of women who are married between the ages of 15 and 19 have three to four children and about 35 % of such women have one to two children.

As of the citizenship rights, a woman does not fall under the descent of the family in Nepal. Therefore, she alone has no right to give any identity to her children as a mother of the child. Citizenship can be acquired either through father or through the husband only. A woman of foreign nationality who is married to a Nepali citizen and who has initiated proceedings for renunciation of her foreign citizenship may acquire Nepal's citizenship. However, a foreign man who has married a Nepali woman is not entitled to ac-quire Nepali citizenship by virtue of such marriage. She even has no right to give the citizenship to her children. Hence, the State obligation to grant women rights equal to that of men with respect to the nationality of her children are denied by the law. Many children who are born of a Nepali mother and a non-Nepali father in Nepal are facing complications arising out of discriminatory laws. Children of unmarried women are also facing severe problem.

Women are still compelled to face marriage-based discrimination in respect of property rights. The daughter has to return her share of parental property upon marriage. Similarly, women were also restricted to dispose their own property. Unmarried daughter were required to take consent of father and mother and widows were required to take the same from their son and daughter. These discriminatory laws were challenged in the Supreme Court by filing public interest litigation. Responding the cases, Supreme Court overturned No 2 of the Chapter on Exclusive Property under the Country Code 1963, and the court issued directive order to amend the No. 1(A) and 16 of the Chapter on Partition.

Section 9 of the chapter on marriage in the Country Code allows a man bigamy even if his first wife is living, if she becomes incurably insane; no child is born or are alive within ten years of marriage or if the children do not survive; turns blind; becomes crippled; is separated after taking share of her husband's property. However, the same rights do not apply to a wife under similar circumstances because women are subject to punishment on adultery. Although polygamy is illegal except abovementioned condition, it is not declared void as Section 10 of the Chapter on Marriage recognizes the second marriage of a man, after a punishment of one to three year imprisonment and payment of a fine or NR5000to 25,000.

Women are provided inadequate maternity leave; even women in informal sector are not provided maternity leave and breastfeeding facility; there is also disparity in providing maternity leave (60 days in government services, 52 days for labor sector except Tea Estates, 45 days for Tea Estate). No provision of leave is provided in case of miscarriage, abortion and also in case of more than two deliveries.

Also, present definition of rape is very restrictive that seems to exclude marital rape. In a case brought to the Supreme Court challenging the validity of the definition of the rape in the Country Code 1963 the court recognized marital rape as a offence but ignored to overturn the provision; rather court issued directive to the government for making necessary legal arrangement to protect women from marital rape. However the law has not been amended to date so marital rape is still exempted from punishment.

Problem is not only felt due to prevalence of discriminatory laws but also due to the lack of effective implementation of positive laws aimed to empower women. For examples: women are not in a position to enjoy right to safe abortion due to the absence of safe abortion facilities throughout the country. Law prohibits female feticide but women are forced to commit sex selective abortion due to lack of monitoring and inspection over the Medical Clinics having technology to detect sex of the unborn baby. As of the maternity protection, laws provide some special measures aimed to strike balance between reproductive and productive function. These include maternity leaves; childcare and breastfeeding facility at the workplace, but implementation status is very weak. Most of the Women employees do not enjoy these rights due to ineffective implementation. On the other hand, employers are found reluctant to hire women employees due to statutory obligations towards maternity protection.

Also one can easily observe legislative vacuum in many areas that is directly or indirectly resulting in violation of reproductive rights. For instances, due to absence of comprehensive laws on domestic violence, problems like forced pregnancy for the sake of producing son, violence on the birth of daughters, low calorie food during pregnancy when the baby is girl, forced abortion to avoid a girl child and violence causing miscarriage are common to most of the Nepali women. Absence of sexual harassment laws is also causing many forms of sexual violence against women along with deprivation of employment opportunities that also negative impact negatively upon mental, emotional and physical health.

Enactment of new laws is also felt urgent in many other areas including marital rape, sexual harassment at work place and public place, family planning, prostitution and maternity protection. Also some customary practices detrimental to the reproductive health of the women including *"chaupadi tradition"* have not been covered up by legislation. The Supreme Court, through several judicial decisions, has already made government alert about the urgency of new enactment in most of the aforesaid areas; nevertheless government is still not found sensitive to initiate the process of enacting new laws.

4. Public Interest Litigation as a Strategic Tool

4.1. Scope of Public Interest Litigation

The constitution not only provides wide scope of empowering women but also paves the way for effective judicial remedy in case of violation of rights. Right to constitutional remedy guaranteed as a fundamental right can be exercised to ensure women's accessibility of justice.

Supreme Court is charged with an obligation and is also empowered to ensure complete justice through enforcing fundamental freedoms and rights at individual as well as collective level under Art 88 of the Constitution.

On the one hand the Supreme Court is empowered to review laws inconsistent with the constitutional provisions; on the other hand, the court can also issue any type of order for the enforcement of fundamental rights and for the settlement of the disputes of public interest. This jurisdiction of the Supreme Court can be exercised to nullify the discriminatory provisions and also to get state obligation under the constitution and other human right instruments enforced. Any public-spirited individual and organization has standing to represent women's issues to the court. In respect of women's rights, Public Interest Litigation Jurisdiction of Supreme Court can be used for fulfilling following purposes:

- To get discriminatory legal provisions eliminated through judicial review those are contradictory with women's rights and freedoms.
- To get appropriate legislative measures adopted in order to fulfill constitutional and international mandate for women empowerment.
- To hold government accountable through issuing appropriate order towards translating the international obligations into domestic laws.
- To accelerate the implementation process of domestic laws those are aimed to promote women's rights and interest.
- To get governmental authorities sensitized in contemporary issues concerning women's rights.

4.2 *Select Public Interest Cases Combating Violence and Discrimination*

4.2.1 *Empowering Women to Enjoy Right to Found Family*

The Supreme Court of Nepal delivered landmark decision in *Meera Gurung V. Department of Immigration* that recognized equal status of men and women in term of right to found family. Petitioner Meera Gurung, a Nepalese national, married an Iranian national, Dr. Reja Mehumudi, while they were pursuing their medical education in the Philippines. In 1991, they came to Nepal. They decided to stay in Nepal and continue their medical practice. However, the Immigration Department refused to grant Dr. Mehumudi a spousal visa for a period beyond four months in a year, on the basis of clause 8 (4) of the Immigration regulations. Under clause 8 (3) of the Immigration Regulations 1976, a foreign woman married to a Nepalese man could obtain a residential visa for the duration of the marriage, and for three months following it's termination; whereas, the foreign husband of a Nepalese woman was not entitled to the same privilege. But, under clause 8 (4) the alien husband was only permitted a four-month visa in one year. Nepalese women and their foreign husbands were therefore not entitled to the privileges given to Nepalese men and their foreign wives under clause 8 (3).

Meera brought the case in Supreme Court challenging the constitutional validity of clause 8(4) of Immigration Regulation. The division bench delivered divided opinion so the case was referred to special bench comprising 3 judges. Finally Special bench of the Supreme Court found the disputed provision discriminatory and declared ultra virus of the constitution. The judgment specially recognized the independent identity of women and upheld the rights of women to marriage and to found a family without any limitation. It also guaranteed women's right against forcible change of citizenship due to marital relationship with foreign husband. In declaring ultra virus the court made very significant observation:

Nepalese man is privileged through the favorable treatment of their wives in matters regarding visas. A foreign spouse is entitled to preferential treatment in the issue of a visa simply through her marriage to a Nepalese man. However, the same privilege is not granted to the foreign husbands of Nepalese women, who are not able to obtain a residential visa. Hence, the said clauses of the Immigration Regulations being discriminatory and as such inconsistent with article 11 of the Constitution of the Kingdom of Nepal are declared null and void. The petitioner's husband is therefore entitled to obtain a residential visa to stay with his wife in Nepal.

4.2.2 Property Rights Cases Resulted in 11th Amendment Aimed to Empower Women in Many Respects

In *Dr. Chanda Bazaracharya V. HMG et al* and *Mira Dhungana et al V. HMG et al,* several discriminatory provisions of Country Code 1963 especially relating to ancestral property were brought to the Supreme Court under Art 88(1) of the constitution. After the promulgation of new Constitution it was the first such case that raised the question of gender discrimination on property rights. The Court went through weeklong hearing and finally concluded that the denial of equal entitlement of ancestral property to daughter contravened the right to equality under Art 11 of the Constitution. The court didn't overturn the unconstitutional provisions; rather, court ordered the government to bring bill in the Parliament within one year in order to reform discriminatory legal provisions. Also, court verdict became objectionable due to its drawback to recognize patriarchal values and norms. The court gave terms of reference to the government to bring law without prejudicing the existing social structure. Despite this drawback, 11th amendment of Country Code came in force due to the judicial intervention.

The amendment not only brought change in property rights but also 11th Amendment has resulted in liberalization of abortion laws; maximization of punishment against some sexual offences; equalization of most of the marital rights and freedoms; elimination of chastity based discriminations; introduction of new offences against women etc. Amongst, it is of great importance that women became entitled to enjoy complete freedom of choice whether or not to abort fetus within first trimester (12 weeks). Additionally, abortion has become permissible with the consent of women up to 18 weeks in case the pregnancy is due to rape or incest. It also legitimizes abortion at any time during the pregnancy with the recommendation of an authorized medical practitioner if the life of the woman is at risk or if the fetus is deformed. Unfortunately, 11th Amendment is not free from criticism as it also legitimized sex-based discrimination in some respects that have been challenged by bringing PIL to the court in subsequent days. Some of the cases are discussed respectively.

4.2.3 Empowering Women to Enjoy Right to Privacy

Though individual aggrieved brought this case to the court but it was of immense public importance. Petitioner had filed a case in Kathmandu District Court against her brother and mother asking for maintenance and marriage expenses because they had made partition of their property in her absence. Replying before the court, respondents had proclaimed that she got married and procreated child. They produced the record of the Hospital in order to prove their statement. District court, during the trail of the case ordered the plaintiff to give presence personally for her vaginal and uterus test by at least three gynecologists of the governmental hospital. Challenging the 'virginity test order', she petitioned at Appellate Court; court didn't allow her appeal. As a final resort she brought the issue before the Supreme Court under the Art. 88(2).

In response to the case *Annapurna Rana V. Kathmandu District Court*, the Court delivered its landmark decision in favor of the petitioner. The court invalidated the 'Virginity Test Order' relying on the ground that the order violated constitutionally guaranteed right to privacy. It was held that gynecologic examination of the private reproductive organ of the petitioner constitutes an interference with the right to respect for privacy under the Art 22 of the Constitution of the Kingdom of Nepal 1990. Significance of the decision also lies in holding state institutions including court accountable towards the observance of fundamental human rights of individual. According to the judgment, even judicial authority cannot enable itself to supersede fundamental rights of an individual by administrating virginity test in the name of collecting evidences. Recognizing the petitioner' sexual freedom and right to control over own reproductive organ, the court interpreted:

"As right to privacy over own body and private organ is guaranteed as inviolable right under the Art 22, if the test of the private reproductive organ is administrated even as per the court order without taking consent, it also results in violation of the right to privacy. The result is same for the petitioner in both conditions: in case of encroachment by other and test performed as per the court order; that is why, the order of the District Court is unconstitutional as it undermine the right to privacy of petitioner".

Court further interpreted that mere sexual relationship does not create any change on the legal status of a woman girl. Before marriage, they may practice cohabitation for years. Emphasized that ipso facto does not establish matrimonial relationship between them. The crucial interpretation of the court is that sexual relationship before marriage does not tantamount to marriage. Also this decision boldly challenged the patriarchal social norms and values that ignore women's sexual autonomy.

4.2.4 Empowering Prostitute Women to Enjoy Equal Protection of Law Against Sexual Offence

Responding the *Sapana Pradhan Malla for FWLD V. Ministry of Law an Justic et al*, the Supreme Court overturned the No 7 of the Chapter on Rape under *Country Code 1963* that constituted discrimination against prostitute by prescribing very nominal punishment in the case of rape on prostitute. In the case, the court upheld women' equal right to freedom from sexual violence irrespective of their character and practice of the profession. The court went on to say that it is unconstitutional to exempt rapist from criminal liability only on the ground that the victim is of loose character. The court further observed that such provision encourage criminal to commit heinous crime like rape against prostitute. And it places prostitute in inferior position then other citizen. The court also made very important remarks about the rape:

Rape is an act that totally deprives victim women from enjoying right to individual liberty and self-determination. It affects victim psychologically, socially and spiritually. It is not only crime against the victim woman but also against society at large. It is an offence of brutal nature; therefore every legal system has strictly forbidden and prescribed the punishment.

4.2.5 Court Order Aimed to Empower Working Women by Maintaining Uniform National Standard of Maternity Leave

Nepal lacks separate legislation dealing with maternity protection. But Several Regulations provide for maternity leaves differently. Despite the similar cause and objective of providing the leave, no uniformity is maintained in providing leave for all working women as women employees are provided 60-days in all government services, 52-days in all enterprises governed under Labor Act and 45-day in tea estates and Royal Nepal Air Line Corporation. On the other hand, the period of maternity leave was also insufficient to harmonize the women workers right to motherhood and their right to work protected under the constitution and international conventions.

In this backdrop, invoking right to equal protection of laws of all working women similarly situated in term of pregnancy and delivery, discriminatory leave provisions were challenged in *Prakash Mani Sharma et al for Forum for Protection of Public Interest (Pro Public) V. HMG Cabinet Secretariat et al*. Also the Supreme Court was called upon to issue mandamus for adoption of uniform national standard of maternity leave. Petitioners also prayed to ask government for providing at least 98 days maternity leave as per the ILO standard as the health of mother and child doesn't permit to work before that.

Responding the case, the Supreme Court issued directive order to the Government for formulating a national standard of maternity leave to be applicable for all workingwomen and make essential arrangement for the maternity protection. The Court also asked the government to take into account the ILO Convention on Maternity Protection 2000, Special Protection Clause of present Constitution, Breast milk Substitute (control of sale and distribution Act) 1992, Labor Act 1991 and Child Act 1992 in formulating such standard. The Court held that it is a matter of state obligation to make proper arrangements concerning nutrition and health care of the women during their pregnancy and post-delivery period. Upholding the importance of the leave in term of maternal and child health the Court went on to say that:

Maternity benefits including maternity leave are provided in order to enable women at work to have complete rest before and after pregnancy and facilitate them to provide proper care for their newly born baby. Weak health status of the women those who are pregnant and mother of newly born baby may result in miscarriage, premature birth and it may also cause risk to the health of fetus and newly born baby. Taking into account the role of women to care and breastfeed baby and the baby' right to be breastfed as well, working women can't be denied the rest period or maternity leave at that condition.

Ridiculously, relying upon the orthodox notion that 'leave is only a matter of facility but not a matter of leave' the court denied recognizing maternity leave as a matter of right. It seems that court neglected to take into account the implication of maternity leave upon the enjoyment of right to work and healthy.

4.2.6 Women's Right to Freedom from Sexual Harassment Upheld

In response to *Sharmila Parajuli for Pro Public V. HMG et al*, the Supreme Court issued directive order to the Government to enact comprehensive legislation in order to ensure women's right to freedom from sexual harassment in work places and public places as well. In issuing directive, though implicitly, Judges relied upon the state obligation under Art 2 of the CEDAW that requires adoption of appropriate measures including legislation to eliminate all form of discrimination.

The case was brought before the Supreme Court taking into account the scenario of the violation of women's right to employment and freedom of mobility. Issuance of judicial guidelines to be applicable was also demanded by petitioners to fill up the gap of law. However, the court didn't agree upon that demand to issue certain guidelines as Indian Supreme Court formulated in *Bisakha's Case*. Anyway, the court recognized the sexual harassment as a sexual violence against women that results in violation of right to dignified life. Also the Court empathetically agreed upon the reality that:

Sexual harassment inhibits women from enjoying constitutionally protected right to equality and freedoms.

Unless and until sexual harassment is fully prevented, it is undisputed fact that realization of the constitutionally protected rights to equality and freedoms of women cannot be materialized in living reality.

4.2.7 Right to Freedom from Marital Rape Upheld

In *Mira Dhungana for FWLD V. Ministry of Law an Justice et a* the court issued radical judgment that stands for women's right to self-determination in deciding whether or not to have sexual intercourse with husband. The Public Interest Litigation was filed at the Supreme Court stating that No. 1 of the Chapter on Rape failed to criminalize rape of a wife committed by her husband using force, threat, fear and duress thereby provided penal exemption to the offenders. Petitioner also contended that such exemption was contrary to right to equal protection of law irrespective of marital status protected under the CEDAW Convention.

Upholding right to dignified life of women the court held the marital rape unconstitutional and denied the husband's ownership over the sexuality of women. Stressing on the implication of "free and full consent" as a recognized ground of marriage upon conjugal life, the court ruled that there must be mutual consent between husband and wife for the sexual intercourse after marriage. Recognizing the independent personhood of women after marriage the court observed:

"Right to self-respect, right to self-determination and right to co-existence are indivisible right provided only for human being; so that, women can also enjoy these rights before and after marriage equally. To get married does not mean that to be transformed into slave; that is why, it is obvious that marital relation does not result in deprivation of women' human right because every human is entitled to enjoy inalienable human right till she/he exist as human. So that, to allow husband to have forcible sexual intercourse with his wife is the same to deny women's coexistence, right to self-determination and right to dignified life".

The court further noted that to compel woman for letting other to use her organ or body result in violation of her right to live with dignity and right to self-determination; that is why, right to privacy has been guaranteed under the constitution.

Finally the court issued directive order to introduce a Bill for providing immediate relief by allowing wife to live separate from or to divorce the rapist husband; prescribing the degree of offence in rape committed in the circumstance of child marriage, and for making complete legal provisions for justifiable and appropriate solution in an integrated manner with regard to marital rape taking into account the special circumstances of marital relationship and position of husband.

5.2.8. Judicial Intervention Aimed to Empower Badi Women and Children

In fact, it was very unfortunate that women from Badi community are forced to involve in prostitution due to social and economic problems. They were further compelled to continue the way of prostitution because of the lack of alternate employment opportunities on the one hand and prevalence of cast based untouchability and social atrocities on the other hand. Those poor, illiterate and ignorant victims of the trap are target group in the flash trade. The people from so-called high caste sexually harass them. Discriminatory laws concerning citizenship and birth also heavily affected this community. Many children from this community are facing problem of citizenship, birth registration and education especially who were born in course of prostitution and sexual exploitation.

Despite the guarantee of gender equality under the constitution, plight of *badi* women remained intact due to the insensitivity of Government. Taking into account the aforesaid plight of Badi Community Pro Public brought public interest litigation to the Supreme Court especially aimed to make the community freed from injustices and discriminations. Demands made by petitioners in this case include enforcement of rights concerning citizenship and birth registration, arrangement of alternate employment opportunities, vocational training, free education and health care facilities.

In this case, initially the Supreme Court asked for written statement from respondent government authorities and placed the case in priority list for disposal. Subsequently, in response to one of the demands of petitioners the court constituted an expert committee that consisted of representatives from victim community, National Dalit Commission and Public Interest Petitioners as well. The Committee coordinated by Joint Secretary of Ministry of Women, Children and Social Welfare was also provided terms of reference by the court. The committee was charged with the responsibility to conduct study overall problems facing by *Badi* community, efforts of HMG towards addressing problems and recommend measures that are essential to be adopted in future for ensuring dignified life of *Badi* Community.

In response to the case the Supreme Court has issued mandamus to the government for the effective implementation of Article 9(2) of the constitution. Under Article 9(2) of the constitution every child who are found within the kingdom of Nepal and the whereabouts of whose parents are not known shall until the father of the child is traced, be deemed to be citizen of Nepal by descent. The Court has also nullified a discriminatory provision of Section 4(1) of the 'Birth, Death and Other Private Incidence Registration Act 1976' that even deprived women from enjoying right to get the birth of the children registered. Nullified provision allowed 'senior member among male family members' to register the birth took place within the family. Similarly, court has also issued directives for the effective implementation of the plan of action submitted by expert committee to the court aimed to uplift *Badi* Community. In fact this litigation has created ray of hope to this community that one day their problems will be taken way.

5.2.9 Government Held Accountable to Reform Dscriminatory Penal Provision on Abortion

In Sapana Pradhan Malla for FWLD V. Ministry of Law and Justice et al the court entered into the rationality and reasonability of penal provisions concerning forced abortion. In this case constitutionality of No. 28 (A) and No. 32 of Chapter on Homicide was challenged. Challenged provisions provided that perpetrator who forces pregnant woman to have an abortion and consequently that results in miscarriage is subject to nominal punishment ranging from 3 to 6 month imprisonment; whereas, under No. 28 a woman who commits abortion voluntarily except in permissible grounds prescribed by law is subject to severe punishment ranging from 3 to 5 years imprisonment.

The Court held that the law that provides different punishment for similar type of offence couldn't in any way be considered rational and reasonable. The Court went on to say that though punishment is a matter of state policy, the court shouldn't refrain from fulfilling it's constitutional obligation towards eliminating discriminatory laws. The Court found said provisions discriminatory and insufficient to protect women's right to freedom from violence. Hence, directive order was issued to the government for amendment of said No 28(A) and 32 so as to make them compatible with the provision under No 28 of the Chapter on Homicide.

5.2.10 Order Aimed to Eliminate Chhaupadi *Tradition Issued*

Responding *Dil Bahadur Bishwokarma et al V. HMG Office of Prime Minister and Council of Ministers et al* Supreme Court issued mandamus to the government to make pro-active intervention including creation of awareness to eliminate *chhaupadi* tradition from society. Simultaneously, the Court also issued directive order to the government for bringing comprehensive laws to cope with the customary practices like *chaupadi* detrimental to health of the women. The Court took serious concern over governmental reluctance towards elimination of such inhuman tradition. The case was brought to the Supreme Court by dozen of Lawyers representing different social organizations challenging the long standing customary practice that was proved detrimental to the reproductive health of the women. In fact, *Chhaupadi* is a superstitious tradition performed specially in time of menstruation and delivery. It mostly exists in far western Region of Nepal where socio economic and educational situation of people is very pathetic. Under this tradition women are placed in a dark room for several days without hygienic foods especially during first menstruation and post delivery period also. Mobility is severely curtailed. Women are treated as untouchable. They are also considered impure, polluted, and not allowed for religious and other social functions.

5.2.11 Directive Issued for the Amendment of Polygamy Law

In *Chandra Kanta Gnywali et al V. HMG, Office of the Prime Minister and Council of Ministries et al*, the petitioners contended that No 9 of the chapter on Marriage contravened the fundamental right to equality under Art 11 of the constitution and demanded the Supreme Court declare it ultra virus of the constitution. Disputed No 9 provided that a man was allowed for bigamy even if his first wife was living, if she became incurably insane; no child was born or was alive within ten years of marriage or if the children did not survive; turned blind; became crippled; was separated after taking share of her husband's property. However, the same rights were not applicable to a wife under similar circumstances because women were subject to punishment on adultery.

In response to the petitioners' plea, a special bench of the Supreme Court observed that the legal provision that allows man to get remarried and disallows woman making her subject to the punishment if she get remarried at the same grounds can be counted as discriminatory against them. Though the court was mainly called upon to eliminate discriminatory legal provisions allowing polygamous marriage based on disability and infertility, Supreme Court seemed much more concerned about provision on adultery that prevents women from getting remarried. The court seemed unwilling to strike gender balance by allowing women for remarriage as court noted that to allow only man for remarriage tantamount to gender discrimination. Most crucial point here is that if women are also allowed to remarriage by making law it further extends the disability-based discrimination.

Notwithstanding the judicial interpretation, the Supreme Court finally didn't dictate particular amendment but left it to the parliament as the court just issued directive to the government for making proper amendment of No 9 as per the constitution and CEDAW Convention. The court also asked government to go through public consultation on the issue before amendment takes place.

4.2.12 Empowering Air Hostesses to Enjoy Equal Employment Right

In *Rina Bajracharya and other V. HMG/Nepal* the Supreme Court delivered landmark judgment not only in term of employment right but also in term of enhancing equality jurisprudence. On the one hand, the court nullified the early retirement provision for Air Hostesses of Royal Nepal Airline Corporation (RNAC) and empowered Air Hostesses to enjoy equal right to equal job security. As per the discriminatory service rule, Air Hostesses were compelled to leave job upon attaining the age of 35 as opposed to male employees who were entitled to enjoy unrestricted employment up to the age of 58. Most significantly the court rejected the contention of respondents that the disputed provision was special provision for women rationalized under Special Protection Clause of the Art 11 of the constitution. Opposed to this contention, the apex court clarified the meaning and intent of 'special protection clause' in a way that it is for the empowerment of women so any provision that inhibits women for the equal enjoyment of rights doesn't fall under the special protection clause. The court further held that 'special protection clause demands positive discrimination in favor of women and it does not allow negative discrimination in the name of special provision.

4.2.13 Empowering Women to Acquire Passport at their Self-Determination

The Supreme Court delivered landmark judgment in response to *Punya Bati Pathak and others V. HMG Cabinet Secretariat and others,* filed by two single women who were not provided passport due to absence of the consent of the guardian. The judgment in this case empowers Nepalese women to acquire passport at their own will. The Court quashed the governmental decision that Imposed disability upon women under 35 in term of acquiring passport as women were compelled to take consent of the guardian. Leveling passport as an integral part of right to fundamental freedom of movement, the court also issued mandamus to the government for providing passport to the women without any hindrance.

4.2.14 Empowering Women to Enjoy Right to Dispose their Exclusive Immovable Property

This case *'Lily Thapa and Others Vs HMG Cabinet Secretariat and Others'* has resulted in Supreme Court judgment having far reaching impact upon women's economic right. The court overturned the discriminatory legal provision, Section 2 of the Chapter on Women's Exclusive Property under National Code 1963that subjected women to the discretion of guardian in term of right to dispose their own immovable property. As per the legal provision unmarried daughters were compelled to take the consent of their father and mother and married women including widow were required to take consent of their son having majority of age.

4.2.17 Empowering Women to Enjoy Inherited Property

Responding the *Mira Dhungana for FWLD Vs HMG Cabinet Secreteriat and Others* The petitioner challenged the constitutionality of Section 12 A of the Chapter on Inheritance added by the Eleventh Amendment to the National Code as being inconsistent with the equality clause of the Constitution of the Kingdom of Nepal and Article 1 of CEDAW. According to the impugned Section 12, unmarried daughter who had earlier received some property in inheritance was no longer entitled to enjoy the inherited property as the remainder of that property shall have to be returned to her heirs belonging to her parental lineage; whereas, a son did not have to return such a property.

Disposing the case, the Supreme Court of Nepal opined that partition share and inheritance was not one and the same thing; rather, they were two entirely different concepts. Recognizing a woman's right to get married as a fundamental human right, the apex court held that the legal provision requiring the return of any property received in inheritance on account of the recipient's marriage was contrary to the constitutionally guaranteed fundamental rights. The apex court, therefore, held the impugned Section 12 A of the Chapter on Inheritance 'ultra virus' of the constitution from the date of decision.

4.2.15 Government Held Accountable to Amend Discriminatory Provision Depriving Women to Enjoy Parental Property

Equal property right is still dream for Nepalese women. Even 11th Amendment of National code 1963 has also retained marriage-based discrimination that hampers women to enjoy right to share of parental property. In response to the case *Prakash Mani Sharma and others for Pro Public Vs HMG Cabinet Secretariat and others* the Supreme Court issued directive to the government for amending discriminatory legal provisions concerning right to enjoy parental property that are inconsistent with the Right to equality under the Art 11 of the Constitution of the Kingdom of Nepal and ratified Convention CEDAW. As per the discriminatory provisions under Chapter on Partition of National Code 1963 the daughter has to return her share of parental property upon marriage. This provision has also resulted in restriction of exercising marital freedom because of the divisibility of property right.

4.2.16 Government Held Accountable to Adopt Legislative Measure for Combating Witchcraft Based Violence

In *Resma Thapa and Others V. HMG Cabinet Secreteriat and Others* the apex court held that women are guaranteed right to live a dignified life as well as freedom from all forms of discrimination and violence against women under the constitution and the ratified conventions. The court further observed that the belief in the existence of the art of witchcraft and the incidents of death caused by it was nothing but an expression of a conservative, superstitions and uncivilized thinking of the society. Therefore the accusation of witchcraft and the resultant cruel and barbaric punishment on that charge were criminal acts. The apex court further observed that the existing laws could not be deemed adequate to deal with the menace of witchcraft. Hence the apex court issued a directive order to the respondents to enact an effective law for the prevention, control and punishment of the acts cruelty and torture in connection with the baseless charge of witchcraft and also to launch an awareness-building program for the eradication of conservative and superstitious belief in witchcraft.

5. Concluding Observations

Nepalese women are no doubt entitled to various rights and freedoms that are explicitly or implicitly protected under the constitution and the international instruments. But, the rights decorated in texts in such way are still observed as dream for most of the women. Even they are not aware about their rights. In practice, violation of women's rights is rampant as most of the women are facing serious problems especially due to existence of discriminatory laws, lack of effective implementation of positive laws and absence of legal protections in many sectors. Hence, gender justice and women empowerment are still seen far from the reach of women who are born in ignorance and die with ignorance.

In this backdrop, exercise of PIL is seemed to have unquestionably created ray of hope to the Nepalese women. Though PIL in Nepal is in its infancy but it has become instrumental in making state accountable towards women's rights protected under the constitution and the ratified conventions. Judicial responses in eliminating legal provisions perpetuating violence and discrimination, in accelerating implementation of positive laws, in holding government accountable for the enactment of gender just laws and amendment of unjust legislations are seemed highly appreciable. Especially exercise of Public Interest Litigation has become fruitful in term of eliminating discriminatory laws. For example, No. 7 of the Chapter on Rape, No. 2 of the Chapter on Women's Property Rights, No. 12(A) of the Chapter on Inheritance of National Code 1963, and Clause 4 of the Immigration Regulation 1976s have been eliminated which were impairing the women empowerment by perpetuating gender discrimination. Additionally, abortions laws, property laws, marital laws and laws relating to sexual offences have been liberalized in many respects as a result of PIL. Another most important achievement obtained through PIL is the judicial recognition to 'the marital rape as a form of heinous crime', 'sexual harassment as a gender based violence', 'virginity test order as a violation of right to privacy', 'right to equal protection of law irrespective of character'. This type of judicial recognition has immense jurisprudential significance in enhancing gender justice and promoting women empowerment. Judicial activism through PIL has also resulted in acceleration of law reform process. Government has been asked by the court to take immediate initiative for amendment of unjust and discriminatory laws, which are preventing women from enjoying right to freedom from violence and discrimination. For example, No 9 of the Chapter on Marriage that allowing polygamy, and No 28(A) and No 32 of the Chapter on Homicide encouraging forced abortion, No 1(A) and No 16 of Chapter on Partition restricting women from enjoying parental property fall under this category. PIL has also played vital role in holding government accountable towards the translation of state obligations mandated by the constitution and the ratified conventions in living reality. Judicial decisions that dictate government to bring laws dealing with 'marital rape', 'sexual harassment', '*Chaupadi* Tradition 'maternity protection', Right to equal share of parental property' and 'witchcraft based violence are counted important in this regard. PIL has also played educative role. It brought many gender issues like marital rape, polygamy, maternity protection and women's sexuality into public consultation and debate. Judges, Law Enforcers, Law Makers, Bureaucrats and general public have got sensitized and educated. Contribution has also been made in term of domestication of treaty provisions. The court delivered most of the judgment specially giving reference to the provisions under ratified conventions that are aimed to protect and promote reproductive rights. Last but not least is the weakening patriarchy due to huge blow given by PIL; in fact, during this period PIL has played tremendous role to get Nepalese women rid of patriarchal norms and values that are responsible to keep men's control over women's sexuality.

Despite the abovementioned achievements some weaknesses could also be observed. In *Maternity Protection Case,* though the court recognized urgent need of adequate maternity leave at workplace for the sake of maternal and child health, the court did blunder by refusing the maternity leave as a right. Likewise, in *Sexual Harassment Case* court declared harassment as a serious violation of women' human rights but denied to formulate judicial guidelines which are needed to enable women for enjoying their rights even during the absence of legislation. In *Polygamy Case* though the court found legal provision discriminatory on the basis of gender but denied to declare such laws *ultra virus* of the constitution. Also the court failed to recognize disability based discrimination as the court made concern to create gender neutrality by allowing women to get remarried rather than by eliminating polygamy.

Besides, various grievances of Nepalese are still left behind where the Public Interest Litigation can really be proven effective tool. But effective exercise of PIL is always expected. The above discussion serves to highlight the need for continued judicial intervention through skilled Public Interest Litigation in the area of women's rights. In a country where large sections of the women population continue to be deprived from enjoying basic rights, the judiciary is very often called upon to intervene in exercise of its primary role as a protector and enforcer of such rights.